A BEGINNER'S GUIDE TO
NEW TESTAMENT EXEGESIS

TAKING THE FEAR OUT OF CRITICAL METHOD

Richard J. Erickson

InterVarsity Press
Downers Grove, Illinois

InterVarsity Press
P.O. Box 1400, Downers Grove, IL 60515-1426
World Wide Web: www.ivpress.com
E-mail: mail@ivpress.com

InterVarsity Press® is the book-publishing division of InterVarsity Christian Fellowship/USA®, a student movement active on campus at hundreds of universities, colleges and schools of nursing in the United States of America, and a member movement of the International Fellowship of Evangelical Students. For information about local and regional activities, write Public Relations Dept., InterVarsity Christian Fellowship/USA, 6400 Schroeder Rd., P.O. Box 7895, Madison, WI 53707-7895, or visit the IVCF website at <www.intervarsity.org>.

Design: Cindy Kiple

Images: TSI/Comstock

ISBNs   0-8308-2771-4
978-0-8308-2771-8

Printed in the United States of America ∞

Library of Congress Cataloging-in-Publication Data

Erickson, Richard J.
  A beginner's guide to New Testament exegesis: taking the fear out
  of critical method / Richard J. Erickson.
    p. cm.
  Includes bibliographical references and index.
  ISBN 0-8308-2771-4 (pbk.: alk paper)
  1. Bible. N.T.—Criticism, interpretation, etc. I. Title.
  BS2361.3.E75 2005
  225.6'01—dc22

                                                                2005012107

| P | 19 | 18 | 17 | 16 | 15 | 14 | 13 | 12 | 11 | 10 | 9 | 8 | 7 | 6 | 5 |
| Y | 19 | 18 | 17 | 16 | 15 | 14 | 13 | 12 | | | | | | | | |

To the memory of my father

Howard Carl Erickson
1921-2004

Ja, må han leva uti hundrade år!

CONTENTS

FIGURES

SIDEBARS

PREFACE

Read Me First!

It's one thing for an enthusiastic Bible student to anticipate with excitement the study of the Scriptures in the original languages. It's another thing for that same student to endure with patience and diligence the long and arduous process of acquiring the necessary tools and skills. It's yet a third thing to practice those skills faithfully throughout subsequent years, especially amid the unpredictable demands of life and ministry. These three "things" provide an object lesson in a maturing sense of reality. The following chapters reflect that sense of reality as it has dawned upon me during the past twenty years of teaching a course in New Testament exegetical method.

From the outset, in 1984, I used Gordon Fee's exceptional *Handbook* as the primary text for the course.[1] Its practical aim, abundance of examples, thorough bibliography and annotations, and triple-level approach combined to make it, in my view, the best tool on the market for the job. Its longevity and successive editions confirm the point. Yet, as parades of eager students passed through my classroom, I found myself frequently on the defensive for choosing this textbook. Not that the students themselves had alternatives to suggest! Still, I gradually realized that the very strengths of Fee's book often worked against its effectiveness.

The practicality of its intentions presents no problem. Instead, what chiefly troubles students are the thoroughness of its approach, on the one hand, and, on the other hand—to a smaller degree—its complex, three-tiered layout. The book may suffer from its attempt to be both an introduction to the work of exegesis and a handbook for future reference. I have no doubt about its enormous value as a reference tool to keep at one's elbow in the regular, ongoing practice of exegesis. In spite of its introductory inten-

---

[1] Gordon D. Fee, *New Testament Exegesis: A Handbook for Students and Pastors,* 3rd ed. (Louisville: Westminster John Knox, 2002). Earlier editions: 1983 and (revised) 1993.

tion, however, its quality as a reference tool can overwhelm a beginner.

Beginners can also feel overwhelmed by the thoroughness of Fee's presentation. In his entirely laudable attempt to give a complete account of the exegete's responsibilities, along with a full listing of the very best resources and tools of the trade, he has unintentionally subjected some unsuspecting students to despair, even terror. The model the book delineates is that of an ideal exegete, realizable only in the best of circumstances (perhaps only in the office of a seminary professor—and not always then!). Most students, however, have neither the time nor the resources required for living up to this admirable model. Nor will they be likely to do so in the future. Many of them are painfully aware of how little their own pastors have made regular use of Greek and Hebrew in preaching and teaching. Fee does indeed acknowledge this edge to reality in the third of the book's three tiers. There he proposes a shortened procedure for producing a sermon in a minimum of ten hours. Students can be grateful for this. Even so, the book's net effect (without doubt, entirely unintended) is all too often to convince students that they will never be able to do a proper job, now that they see all that is involved. In other words, as I have experienced it from a teacher's perspective, Fee's *Handbook* gives too much meat to beginners in need of milk.

This book, therefore, attempts to provide a more digestible diet for beginning exegetes. It intends to leave students encouraged, enthused and ready to move on to new stages of active exegetical life, at whatever level their real circumstances allow. It reasons that doing any honest, open and original exegesis on a realistically regular basis is better than doing no original exegesis out of fear of doing it inadequately. To this end, it distinguishes between professional, scholarly exegesis and professional, pastoral exegesis. It does not elevate one over the other but recognizes the place each occupies in the work of God's kingdom. Students are invited to relax and enjoy the learning process as a prelude to enjoying—*finding joy in*—original exegesis done at whatever level they can do it. Once they get their exegetical feet solidly on the ground, once they develop some personal confidence for the task, they can do themselves no greater favor than to pick up Fee's *Handbook* as a refresher and as a guide to improving their technique. In any case, the present book owes a great deal to Fee's, as will be evident to anyone acquainted with both.

The course out of which this book has grown is one I have taught regularly for two decades at Fuller Theological Seminary Northwest in Seattle, Washington. Fuller operates on the quarter system (rather than the semester system), which accounts for the ten (weekly) chapters. But as students routinely remind me, the amount of material covered in the course could easily be stretched out over a longer period, even to accommodate a semester course of thirteen or fifteen weeks. A creative teacher could easily expand the chapters on specific genres (letters, narrative, apocalypse), as well as those devoted to structural and historical-cultural analysis.

Although the ultimate goal of the book is to lay a groundwork for the exegesis of the *Greek* New Testament, all references to Greek and Greek texts are provided also in English, in order to enable anyone familiar with English to use the book and benefit from it. Thus the book can be used effectively at both the college and the seminary level. Indeed, anyone with a desire to gain a footing in serious, responsible study of the biblical text can use it with profit.

Additional exercises and supplemental material (arranged according to the appropriate chapters) are available on the InterVarsity Press website, <www.ivpacademic.com>, and can be found by searching for this book's title. Instructors and students alike are invited to make free use of these materials in order to enrich the content of the various chapters of the book. Suggestions for improving both the book and the webpage are welcome; see the link designated for suggestions.

Students working individually or in small groups, without a "teacher," can also make effective use of this book and the webpage. It is always good to have an experienced person on hand, one who can answer specific questions. Nevertheless, the book is (I trust) sufficiently readable and (except for a few places, perhaps) plain enough that most of it can be grasped and mastered without the benefit of a live teacher at one's elbow.

An innumerable cloud of witnesses has kept me encouraged in the ongoing exegetical task: former professors, colleagues, congregations of churches I have served and preached in, family and friends, and a crowd of students. Many of these people in recent years have contributed directly to the writing of this book, chiefly by reading and criticizing some or all of it in earlier stages of its development, or by challenging me (intentionally or not) to rethink this or that feature of its argument.

Those who have been particularly helpful deserve to be mentioned by name. I list them alphabetically: Mike Evans, Cathy Johnson, Mike Moore, Joel Nordtvedt, Tom Parker, Art Patzia, Charlie Scalise and Steve Young. I hope I haven't forgotten anyone! InterVarsity Press editor Dan Reid has walked me through the entire process, bucking me up along the way, assuring me that it will all have been worth doing.

I give special, heartfelt thanks to Randee, my beloved and faithful wife, a close companion for over thirty-five years, and to Ingrid Steele, our recently wedded daughter. Both of them have made it clear in no uncertain terms that they love me. Who could wish for more?

Finally, I dedicate this little book to the memory of my father, Howard Carl Erickson, a very funny man, who died with his family around him. He taught me, among many other things like baiting hooks and trolling slowly, that in the end, people are worth it, whatever *it* is. People and their everlasting worth are the only reason I have bothered to write at all.

1

FRAMING YOUR MIND, OR HOW TO PRONOUNCE ZMRZLINA

"Simon son of John, do you love me?"
Peter felt hurt because he said to him the third time, "Do you love me?"
And he said to him, "Lord, you know everything; you know that I love you."
Jesus said to him, "Feed my sheep."
JOHN 21:17

In my view there is scarcely anything more important to the health and welfare of the Christian church than a firm grasp of the message embedded in the Holy Scriptures. This message comes to us wrapped, like the Holy Infant, in the swaddling clothes of history, language and culture. We need an ever-renewed army of preachers and teachers, dedicated exegetes, to help us unwrap that message. We need exegetes who know their work and how to do it. This book intends to help equip that army.

Two things I wish to say as we begin. First, after teaching New Testament exegetical method to hundreds of students over the last twenty years, I have come—I think—to understand much of what excites them about it and much of what terrifies them about it. I have written especially with those issues in mind. Second, I am a Christian. I have written for the direct benefit of other Christians, for the church of Jesus Christ. I therefore take the liberty of assuming certain things are true without feeling the need to defend myself, apart from saying so right now, of course, somewhat defensively. Here is a list of these assumptions.

1.1 SOME ASSUMPTIONS AT THE OUTSET

1.1.1 The Inspired Word of God

I assume, for example, that the Bible, in both Old and New Testaments, is the inspired Word of God, communicated not only to the original audiences but also to all other human communities in all of history. As an heir of the Protestant tradition, I confess my allegiance to the Protestant Bible, but I find much to appreciate in the books that make up what Protestants call the Old Testament Apocrypha and that Roman Catholics regard as deuterocanonical Scripture (books such as Tobit, Judith, the Maccabees and the Wisdom of Sirach). In fact, I regard them as essential reading for anyone who wants to understand the New Testament more fully.

1.1.2 Holy Scripture and the "Word of Life"

I also assume that the Bible, as God's inspired word, is a primary medium of life and understanding for the church and the world. I say "*a* primary medium," because I do not for a moment deny the significance of what Jesus says about himself, according to the Gospel of John: "I am the way, and the truth, and the life" (Jn 14:6). I freely confess Jesus of Nazareth, the crucified and risen Messiah, as the ultimate source of life and truth. Nevertheless, I immediately remember that I know this about him *only through the words of the Bible.* In fact, in all of the Bible only Paul (Phil 2:16) and "John" (1 Jn 1:1; the author doesn't actually identify himself) use the phrase "word of life" (λόγος [τῆς] ζωῆς), though they apparently do not use it to refer to the same phenomenon. Paul speaks of communicated teachings, whereas John has in mind the incarnated manifestation of God in the human person of Jesus. Yet in both cases we can understand the expression *word of life* to mean the word or message that provides life. Jesus the human being came as God's incarnated, life-giving *word* to the human race. Paul and John restate that "word of life" each in his *own* words—as do Matthew, Mark and Luke. These restated interpretations we now find deposited in the written *words* of Scripture. Today we must consult these written words of Scripture when we want to understand what God has said to us in his mighty acts and through his Son. (Of course, both Pastor Bob and your mother restate the "word of life" in their own words, too, but we do not regard their restatements in the same reverent way as we do those of Paul, John, Matthew, or the others.)

Paul himself demonstrates awareness of this dynamic of restatement. After a devastating critique of humanity, both Jewish and Gentile, he proclaims the bold solution: God has simply intervened in mercy toward us (Rom 3:21). Taking things into his own hands, God resolved the unnatural alienation between us human beings and himself by providing a way out through faith in Jesus of Nazareth, the Messiah, crucified and raised again, not just for Jews, but for Gentiles, too. Such a Gentile-friendly perspective alarmed and annoyed the Jews of Paul's day, including Jewish Christians. In order to argue his point, Paul turns to Scripture. This is not the first time he does so, of course, but now he does so with a rhetorical question carrying as much force today as it did for Paul himself: τί γὰρ ἡ γραφὴ λέγει; "For what does the Scripture say?" (Rom 4:3). By appealing to Genesis 15, Paul shows his readers that even the life of the Jewish patriarch Abraham illustrates God's openness toward all nations of the world. Abraham's acceptability before God, attested in the Scripture, is based not on any of his deeds, not even on his Jewishness (after all, at Gen 15:6 he was not yet "Jewish"!), but on his faith in God and in God's promise, a faith open to all human beings, Jewish or not.

Of course, for Paul, Abraham was dead and gone. All that Paul had left was the text, ἡ γραφή. For this reason, he insists a few verses later that these words about the ancient forefather were written for "our" sake, too (Rom 4:23-24). Today, for us, Paul himself is gone. All *we* have left is the text. Until the coming "new day," for us as for Paul the text remains the final court of appeal.

1.1.3 Flocks and Shepherds

Third, because of the importance of Scripture for the life of the church, I assume that every local manifestation of the body of Christ on earth needs someone dedicated to studying that Scripture and to communicating its message to the flock as completely and accurately as possible. Of course, all who can read may study the Bible for themselves, at least in translation. There is nonetheless a great deal involved in reading and hearing the Bible completely and accurately. The message of Scripture is simultaneously simple enough for a child to grasp and complex enough to keep schools of scholars fully occupied. We will soon see why.

1.1.4 The Holy Spirit as Interpreter

Nothing I say here, however, denies or overlooks the interpretive power of the Holy Spirit. For this reason, I assume, finally, that the Spirit himself is at work both in the heart of the child and in the heart of the scholar. Still, in his inscrutable wisdom, God has apparently seen fit to reveal his message, his mysteries, through the medium of human blood, sweat and tears. Prophets spoke the word and wrote it down—sometimes at the cost of their lives. We read it today and struggle to puzzle it out, working together to grasp its significance for our own time and place—sometimes even *without* acrimony.

From these basic assumptions we may draw several conclusions about the task laid out in the coming chapters. They will help us to see what we are doing here. Many of them speak to our attitudes, our frame of mind, in approaching the Bible as exegetes.

1.2 AN EXEGETICAL FRAME OF MIND

My father used to tell me, "Nothing good comes easy." As a kid, I never truly appreciated this bit of his homespun wisdom, usually because he delivered it when I was least receptive to it (and I was least receptive to it when I needed it most). Yet now, years later, I see how right my father was. In fact, I see that the maxim applies no less to exegesis than to anything else. In her hilarious and insightful guide for aspiring writers, Anne Lamott urges her readers to adopt "the writing frame of mind."[1] She leaves us under no misconceptions! Writing is hard work. So is exegesis. Anyone who thinks otherwise has probably never really done it. Yet, the fruit of exegetical labor is glory; and by the word *glory,* I do not mean fame.

1.2.1 The Priority of Exegesis

If in one sense the biblical text is all we have, then understanding the text is of paramount importance to those of us who pin our ultimate hopes and expectations on its message. We confess that the Creator of the universe, the Judge of all humanity, has revealed himself to us in his dealings with Israel and in his Son, Jesus of Nazareth. If the stories of Israel and of Jesus are deposited authoritatively in the words of the Bible, then understanding those words rightly is essential for understanding the nature of our Creator and Judge, something well worth doing, considering the stakes.

Those words of Scripture, however, are *foreign* words. The text spoke first to a *strange* culture, strange to us at any rate. Thousands of years, unfamiliar languages no longer spoken, and tremendous cultural gaps separate us from the message embodied in the Bible. It can be difficult enough to understand what someone in our own family tries to say to us. The difficulty increases—almost beyond comprehension, so to speak—when we try to understand a message directed to an ancient tribe of Semites or to a gaggle of first-century Corinthians recently converted from outright paganism. Yet even this is not enough; we cannot be content with understanding just the ancient message. We need to make sense of it as a message relevant to us today. We who look to the Bible for

---

[1]Anne Lamott, *Bird by Bird* (New York: Anchor, 1994), p. 95.

a word from God need first to hear that biblical word in its original context. At least, someone needs to hear it for us in that way and to help us see what it meant. But this means doing whatever we can to project ourselves back into that ancient original setting in order to hear those ancient words, as well as we can, with the ears of their first audiences. That is the task of exegesis: *to project us back into that ancient world*. Without exegesis, we can easily "hear" something completely different from the message first delivered. Sound, backward-projecting exegesis begins with the languages.

1.2.2 The Importance of the Original Languages

Speaking of them as the "*original* languages" does not imply that Adam, Eve, Cain and Abel sat around the campfire at night singing Hebrew folk songs or spent their afternoons inventing new conjugations for the Greek contract verb. Instead, we mean that the biblical texts as we have them from antiquity survive in Hebrew, Aramaic and Greek. It is a safe assumption that most of these documents, if not all of them, first appeared in those very languages—that Paul, for instance, actually wrote to Corinthian Christians in everyday first-century Greek, what we today call *koine* Greek. This can be frightening, but it is actually very convenient. Having the *very words* that Paul, Matthew or Luke wrote to specific people in specific situations gives us a tremendous advantage in determining what those authors meant to say with those words.

In contemporary English-speaking cultures, we have an embarrassing wealth of Bible *translations*. If we dislike the way a particular version renders a passage, we can choose another; and if we find our second choice no better, we can try a third or a fourth. The hidden problem in this privileged scenario is the unspoken question, how do we decide whether one translation is better than another? What do we mean by "better"? If we base our preferences on whether a translation supports or fails to support our chosen doctrinal orientation, then what have we learned from Scripture that we did not already know? We assume that the message of the Bible, properly understood, speaks prophetically, critically and "life-givingly" to us today. But how can the Bible possibly critique us (and thereby offer us life) if we ourselves determine in advance what it is allowed to say?

Another matter related to this issue of languages is a virtual no-brainer. Suppose we enroll in a university to study French literature and none of our professors can read French. Suppose they depend entirely on English translations of Molière and Camus. Yet we often hear, and sometimes experience firsthand, that many Bible teachers and preachers in churches across this continent make precious little use of the Greek or Hebrew they once learned in seminary, if they use it at all. There may be many reasons for this, some justifiable. In any case, I have no doubt the Spirit of God preserves for himself a faithful testifying community in spite of their inability to drink as deeply from the biblical well as sound exegesis might enable them to do. But that is just the point: sound biblical exegesis cannot reach its full potential without appeal to the original languages. I have noticed that most of those who remain skeptical about the value of doing original work in the Greek text of, say, Matthew have actually done very little of it or none at all. We may resist diving into cold water; yet, once we're in it, the water refreshes and invigorates us. The joy of discovery and the enriching results of seeing things invisible in translation soon outweigh the time and effort we spend in devoting ourselves to this kind of linguistic study. Chapter ten discusses the necessary balance between this prophetic responsibility and the demands of everyday life and ministry. But it needs to be said here and now that there is no adequate substitute for, and nothing more thrilling than, seeing the message of God come alive in the ancient words of its first authors. The enthusiasm of a "thrilled" exegete-preacher/teacher has the potential to electrify a group or a congregation with the power of God's message brought forward for them from its ancient context. An enthusiastic chef who serves up a home-cooked gourmet meal gets better results than one who heats up canned beans and frozen Swiss steak. Do not let the television commercials fool you; it is *not* the same.

1.2.3 Commitment and Openness

We may indeed count ourselves among those who love the Lord Jesus Christ and are committed to the Word of God. Yet, even for us there is a time to exult in that Word and a time to dissect it, a time to glory and a time to think hard, a time to embrace and a time to refrain from embracing, a time for commitment and a time for openness. In fact, commitment to the Word of God *implies* openness to it. There are perhaps those gifted folks who can preserve an attitude of warmly devoted commitment to Holy Scripture and simultaneously pursue a hard-line, critical analysis of it. Many of us cannot.

Only with conscious effort can we distinguish between what we *believe* the Scripture says and what the Scripture does *in fact* say. We usually exult over and glory in what we believe it says or in what our authority figures have taught us to believe it says. This is completely natural and normal; otherwise, we could not exult or glory in it at all. Yet all of us believe that many passionate Christians are anywhere from slightly to grossly mistaken about what Scripture teaches. In fact, for many of us, passion itself prevents us from listening to any point of view different from our own.

Exegesis is the *discipline* of temporarily distancing ourselves from the text, of setting aside our passion for it and our glorying in it. We do this in order to see more clearly what our passion might otherwise prevent us from seeing: *another point of view*, one different from and perhaps even threatening to our own more comfortable position. We may eventually reject that other, threatening point of view, but it always deserves a dispassionate hearing, unless—God forbid—we are convinced in advance that our perspective and ours alone is the right one. We need not be afraid to seek the truth. That search by itself will not rob us of our love for God and Scripture. Only persons who for other reasons are seeking a way out from under the "oppression" of Scripture are in danger of losing their love and passion for the Word. For those who truly love the Bible and the Bible's Lord there is little risk of losing the passion by listening to what others think. These people love Scripture so much that they are willing to risk what they believe the biblical text says in order to discover more accurately what in fact it does say.

We may be passionately in love with Pastor Bob's interpretation of a text. In the process of exegesis, however, we temporarily distance ourselves from his view of things in order to reexamine the text for ourselves. (Remember the "more receptive" Beroeans, in Acts 17:11?) Then we discover, perhaps with dismay, that the text actually supports a different interpretation. We now become passionate about our new understanding of the text. After all, our ultimate concern is to be passionate about what the text actually does teach, to the degree we can discern it, rather than about what we *want* it to teach.

Consider a woman's love for her husband. In order to understand him more accurately, can she love him enough to risk "doubting" some precious notion she has always held about him—that he likes gardening, for example? What would she have to do in order to entertain a new, revised notion? Would admitting to herself that he hates gardening make her love him less devotedly? Is it the person as he *really* is that she loves, or is it only her preconceptions about him? Will passion help or hinder her in getting to know him better? Will getting to know him better destroy her passion, if she truly loves *him*? Passion, certainly appropriate in its place, needs to be set aside for a time in certain other settings, almost as a prerequisite, a first step to improved understanding. Scripture exegesis is one of those settings. Nevertheless, the goal of exegesis is to find something to be passionate about; it seeks the truth regarding what the Scripture says.

Take a real example from my own exegetical life. For many years, I believed God distributed forgiveness of human sins on a person-by-person basis. Once an individual "believed," or "accepted Christ as personal Savior," then and only then that person received God's forgiveness of sins. If souls "went to hell," it was because they had failed to seek or to find God's forgiveness. The damned went to hell unforgiven—in fact, *because* they were unforgiven. The evangelistic message of the church, then, called people to come, one at a time, to ask God for forgiveness. One year, however, as I was preparing an extended study of Paul's letter to the Romans, I made a discovery that stunned me. Romans 5:12-21 appeared to be teaching that just as Adam represented all humanity for condemnation, in the same way Christ represented all humanity for justification. At first I tried to make sense of this idea within the context of my inherited doctrinal position. Yet the more I analyzed the text, and the more I compared it with other biblical texts, the more I became convinced that I had had it backward all along. I came to a new understanding of God's ways with humanity. I gradually realized that God's forgiveness, entailed in his justification of humanity, was the foundation of his invitation to repentance. The message of the gospel was not "come to God in order to *gain* forgiveness" but rather "come to God because he *has already* forgiven." Christ represents all humanity, and thus, thanks to him, even the damned who "go to hell" go to hell fully forgiven! By the same token, Adam too is our representative; thus, thanks to him, even the forgiven who "go to heaven" go to heaven fully damned. My point here is not to convince anyone of my exegesis of Romans 5, but to demonstrate that exegesis, if done "from a distance" and with rigor, has the power to change our understanding of even a precious doctrine. It should. It did for Paul. It did for Martin Luther. It may for you. Do not worry about this, however! You are never alone in it. This is a community project, something we will return to in a moment.

Meanwhile, we may rest assured that we need not lose our passion by being rigorous. Instead, our passion may mature into deeper appreciation and love for the Word of God. Passion and listening are by no means mutually exclusive. Although they are difficult to practice well simultaneously, they lead into one another. True passion (as opposed to blind passion) drives us to investigate more completely—from a "distance"—what we are passionate about. That kind of listening, the kind that seeks the truth, will fire renewed passion within us. This book is about the sober, rigorous pursuit of an accurate understanding of the written Word of God, whether or not we always—or ever—perfectly attain that goal. We carry out this "sober" pursuit *because we are passionate* about the Word of God. Nevertheless, in carrying it out we set our passion aside for the moment in order to see that Word more clearly. The act of setting passion aside, the act of distancing, is fundamental to exegesis. Exegesis requires *openness* toward hearing the message of the Bible, the Bible to which we are passionately *committed*. Exegesis remains a perpetual quest, a never-ending pursuit. There are no guarantees of a final answer, one which forever makes further exegesis superfluous. Yet without the ongoing quest, we grow stale and die. This textbook is about the methods for pursuing that exegetical task.

1.2.4 Community Exegesis

As I said a moment ago, we are not alone in this task. Part of the process of seeking a more accurate understanding of the written revelation of God is participating in a grand conversation with other readers. These other readers include both those alive and active now and those who have had their say and gone on before us into the Future, perhaps centuries ago. It even includes those yet unborn. It includes both those we know and love and those we do not know, both those with whom we find ourselves in basic agreement and those with whom we disagree, perhaps profoundly. A few of us among these conversation partners may have consciously forced our interpretations of biblical texts to conform to what we wish those texts to teach. But the vast majority of us have done our interpretative work in good faith, only *unconsciously* forcing Scripture to suit our expectations. Thus we find ourselves often enough in direct conflict with one another. We may feel frustrated about God's allowing such confusion within the church, but there it is nonetheless. Our role in the kingdom of God is not to be always right, nor to be always in agreement with each other, but to love each other, even in our disagreements (Jesus calls it *his* commandment: Jn 15:12). More than that, it is to give each other a fair and sympathetic hearing. Not to do so is to determine ahead of time—often passionately—that God has no more to teach us. This is not a good thing.

Coming to the table with the rest of the exegetical community—be they dead or alive, male or female, lay or professional, humble or arrogant, brilliant or ordinary—raises some other issues, too. Suddenly we are on stage. It is one thing to mumble away in our little private studies, but to speak up in the community and give voice to our opinions potentially exposes us to anything from ridicule to admiration. (Which is worse, ridicule or admiration, is hard to say.) We may feel acute intimidation when we find ourselves in the presence of world-class scholars or their books. We may think that we ourselves have nothing of value to contribute to this grand conversation, since one or another of the giants has already said everything worth saying about a given text. We may regard ourselves as incompetent compared with the experts. We fear we will never be as learned as F. F. Bruce, Morna Hooker or N. T. Wright. We may be right about that, but *it is hardly the point.*

The point is rather that, in the face of such intimidation and failure of nerve, we may be tempted to resort to complete dependence on what the experts say. In place of doing our own exegesis, we may simply quote someone else's. We may forfeit our birthright for a mess of warmed up beans. God knows we can find plenty of additional excuses to go this route. The truth is that we will always face this sort of intimidation, and that is not a bad thing. Insecure creatures that we are, we turn our communities into arenas of competition. We find standards against which to measure each other (and ourselves), and where we cannot find them, we invent them. But rather than competing for positions of greater and greater honor at the exegetical table, we simply need to find a place there—any place—and start working. All who are called to this task (and many of those not called to it!) have as much native ability and common sense as do any of the big shots. Every one of them once stood where you now stand. If you are reading a book like this one, it is highly probable that God has called you to this work. Whom he has called, he will also equip, and whom he equips, he will use! You may often feel intimidated (as I do), but know this: you are also empowered. You may doubt that you will ever have the requisite expertise, but know this: you are competent. You are competent to listen and competent to teach what you learn from listening. You are a gift of God to his people and to the world. *That* is why you are here.

There is also a "good" side to the intimidating aspect of the community: it helps prevent us from becoming bullies. It can be a heady experience when a congregation regards us as the oracle of God. We may even come to believe it ourselves. The pages of church history teem with stories of leaders who have fallen into this trap. As particularly flagrant examples from recent times, Jim Jones and David Koresh come to mind. There are doubtless thousands more we have never heard about. Indeed, some prominent evangelical scholars publish volume after volume of their authoritative expositions of the Word of God, which their admiring disciples take to be the final statement on the subject. In one sense it is wonderful when the saints in the pews listen raptly to the proclamation of the Word of God, perhaps even scribbling notes fast and furiously. Scenes like this, however, can all too easily degenerate into unhealthy dependence on a lone ranger's reading of the Bible. For such situations, there is scarcely any better remedy than the international, transmillennial, transconfessional conversation at the exegetical table. Study groups, refresher courses, conferences, commentaries and reading the classics all help in this regard. We will take up many of these in the coming chapters. Do not forfeit your birthright! Forfeit neither your right to listen nor your right to speak. Listen to the Bible and listen to the church's discussion. Be willing to make your contribution, and be willing to hear the contributions of others. Be willing to hold your ground, and be willing to change your mind. Know when to hold them; know when to fold them. Be a part of the church.

1.2.5 Levels of Engagement

In other words, exegesis engages us on many levels. It is neither simply a tool for scholarly study of the Bible, nor it is merely a stage in preparing sermons. It is primarily a listening device, a systematized process we can use for projecting ourselves backward into the cultural settings out of which the biblical documents arose. Once there, we can more accurately hear the message as its authors first delivered it. And once that or something close to it is clearer to us, we are all the more likely to hear the message the Scripture has for us in our own settings. It might speak to me personally, reassuring me of God's unchanging love for me or convicting me of speaking sharply to my spouse this morning, or both. It might speak to my congregation and to me, reminding us of our role as the "light of the world," reorienting our perspective on our present purpose and our ultimate destiny and on how generous God must feel toward those who hate him. It can engage us at the level of scholarship, where sometimes heated, sometimes pedantic and sometimes illuminating discussion of exegetical minutiae can throw new light on ancient practices, attitudes or expectations. Yet no matter at what level we engage Scripture or it engages us, exegesis provides the processes we need for listening to it.

This abbreviated list of issues and attitudes makes up some of what we might call, with thanks to Anne Lamott, the exegetical frame of mind. A friend of mine who grew up in Prague once told me that to speak Czech, one needed to get one's mouth set in a certain position. (I can't tell you what it is!) The reason people from America speak Czech with an American accent is partly their failure to get their mouths set right. It is a lot like that for the business of exegesis, only now we must get our minds set right—framed right, so to speak. So taking up the actual exegetical tools with this frame of mind is a bit like trying to pronounce the word *zmrzlina* in order to ask for ice cream in Prague.

1.3 A VIEW FROM THE TOP

Before taking up the various specific tools of New Testament exegesis, we can wrap up this introductory chapter by surveying the interpretive task from the top down. Figure 1.1 graphically represents the larger interpretative process, at least as this book conceives it. The diagram there may serve as a map, a "big picture" of that larger process and the place exegesis occupies within it. A few comments take us through it.

For one thing, the diagram presupposes the assumptions acknowledged above in section 1.1, particularly that the New Testament (like the Bible as a whole) speaks God's message to humanity in any cultural setting. We regard this as true even though that message originally came to very particular groups of people in very specific historical-cultural circumstances. The process depicted in figure 1.1 is theoretically applicable also to Caesar's *Gallic Wars* or to Chaucer's *The Tale of the Wife of Bath*. We do not usually understand those literary pieces, however, as having the same significance for contemporary communities as Christians claim for the New Testament. Rarely will critics of Caesar or Chaucer attempt to draw out a message for, say, the Hakka people of Taiwan in the way a Christian missionary to the Hakka people may try to do with New Testament material. With that caveat, we can look at the diagram itself.

It begins with an ancient message contextualized for an ancient people, a message more or less incomprehensible to modern readers unfamiliar with that ancient context. It ends with the *same message* now re-contextualized in terms relevant to some other culture and people. To get from the one form of the message to the other requires two major steps. One of them is exegesis. Before even embarking on the exegetical step, however, an interpreter must acknowledge entering a strange world where little is predictable in terms of his own world. The ancient writer may or may not take it for granted that the earth is round or that the government should outlaw slavery immediately. This sort of hermeneutical preorientation will pave the way for the interpreter to listen to the ancient text with sympathy and humility. It forms part of the exegetical frame of mind.

With the right hermeneutical attitude, then, the first stage in moving from ancient text to contemporary significance is to hear as accurately as possible what that ancient text actually said to its first readers. The interpreter sends the text through an exegetical grid. What is really happening, however, is that the interpreter sends *herself* through the exegetical grid. She uses the tools of exegesis to project herself back into the ancient culture, reconstructing around her, *as well as she can*, the elements constituting that first setting, beginning with the text and the language. The various exegetical "criticisms" listed in the large upper oval of the diagram indicate many of the more important pieces of the exegetical task. The result of this process is the biblical message exegetically analyzed—understood, that is, by the interpreter who has entered that ancient context by means of the exegetical tools.

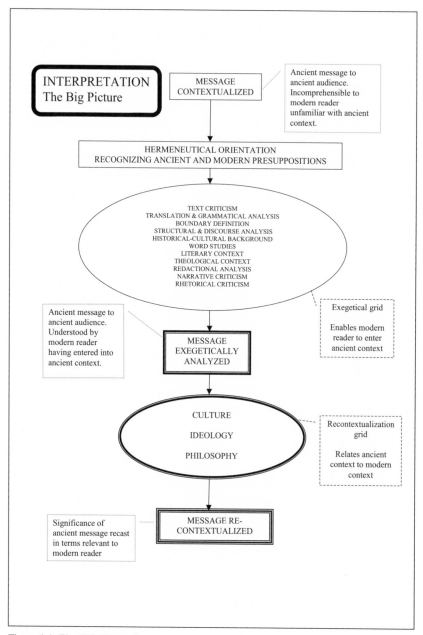

Figure 1.1. The "Big Picture"

With an exegetically improved grasp on the original message that Paul, for instance, delivered to the Corinthian Christians, an interpreter passes the results through a "recontextualization grid" meant to relate the ancient and modern contexts to one another. In this process, the interpreter takes into consideration the relevant points of similarity and contrast between first-century Corinthian culture and his own contemporary culture. Issues of language, sociopolitical circumstances, philosophy, ideology, economics, cultural values and many other factors, as they are relevant to the question at hand, are brought to bear on the process. The desired result of this is the biblical message appropriately applied to a new people in their own cultural setting. The process "recontextualizes" the significance of the ancient message to Corinth, recasting it in terms that speak meaningfully to the new setting, yet in a way compatible with that original message.

It is important, however, to keep well in mind that the results of both major steps in the interpretive process (the exegetical and the hermeneutical) are always subject to review by the community. There can never be absolute certainty about those results in any mathematical or philosophical sense. We are always dealing with the fundamental characteristic of historical study: the weighing of probabilities.

The lion's share of this book is devoted to the first of these two major stages of interpretation. The reason for this is twofold. For one thing, the exegetical process, properly done, is highly complex, more than can be fully described even in a book like this. In fact, comparatively few people ever approach full mastery of exegetical technique. Almost as soon as they do, some new development emerges, appearing to render everything else obsolete! Simply *introducing* exegetical method will be enough for now. By the same token, the other reason for focusing primarily on exegesis, rather than on the hermeneutical stage of interpretation, is that the latter is also complex enough—and controversial enough—to merit more space than half this book can provide. Still, in chapter ten, we will look ever so briefly at the subject. Now, however, we are ready for a systematic look at exegetical method.

1.4 A LOOK AT WHAT'S TO COME

The remainder of this book falls broadly into two complementary parts. Chapters two through five cover exegetical issues relevant to all New Testament literature, whereas chapters six through nine deal with issues pertinent to specific genres of the literature. Chapter two takes up the question of what we have to work with: text and tools. It discusses textual criticism and introduces the use of tools such as concordances, commentaries, dictionaries, synopses and so on. Chapter three is concerned with the way texts are constructed from smaller parts, which themselves are constructed of even smaller parts. The relation of the parts to the whole, and the whole to the parts, has powerful implications for a text's meaning. Built on the insights gained in chapter three, chapter four deals with analyzing the structure of the whole, whether by "the whole" we mean an entire book or a mere phrase in a sentence. Texts have ways of tying "wholes" together as coherent units, and this fact too has important influence on meaning. Both chapters three and four have to do with this sort of literary and linguistic context. Chapter five then turns to the subject of historical and cultural context. The New Testament texts all addressed specific, historically real people and specific, historically real settings. In order to understand these texts today, we need to pay close attention to the history and cultures represented by those specific times and places.

In the second half of the book, the discussion turns to specific genres and special considerations pertinent to each one. Chapter six focuses attention on New Testament epistles. Narrative material in general (the Gospels and Acts) occupies us in chapter seven, and specific subgenres of narrative texts come up for treatment in chapter eight. The strange world of New Testament apocalyptic literature is the subject of chapter nine. Finally, chapter ten raises the question, what now? What are we to do with all this information, not to mention the results of our exegesis? How are we realistically to keep laboring away as exegetes for the rest of our natural lives, and why should we?

So now, what do we have to work with?

TEXT AND TOOLS

Mowing the New Testament Lawn

When you come, bring the cloak that I left with Carpus at Troas,
also the books, and above all the parchments.

2 TIMOTHY 4:13

In my early teens I made spending money by mowing lawns in the neighborhood. The first requirement for a job was that there had to *be* a lawn. No lawn? No job—and no pay! The second requirement was access to tools. Nobody envisioned me on my hands and knees snipping off individual blades of grass with my fingers. Employers provided mower, rake, clippers and broom—the tools of the trade. As exegetes of New Testament texts, we have a job to do and tools for the job. No text? No exegetical task—and no message! But there *is* a text! The question is, what is this text like? We have plenty of resources for the task, but what are these resources like? What do they do for us as we carry out the task? This chapter takes a long look at the text, followed by a short look at some of the available exegetical tools. What, in fact, do we have to work with?

2.1 THE NEW TESTAMENT TEXT: ORIGINALS, COPIES, TRANSLATIONS AND EDITIONS

What is the Word of God, anyway? What is the Bible, or (for our purposes in this book) the New Testament? Are the New Testament and the Word of God in some sense the same thing? If so, how should we understand John 1:14, which tells us that the Word became flesh and lived, as in a tabernacle, among us? If we need to make a distinction between the New Testament and the Word of God, how should we describe that distinction? What qualifies as the New Testament? Is it the King James Version (KJV)? If so, which edition? Or is it Luther's German Bible? How about the original Greek text? Is the true Word of God only the original "autographs," right from Mark's pen or Paul's? Or is it instead some surviving ancient copy, like Codex Vaticanus, or some particular modern edition, like Nestle-Aland (which we'll return to presently)? If the "real" New Testament is in fact a hypothetical collection of the original autographs, which are now lost, then what is the attraction of this book, Greek or otherwise, that we carry around with us to church or to class?

If we claim that the New Testament is in any sense God's word to us, we should try to answer questions like these. No matter how we answer them, however, it is important to grasp the distinctions among *originals, copies, translations* and *editions* of the New Testament text. The *original* New Testament documents, the ones actually held in the hand by their authors (the "autographs"), are—apparently—gone forever. That is probably a good thing, since we would worship them and fight over them if we still had them. What have survived instead are some three thousand *copies* (or copies of copies) of those lost Greek originals, preserved and handed down to us—still in Greek—over the last nineteen centuries or so. We also have some two thousand other ancient written witnesses. These include copies of *translations* (or *versions*) in which the message of these Greek documents has been rendered into different languages for the benefit of those who do not understand Greek. People have been translating New Testament literature since very early in the church's history (Latin versions, for example, appeared at least as early as the second century), and new translations continue to appear in our own day. Some languages, notably English, boast many different translations of the New Testament, while other languages may have only one version, or a portion of one. Finally, we also have *editions*. There are various editions of translations, for example. The Revised Standard Version (RSV), completed in 1952, appeared in a new "version" in 1989, known as the New Revised Standard Version (NRSV). This new version itself came out in a study *edition* in 1991 and again in 1994. Likewise, the Greek New Testament has seen numerous editions over the centuries; the Nestle-Aland *Novum Testamentum Graece* appeared in over twenty-five editions during the twentieth century alone.[1]

To put it another way, thousands of handwritten *copies* of the Greek New Testament ultimately go back to the *original* documents. Based on surviving copies, various *editions* of the Greek New Testament have appeared. Likewise, based on copies (in earlier times) and on editions of the Greek New Testament (more recently), scholars have given us hundreds of *translations*, including many in English, most of them printed in thousands—even millions—of cop-

---

[1] *Novum Testamentum Graece: post Eberhard et Erwin Nestle,* 27th ed., rev. by K. Aland et al. (Stuttgart: Deutsche Bibelgesellschaft, 1993, c. 1898); commonly abbreviated NA²⁷.

ies. Many of these translations have appeared in various editions, each presumably improving on the last, or providing some feature others do not. Students of the New Testament who cannot read Greek must depend on translations and various tools that help make the Greek text semi-accessible. Yet, any modern reader dependent on a translation of the New Testament already stands at five degrees of separation from the New Testament authors and their messages: author, original autograph, copies in Greek, editions of the Greek text, translation, modern reader. Greek-reading students can reduce that distance by at least one degree.

Does eliminating that one degree make a difference? It does indeed, though it would be outrageous to claim that only those with Greek skills can interpret the New Testament properly. Instead, interpretation is often a matter of nuances. Of course, readers can find many of those Greek-based nuances explained in Bible commentaries. Nevertheless, there is scarcely any joy like that of discovering the New Testament message for ourselves. In any case, without access to the Greek text, we have no effective way of evaluating what a commentary says or fails to say—or for that matter, of evaluating the accuracy of a translation. For these reasons alone, students of the New Testament ought to do everything they can to learn New Testament Greek.

What most of us have to work with in studying the New Testament, then, is at least a translation and at best an edition of the Greek text. Yet, how reliable is that edited Greek text? Users of the New Testament in translation sometimes notice footnotes or marginal references to alternative readings, often worded something like "other ancient authorities read . . . ." Notations of this kind alert readers to the problem of *textual criticism*, which we are about to take up. It will not be easy for readers to evaluate these marginal notes in their Bibles, unless they can refer to and use a recent edition of the Greek New Testament. Even without Greek skills, however, readers can gain an appreciation for the issues behind these difficulties. They can learn why, for example, the proviso in the KJV rendering of Romans 8:1 ("who walk not after the flesh, but after the Spirit") is absent from many later translations.

2.2 TEXTUAL CRITICISM: ESTABLISHING THE TEXT FOR EXEGETICAL PURPOSES

Here, then, is the problem. We have inherited from antiquity so many thousands of New Testament manuscripts with so many thousands of differing readings for various New Testament passages that we cannot immediately tell what it was that Mark, Paul or John originally wrote. The densely packed "footnote" material *(textual apparatus)* at the bottom of any page of NA[27] or of the fourth edition of the United Bible Societies' *Greek New Testament* (UBS[4])[2] is intended to help us recover those original readings through the "science" of textual criticism. (See figs. 2.1 and 2.2.) That material can look like computer-generated gibberish, which highlights the fact that textual criticism can be an intimidating and, at the least, a confusing subject.

Therefore, hear this, now, from the beginning! *Do not be afraid!* No one expects you, personally, to reconstruct the entire text of the New Testament in order to be a faithful exegete! This enormous task has been in the hands of many coworkers over the centuries and will probably continue to be until the day we no longer need a Bible. Some of these people pursue textual criticism as a profession, devoting much of their working life to the subject. Others (and this includes the vast majority of exegetes) do not have the necessary time or training to pursue it at that level, but they use it as they are able in what we could call "pastoral exegesis." We can define "pastoral exegesis" as exegesis done for the purposes of personal Bible study or for the production of an exegesis paper, a sermon or some other presentation. The task of reconstructing the New Testament text does not rest on any one person's shoulders, certainly not on yours or mine. For most of us, exegesis is more a pastoral pursuit than a strictly academic one. In another sense, of course, even the professional textual critics render an invaluable *pastoral* service to the church through their work, but our text-critical questions will be less complex than theirs are.

Still, this is *our* text, and we are the experts on it for whatever flock of believers we serve. For this reason we must at least understand the issues involved and have an elementary grasp of the procedures scholars use for dealing with the problem. We can largely depend on the New Testament text as the editors of NA[27] and UBS[4] have established it for us, but they provide us a rationale for their decisions on the various problem points. Much of their rationale is deposited in the textual apparatus found at the foot of any page in these two standard editions of the Greek New Testament. The information the editors provide there is embedded in an ingenious system of symbols and abbreviations, a system that has evolved over many years and is explained in the introductions to the Greek New Testaments.

In a way, these editions of the Greek New Testament contain both lawn and lawn mower in one package. They provide the text, but they also serve as a primary tool for investigating it. The smart thing to do after purchasing a new John Deere riding mower is to study the instructions. *There is simply no substitute*

---

[2] *The Greek New Testament,* 4th ed., ed. B. Aland et al. (Stuttgart: United Bible Societies, 1993); commonly abbreviated UBS[4].

615   ΙΩΑΝΝΟΥ Α΄   1,1–7

καὶ ᶠγνώσει τοῦ κυρίου ἡμῶν καὶ σωτῆρος Ἰησοῦ Χρι-   1,2! Ph 3,8! ·
στοῦ ᵀ. αὐτῷ ἡ δόξα ⸀καὶ νῦν καὶ⸃ εἰς ᶠἡμέραν αἰῶνος⸃.   1,11! ·
                                                          R 16,27! · Sir 18,
ᵒ[ἀμήν.]   10

⸀ΙΩΑΝΝΟΥ Α΄⸃

1 Ὃ ἦν ἀπ᾽ ἀρχῆς, ὃ ἀκηκόαμεν, ὃ ἑωράκαμεν τοῖς   2,13 J 1,1; 15,27
   ὀφθαλμοῖς ἡμῶν, ὃ ἐθεασάμεθα καὶ αἱ χεῖρες ἡμῶν   Is 43,13 ⑹ · Act
                                                          4,20 J 1,14; · 20,20.
ἐψηλάφησαν περὶ τοῦ λόγου τῆς ζωῆς – 2 καὶ ἡ ζωὴ   25 L 24,39
ἐφανερώθη, καὶ ᵀ ἑωράκαμεν καὶ μαρτυροῦμεν καὶ ἀπαγ-   4,9 J 1,4 R 3,21
γέλλομεν ὑμῖν τὴν ζωὴν τὴν αἰώνιον ἥτις ἦν πρὸς τὸν   5,20
πατέρα καὶ ἐφανερώθη ἡμῖν – 3 ὃ ἑωράκαμεν καὶ ἀκη-   J 1,18
κόαμεν, ἀπαγγέλλομεν ᵒκαὶ ὑμῖν, ἵνα καὶ ὑμεῖς κοινω-   7
νίαν ἔχητε μεθ᾽ ἡμῶν. καὶ ἡ κοινωνία ᵒ¹δὲ ἡ ἡμετέρα   Ph 1,5
μετὰ τοῦ πατρὸς καὶ μετὰ τοῦ υἱοῦ αὐτοῦ Ἰησοῦ Χρι-   1 K 1,9
στοῦ. 4 καὶ ταῦτα γράφομεν ⸀ἡμεῖς, ἵνα ᵀ ἡ χαρὰ ᶠἡμῶν   5,13 · J 15,11! 2 K
                                                          1,24 2J 12
ᾖ πεπληρωμένη.

   5 Καὶ ⸉ἔστιν αὕτη⸊ ἡ ⸀ἀγγελία ἣν ἀκηκόαμεν ἀπ᾽ αὐ-   3,11; 2,25; 5,11 ·
τοῦ καὶ ἀναγγέλλομεν ὑμῖν, ὅτι ὁ θεὸς φῶς ἐστιν καὶ σκο- Jc 1,17
τία ⸉¹ἐν αὐτῷ οὐκ ἔστιν⸊ οὐδεμία. 6 Ἐὰν εἴπωμεν
ὅτι κοινωνίαν ἔχομεν μετ᾽ αὐτοῦ καὶ ἐν τῷ σκότει περι-   2,11 J 8,12! ·
πατῶμεν, ψευδόμεθα καὶ οὐ ποιοῦμεν τὴν ἀλήθειαν· 7 ἐὰν   2,4! · J 3,21

18 ⸀ πιστει P 69 pc | ᵀκαι θεου πατρος 630. 1505. 1852 al sy | ⸃ 2 3 K 2464 al vgᵐˢ ¦ κ.
το κρατος νυν κ. Ψ (pc) ¦ νυν κ. αει κ. 623 (syᵖʰ) | ⸀-ρας -νος 630. 1241. 1505 pc vgᵐˢ
syⁱᵖʰ·ʰ sa ¦ -ραν -νος θεου πατρος 614 ¦ τους αιωνας των αιωνων 623 pc | ᵒᵀ B 1241.
1243. 1739*. 1881. 2298 pc vgᵐˢˢ ¦ txt 𝔓⁷² ℵ A C P Ψ 33. 1739ᶜ 𝔐 vg sy co

Inscriptio: ⸀ Ι. επιστολη (+ καθολικη 323. 614 pc) α´ (ℵ) Ψ 33. 69. 81. 945. 1241. 1739 al
(K 614. 630. 1505 al) ¦ επ. καθ. του αγιου αποστολου Ι. (L 049) al ¦ Ι. του ευαγγε-
λιστου (θεολογου pc) και αποστ. επ. α´ P pc ¦ txt (ℵ A B)

¶ 1,2 ᵀ ὃ B pc • 3 ᵒ 𝔐 t vgᶜˡ·ʷʷ saᵐˢ bo ¦ txt ℵ A B C P Ψ 33. 81. 945. 1739 pc z vgˢᵗ
syᵖ·ʰ** saᵐˢ bo ¦ ᵒ¹ C* P 33. 81. 323. 630. 945. 1505. 1739 al syʰ sa • 4 ⸀υμιν Aᶜ C 1739
𝔐 t vg sy saᵐˢ bo ¦ txt ℵ A*·ᵛⁱᵈ B P Ψ 33 z* saᵐˢˢ ¦ ᵀ gaudeatis et vgᶜˡ·ʷ ¦ ᶠυμων A C K P
33. 81. 323. 614. 630. 945. 1505. 1739 pm t vgᶜˡ syʰ bo; Aug ¦ txt ℵ B L Ψ 049. 69. 1241 pm z
vgˢᵗ·ʷʷ syᵖ sa • 5 ⸉ A 33. 81. 323. 945. 1241. 1739 al syʰᵐᵍ ¦ ⸀επαγγελια C P 33. 69. 81.
323. 614. 630. 945. 1241. 1505. 1739 al saᵐˢ bo ¦ αγαπη της επαγγελιας ℵ² Ψ ¦ txt ℵ⁽*⁾·¹ A
B 𝔐 | ⸉¹ 3 4 1 2 B 33. 69. 81 z: Orᵖᵗ Eus

Figure 2.1. Sample page from NA²⁷ (1 Jn 1:1-6) (Used by permission.)
The lower, "footnote" material is the textual apparatus; on this page it is divided
between comments on the last words of 2 Peter, which ends on this page, and those on the
opening of 1 John, beginning with the variants for the title *(inscriptio)*. The right hand margin,
down to the apparatus, contains the marginal references. The remainder of the page contains
the Nestle-Aland preferred text.

ΙΩΑΝΝΟΥ Α

The Word of Life

1. Ὃ ἦν ἀπ' ἀρχῆς, ὃ ἀκηκόαμεν, ὃ ἑωράκαμεν τοῖς ὀφθαλμοῖς ἡμῶν, ὃ ἐθεασάμεθα καὶ αἱ χεῖρες ἡμῶν ἐψηλάφησαν περὶ τοῦ λόγου τῆς ζωῆς – **2** καὶ ἡ ζωὴ ἐφανερώθη, καὶ ἑωράκαμεν καὶ μαρτυροῦμεν καὶ ἀπαγγέλλομεν ὑμῖν τὴν ζωὴν τὴν αἰώνιον ἥτις ἦν πρὸς τὸν πατέρα καὶ ἐφανερώθη ἡμῖν – **3** ὃ ἑωράκαμεν καὶ ἀκηκόαμεν, ἀπαγγέλλομεν καὶ ὑμῖν, ἵνα καὶ ὑμεῖς κοινωνίαν ἔχητε μεθ' ἡμῶν. καὶ ἡ κοινωνία δὲ ἡ ἡμετέρα μετὰ τοῦ πατρὸς καὶ μετὰ τοῦ υἱοῦ αὐτοῦ Ἰησοῦ Χριστοῦ. **4** καὶ ταῦτα γράφομεν ἡμεῖς[1], ἵνα ἡ χαρὰ ἡμῶν[2] ᾖ πεπληρωμένη.[a]

God is Light

5 Καὶ ἔστιν αὕτη ἡ ἀγγελία ἣν ἀκηκόαμεν ἀπ' αὐτοῦ καὶ ἀναγγέλλομεν ὑμῖν, ὅτι ὁ θεὸς φῶς ἐστιν καὶ σκοτία ἐν αὐτῷ οὐκ ἔστιν οὐδεμία.[b] **6** Ἐὰν εἴπωμεν ὅτι κοινωνίαν ἔχομεν μετ' αὐτοῦ καὶ ἐν τῷ σκότει περιπατῶμεν, ψευδόμεθα καὶ οὐ ποιοῦμεν τὴν ἀλήθειαν· **7** ἐὰν δὲ ἐν τῷ φωτὶ περιπατῶμεν ὡς αὐτός ἐστιν ἐν τῷ φωτί, κοινωνίαν ἔχομεν μετ' ἀλλήλων καὶ τὸ αἷμα Ἰησοῦ τοῦ

---

[1] **4** {B} ἡμεῖς א A*vid B P Ψ 33 itz copsamss ‖ ὑμῖν Ac C 81 322 323 436 945 1067 1175 1241 1243 1292 1409 1505 1611 1735 1739 1844 1852 1881 2138 2298 2344 2464 *Byz* [K L] *Lect* itar. t vg syrp. h. pal copsams. bo arm eth geo slav Augustine

[2] **4** {A} ἡμῶν א B L Ψ 322 436 1067 1175 1241 1409 *Lect* itar. z vgww. st copsa geo ‖ ὑμῶν A C 33 81 945 1243 1292 1505 1611 1735 1739 1844 1852 1881 2138 2298 2344 2464 *Byz* [K P] *l* 422 *l* 598 *l* 938 *l* 1021 vgcl syrh. pal copbo arm eth slav Augustine Bede ‖ ἡμῶν ἐν ὑμῖν syrp

---

[a] **4** NO P: TR ‖ P: WH AD M NRSV ‖ MS: NJB [b] **5** SP: WH NA

---

1 Ὃ ἦν ἀπ' ἀρχῆς Jn 1.1, 2; 1 Jn 2.13, 14 τοῦ ... ζωῆς Jn 1.1, 4, 14 **2** ἡ ... ἑωράκαμεν Jn 1.14 **4** ἡ ... πεπληρωμένη Jn 15.11; 16.24 **5** ὁ θεὸς φῶς ἐστιν 1 Tm 6.16; Jas 1.17 **6** 1 Jn 2.4 ἐν ... ἀλήθειαν Jn 3.21 **7** ἐὰν ... φωτί Is 2.5 τὸ ... ἁμαρτίας He 9.14; Re 1.5; 7.14

Figure 2.2. Sample page from UBS[4] (1 Jn 1:1-7) (Used by permission.)
The top portion of the page contains the preferred text for UBS[4], identical to that of NA[27].
The lower portion is divided between (a) textual apparatus, (b) symbols for the readings of various translations and editions, and (c) marginal (cross-)references.

for reading carefully through the introduction to NA²⁷ or UBS⁴. (Note that NA²⁷ provides both German and English introductions, just as many tools and gadgets sold today come with instructions in multiple languages. It's always a relief to realize that I have to read only five pages of text about my new camera instead of all fifty-nine pages in the booklet.) Doing this will take a little time, but once you get a feel for what is going on, and a sense of where to turn when you forget something, much of the potential for intimidation and confusion will evaporate. What we discuss in the following paragraphs *assumes* that you have read the introduction to your Greek New Testament. Nevertheless, it will help us in sorting this all out if we clarify a few things up front.

2.2.1 Clarifying Some Terms and Concepts

Visualize for a moment an Arthur Conan Doyle mystery: there is a murder and several suspects; Sherlock Holmes investigates, accompanied by Dr. Watson. Visualize also a parallel universe in which a New Testament text, say Matthew 1:18, survives in more than one form in ancient biblical manuscripts and other written "witnesses." You are the investigator. You must decide which of the existing optional readings for a given *problem point* in a biblical text is most likely the original one. This begs the question, of course, why the original reading is so important, and even what we mean by "original reading." We already assumed in chapter one that in one sense the message of God resides in the texts of the Bible. By that we mean the texts as composed by the original authors (or editors) of a book. Yet those original autographs are now lost, and during centuries of copying and recopying, the wording of their text was altered in some manuscripts. We have to ask, then, which manuscripts preserve the original wording for a particular text. That text needs reconstructing if we are to have any confidence that we actually do possess it in something like its original form. Naturally, perfection will elude us, but we do the best we can with what we have. This takes us back to Sherlock Holmes.

Textual problem, or problem point. A *textual problem* is like the mystery, the murder. (People also call it a "textual *variant*"—but I think this becomes confusing, since the term *variant* is used to refer to an alternate reading as well. We will return to this in a moment.) A textual problem is a particular, single *problem point* in a text's preservation that needs to be resolved, like the one involving the third and fourth words of Matthew 1:18. (See fig. 2.3; English-only readers, please bear with us here!) Holmes wants to know which of several suspects is the murderer; we want to know which of the two or more optional readings for a particular text is the correct one. Did the original text of Matthew 1:18 read "Jesus Christ" or "Christ Jesus" or "Jesus" or "Christ"? The ap-

```
18-25: L 2,1-7      18 Τοῦ δὲ ⸀Ἰησοῦ Χριστοῦ⸃ ἡ ⸉γένεσις οὕτως ἦν. μνη-
    L 1,27      στευθείσης τῆς μητρὸς αὐτοῦ Μαρίας τῷ Ἰωσήφ, πρὶν
  20 L 1,35      ἢ συνελθεῖν αὐτοὺς εὑρέθη ἐν γαστρὶ ἔχουσα ἐκ πνεύ-
                  ματος ἁγίου. 19 Ἰωσὴφ δὲ ὁ ἀνὴρ αὐτῆς, δίκαιος ὢν
                  καὶ μὴ θέλων αὐτὴν ⸀δειγματίσαι, ἐβουλήθη λάθρᾳ
    2.13.19      ἀπολῦσαι αὐτήν. 20 ταῦτα δὲ αὐτοῦ ἐνθυμηθέντος ἰδοὺ
                  ἄγγελος κυρίου κατ' ὄναρ ἐφάνη αὐτῷ λέγων· Ἰωσὴφ
                  υἱὸς Δαυίδ, μὴ φοβηθῇς παραλαβεῖν ⸀Μαρίαν τὴν
                  γυναῖκά σου· τὸ γὰρ ἐν αὐτῇ γεννηθὲν ἐκ πνεύματός
  18! | Gn 17,19  ἐστιν ἁγίου. 21 τέξεται δὲ ᵀ υἱόν, καὶ καλέσεις τὸ ὄνομα
  L 1,31; 2,21    αὐτοῦ Ἰησοῦν· αὐτὸς γὰρ σώσει τὸν ⸀λαὸν αὐτοῦ⸃ ἀπὸ
    Ps 130,8      τῶν ἁμαρτιῶν αὐτῶν. 22 τοῦτο δὲ ὅλον γέγονεν ἵνα
    Act 4,12
```

11 ᵀτον Ιωακιμ, Ι. δε εγεvν. M Θ *f*¹ 33 *al* syʰ**; Irˡᵃᵗ ᵛⁱᵈ ¦ (*ord. invers.* του Ιεχονιου του Ιωακιμ του Ελιακιμ *add.* Dˡᵘᶜ, *i. e.* L 3,23-31) • 16 ⸀ω μνηστευθεισα παρθενος (– q), Μαριαμ εγεvν. Ιησουν τον λεγομενον χριστον Θ *f*¹³ it ¦ , Ιωσηφ, ω μν-θεισα ην M. παρθ., εγεvν. Ι. τ. λ. χρ. syˢ ¦ ω μν. ην M. παρθ., ἧ ετεκεν Ι. χρ. syᶜ ¦ *txt* 𝔓¹ ℵ B C L W (*f*¹) 33 𝔐 aur f ff¹ vg syᵖˑʰ co • 18 ⸉ 2 / B ¦ / W ¦ 2 *pc* latt sʸˢ·ᶜ; Irˡᵃᵗ ¦ ⸉γεvνησις L *f*¹³ 33 𝔐; Ir Or ¦ *txt* 𝔓¹ ℵ B C P W Z Δ Θ *f*¹ *l* 2211 *pc*; Eus • 19 ⸀παραδ- ℵ*² C L W Θ *f*¹³ 33 𝔐; Eus ¦ *txt* ℵ¹ B Z *f*¹ • 20 ⸀ Μαριαμ ℵ C D W Z Θ *f*¹³ 33 𝔐 ¦ *txt* B L *f*¹ 1241 *pc* co • 21 ᵀσοι sʸˢ·ᶜ ¦ ⸀κοσμον syᶜ

Figure 2.3. Mt 1:18-21 in NA²⁷ (Used by permission.)

paratus tells us that all four of these options show up here in the ancient manuscript tradition. We want to know which of these four "suspects" is "guilty" of representing the author's original wording. (Look, I know this creates an odd analogy between a murderer and the Holy Word of God. But stick with me here; it's only an analogy!)

Wherever you see one of the textual symbols in the NA²⁷ text (º □ ᵀ ⸀ ⸆, etc., described in the introduction!) or a footnote marker in the UBS⁴ text, there you have a "textual problem," a "problem point"—the site of a "murder," so to speak. There are actually *two* "murders" in Matthew 1:18. Referring to figure 2.3, see if you can identify the second one and determine how many "suspects" there are for it. (If you find two suspects, you are right.) In this verse, *both* NA²⁷ and UBS⁴ treat *both* textual problems. This is not always the case. In Matthew 1:19-25, NA²⁷ notes no fewer than twelve problem points, whereas for the same stretch of text UBS⁴ cites only one, in verse 25. The reason for this difference is that the UBS text is designed primarily for the use of Bible translators, and it therefore treats only those textual problems the editors feel will be significant in the process of Bible translation. In Matthew 1:19, for example, the editors of UBS⁴ simply ignore the variant reading παραδειγματίσαι ("publicly expose to shame") read by some ancient manuscripts in place of δειγματίσαι. UBS⁴ considers the meanings of these two words as too similar to one another in this context to make any real difference *in translation*. The NA text (all editions), however, includes for us as many textual variants as possible, given the constraints of space. It does so because this edition has the needs of New Testament scholars in mind, and thoroughness is a mark of good and faithful *scholarship*.

Variant readings. For any given textual problem point, each of the preserved optional readings (suspects in a "murder") is a *variant*, or a *variant reading*. This includes the editors' *preferred reading* printed in the body of the NA[27] and UBS[4] texts (whereas the rejected options are printed in the apparatus at the bottom of the page). All these variant readings are the "suspects" from which we must select one as most likely to be the "guilty" original.

If Professor Moriarty confesses to murdering Miss Marple (anachronistically, of course) and there are no other suspects to consider, then Holmes has no mystery, no "problem" to solve. On the other hand, if Moriarty and his butler are both individually suspected of the crime, and neither confesses, then Holmes does have a problem: Who actually did it? The plurality of suspects is what creates the mystery. In the same way, a particular textual problem point is in fact a problem precisely because the ancient witnesses preserve at least two different (variant) readings for the text in question. If there is only one serious contender for the original reading, there is no serious textual problem to solve.

Preferred reading (the "text") and alternative variants. Of the two or more variant readings for a given textual problem, we call the one preferred by a particular "inspector" (you, Nestle, Aland, Metzger, a committee, anyone else) *the preferred reading* naturally. A particular inspector, like Holmes, prefers it above all the other variants, or "suspects." Of course, Watson may prefer one of the other suspects. NA[27] and UBS[4] print their preferred readings as the "text" (like verdicts) and relegate all the other presumably innocent "suspects" to the critical apparatus at the bottom of the page. All the "acquitted" suspects in a given inspector's theory are *alternative variants*, rather than *preferred* variants. Because of their differing purposes, NA[27] investigates many more mysteries than UBS[4] does; yet, the (partially overlapping) editorial committees of NA[27] and UBS[4] have agreed to "prefer" the same readings throughout the Greek New Testament. Even though the designs of their respective critical apparatuses differ, their preferred texts are identical. Other contemporary critics of the Greek New Testament text come to different "preferred" results. In fact, so did earlier editions of the NA and UBS texts. Theoretically, the question remains an open one at every textual problem point, and it always will.

2.2.2 Answering the Question

What do we do, then, when we encounter a textual problem in a passage we are studying? That is, how do we resolve it? As we will see in a moment, not every textual problem is in fact worthy of our attention. Identifying the worthy ones, however, requires some understanding of the process. As it happens, the art and science of recovering the most likely wording of the original New Testament documents is exceedingly complex, requiring far more space to explain fully than can be devoted to it here. (In addition to the introductions in editions of the Greek New Testament, we have full-scale standard introductions, such as those by Metzger and Ehrman and by Aland.)[3] What we will provide here, however, is a survey of the main considerations scholars make in determining which one of a set of variant readings is most likely the original. These considerations organize themselves according to external and internal evidence; we will look first at the external evidence, the so-called textual *witnesses.*

External evidence: The witnesses. The enormous mass of ancient data from which textual critics reconstruct the text of the New Testament astronomically exceeds what has survived for any other ancient writing. This mass of ancient materials sorts itself into *four main categories:* (1) Greek New Testament manuscripts, (2) manuscripts of ancient translations (versions) of the New Testament, (3) quotations of New Testament texts by early theologians (the church fathers), and (4) selected New Testament texts preserved in ancient church lectionaries (lists of liturgical readings from Scripture). While there are many exceptions, the general rule is that Greek texts carry more weight than translations do, and copies of biblical books carry more weight than do quotations from them in lectionaries and in the writings of the church fathers.

The exceptions to this general rule include the possibility that a carefully done translation or quotation was made from a Greek manuscript (now lost) whose text preserved the original wording more faithfully than does the text of some other Greek manuscript we may wish to compare with it. For example, suppose that the church father Origen, writing a commentary on John's Gospel, carefully quoted passages from the Gospel here and there throughout the commentary. Suppose too that Origen's copy of John was a very early one, quite close in wording to the original, but that this copy of John used by Origen is now lost to us forever. Meanwhile, we have another ancient copy of

---

[3]Bruce M. Metzger and Bart D. Ehrman, *The Text of the New Testament: Its Transmission, Corruption, and Restoration,* 4th ed. (New York/Oxford: Oxford University Press, 2005); B. Aland and K. Aland, *The Text of the New Testament: An Introduction to the Critical Editions and to the Theory and Practice of Modern Textual Criticism,* 2nd ed. (Grand Rapids: Eerdmans, 1995).

John's Gospel, one that frequently disagrees with Origen's quotations. Should we simply "follow the rule" and go with the wording of the Gospel copy, setting aside the commentary's quotations as of less weight? Not necessarily. For not every Greek manuscript is of equal value. Some preserve a better text than others do, even if all that survives of a better one are quotations that Origen, or some other ancient writer, has left us.

As you have seen (by now) in the introduction to your Greek New Testament, the ancient Greek manuscripts divide themselves into three subgroups: (a) "papyri," written on papyrus (the "paper" of the ancient world), (b) "uncials," written usually on parchment (specially prepared animal skins) and using only capital letters, and (c) "minuscules," written in cursive Greek. Only a very few manuscripts contain the entire New Testament or even most of it. Some contain as little as a few verses from a single book, and others the collection of a single author's writings (Paul's, for instance) or one or more of the Gospels. Many are damaged, missing smaller or larger sections from their original state. Minuscule manuscripts outnumber papyri and uncials combined by more than eight to one, but very few minuscules predate the tenth century. As a group, papyri generally predate uncials by one or more centuries (and predate minuscules by at least six or seven). Papyri therefore enjoy more authority as a group, on the principle that fewer errors will have time to creep in if there is less time for that to happen. In other words, *the older a witness is, the more likely it is to be reliable.*

There are many reasons for making exceptions to this rule, too. We must apply it with our eyes open. This is because copies of New Testament texts sort themselves into groups (or "families") representing different "text-types," each characterized by a loosely associated selection of variant readings. Errors made in one manuscript, unless caught and corrected, tended to reappear in subsequent generations of manuscripts based ultimately on that faulty parent manuscript. Textual critics give names to these text-types—such as Alexandrian, Western, Byzantine and sometimes Caesarean—and they rate them for relative reliability. Their names also highlight the *geographical* element in their history; the Alexandrian readings appear mostly to be associated with Egypt, while the Western readings center more or less around Rome. Western readings tend to be fuller and more wordy, and for that reason are held in more suspicion than the leaner, cleaner Alexandrian readings. Thus a manuscript with a Western text-type may predate another with an Alexandrian text-type, but the later Alexandrian reading might trump the earlier date of the manuscript with the Western reading. *In other words, the age of a manuscript may carry less weight than its family text-type, and vice versa.*

The vast *majority* of individual witnesses, including most minuscule (cursive) manuscripts, belong to the Byzantine text-type; but as a family, they tend by far to be the least ancient. The textual apparatus often refers to witnesses of this text-type as the "Majority Text" (obviously, since there are so many of them!) and usually symbolizes them with a gothic 𝔐. For the most part, manuscripts representing the somewhat less reliable Byzantine text-type date at the earliest from the tenth century. Thus ironically (but not surprisingly) the younger, less reliable text-type survives in the majority of manuscripts. This fact illustrates the principle that *the decision about a particular variant reading's originality cannot be settled by counting manuscripts like votes.* Of a thousand witnesses, one might be right and 999 wrong.

Of course, knowing about text-types is relatively useless for "reading" the textual apparatus in a Greek New Testament, unless we have some idea about which witnesses (manuscripts especially) belong to which text-types. In fact, text-type can vary even within a single manuscript, since various parts of a manuscript (individual books, for example) may ultimately derive from *exemplars* of different text-types. (An "exemplar" is the copy from which a scribe makes a new copy.) Codex Sinaiticus (symbolized as ℵ or 01, and dating from the fourth century) contains the entire Greek New Testament, and for the most part represents the Alexandrian text-type. (The term *codex* refers to what we would call a book, with pages and spine, as opposed to a rolled up scroll.) Yet in the opening eight chapters of John's Gospel, Codex Sinaiticus reads more like the Western text. Those of us who practice "pastoral exegesis" will need to get this kind of information from partial lists prepared by experts in

	Papyrus manu-scripts	Uncial manu-scripts	Minuscule manu-scripts	Ancient versions	Church Fathers	Lectionaries
Alexandrian text-type	𝔓 46 𝔓 66 𝔓 75	ℵ B	33 81 579 892 1739	Sahidic (in part) Boharic	Clement/ Alex Origen (in part)	
Western text-type	𝔓 69 𝔓 29 (Acts)	ℵ (Jn 1-8) D W (Mk 1-5)	383 614 1739 (all in Acts)	Old Latin Curetonian Syriac	Tertullian Irenaeus Ephraem	
Byzantine text-type	None	A G Π Ω Gospels: E F	most minuscules belong here	Peshitta Gothic	Chrysostom	most lectionaries belong here

Figure 2.4. Sample textual witnesses and text-types
[**Sources: Metzger,** *Textual Commentary,* **pp. 14*-16*; Black,** *New Testament Textual Criticism,* **pp. 63-65; see bibliography**]

the field. Figure 2.4 illustrates the basic categories of textual witnesses and an example or two for each.

These are some of the main issues critics take into consideration with regard to the manuscript evidence. However, this *external* evidence regarding the witnesses to the text is only half the picture. Alongside evidence from external manuscript tradition for a given textual problem is evidence of a different type. Here we ask which variant reading does a better job than any of the others do of explaining how those others arose. This kind of consideration deals with *internal* evidence. A strong confluence of external *and* internal justification for a particular variant reading provides a reasonable ground for preferring that reading in place of others.

Internal evidence: The scribes. Critics sort the testimonial value of internal evidence into two kinds: (1) transcriptional probability and (2) intrinsic probability. *Transcriptional* probability has to do with the way scribal copyists did their work and the sorts of errors they were prone to make. Some of their errors were *unintentional,* such as skipping a section of text because two lines in the exemplar were similar in some way, often in their endings or beginnings. Likewise, a scribe may have absent-mindedly added a word or phrase familiar to him from the Septuagint (or LXX, the Greek translation of the Old Testament) or from a parallel passage in a Gospel other than the one he was copying. Other errors were *intentional,* as when a scribe felt something was missing, or—worse—felt the theology of a particular text needed improvement (as possibly in the example from Rom 8:1, mentioned above). Often, apparently, a scribe who encountered a marginal note in the exemplar faced a dilemma. Did an earlier copyist accidentally omit this bit of text, or was it merely a helpful interpretive remark? To play it safe, the puzzled scribe might incorporate the marginal note into the body of his new copy. This is what may lie behind the note in John 5:4 (KJV) about the angel who troubled the water of the pool of Bethesda. To cope with these and similar possibilities, textual critics tend to prefer the *more difficult readings* (reasoning that scribes would wish to make things easier, not harder, to read) and *the shorter readings* (reasoning that scribes would be more likely to add text than to omit it). These are examples of weighing transcriptional probability.

Intrinsic probability has to do with how well a given variant reading fits the context and the author's (or genre's) overall vocabulary, style and literary tendencies. A variant for a textual problem in Romans, for example, may resemble the sort of thing Paul frequently says elsewhere, while another variant may be foreign to Paul's usage elsewhere. This would appear to support the probability that the first variant is original. Obviously though, a scribe finding

WHERE DID SHE GO?

One of the more familiar Gospel stories relates the encounter Jesus has with a woman caught in adultery and her accusers (Jn 7:53—8:11). The image of Jesus writing something in the dirt with his finger has intrigued us for centuries, and "casting the first stone" has become proverbial. Yet most modern translations of the New Testament omit this story from John; if they keep it, they place it within brackets to show that it probably should not be there. Consider why:

- Early and widespread manuscript tradition does not include the story.

- Not all manuscripts that do include the story have it in the "usual" location. It also shows up variously at John 7:36; 21:24; Luke 21:38; 24:53.

- Many manuscripts and ancient commentators express doubt about the story through comments and by tagging it with asterisks or other marks.

- It displays considerable stylistic difference from John's usual way of expressing himself.

- If we leave it out, John's account runs smoothly from 7:52 to 8:12. In fact, the story does not quite fit the context at 7:52.

Considerations like these make it highly probable that the story, which may very well preserve a genuine incident from Jesus' life, did not originally belong in John's Gospel.

something "odd" in his exemplar of Romans might wish to smooth it over so that it reads more like the rest of Paul's letters. Thus intrinsic probability as a criterion for originality *can sometimes actually end up in conflict* with the "transcriptional" rule that the more difficult reading is preferable to the easier one!

2.2.3 Textual Problems and Exegetical Significance

Most discussions of the science of New Testament textual criticism focus on the broader question of reconstructing the entire text of the New Testament, regardless of the importance of the variants in other respects. This is indeed a crucial service to the church. However, not every textual problem has *exegetical* significance, and for pastoral exegesis—as opposed to the work done by a professional textual critic—this is an important point. It helps keep the pastoral-exegetical task reasonably manageable.

We have already seen that UBS[4] cites only the textual problems having significance for Bible translation. This by itself tips us off to the fact that in pastoral exegesis it will not be necessary to tackle and solve the problems raised by every single variant we find at the bottom of a page in a Greek New Testament. *Only those problems that have a bearing on the meaning and interpretation of the text need our attention.* But how do we decide which of the many textual problems are important enough to deal with? We face this question even if we use the more selective UBS[4]; not every variant making a difference in *translation* (the focus of the UBS apparatus) will also make an *exegetical* difference. (However, the reverse will likely be true: an exegetically significant variant will also have translational significance.) We will see some examples in a moment.

For the purposes of pastoral exegesis, there are *three main categories* of textual problems. We can visualize this graphically with the diagram in figure 2.5. The diagram sorts variant readings both for exegetical significance (or not) and for sufficient (or insufficient) textual support.

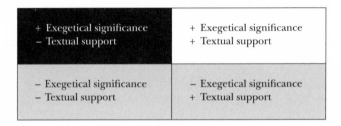

+ Exegetical significance − Textual support	+ Exegetical significance + Textual support
− Exegetical significance − Textual support	− Exegetical significance + Textual support

Figure 2.5. Exegetical significance of textual problems

Textual problems for which the variant readings make no exegetical difference in the text's meaning. In most cases, for exegetical purposes, it does not matter whether we, the exegetes, solve the textual problem, since the various alternative readings for those cases would make little or no exegetically significant difference if substituted for the preferred reading (see the lower tier of the diagram). Referring to NA[27], note the instances of inverted wording represented by the variant readings for 1 John 1:5a (ἔστιν αὕτη vs. αὕτη ἔστιν, both of which mean "this is"), 5c, 8b and 10b. Textual problems like these are most likely negligible for "pastoral" purposes. So is the problem at 1 John 1:9a, where some witnesses unnecessarily insert the possessive pronoun ἡμῶν "our," apparently to clarify that the sins of which we are forgiven are our own. Similar, perhaps, are the problems at John 9:35 and 37, where manuscripts sometimes insert and sometimes omit the definite article "the" before the name Jesus. Other negligible problems with variants involve spelling discrepancies.

Conceivably, spelling variations may have *historical* significance, and if linguists develop a sound theory of the use of the article and the role of word order in Greek discourse, some of these exegetically "negligible" variants may become more important. For now, however, we may pass them by without comment, even in an exegesis paper, and even if they have strong textual support.

Some variant readings making little or no *exegetical* difference in a given textual problem could nevertheless require a different *translation*. For example, the NA^{27} text of 1 John 1:7c can be translated as "of Jesus his son"; the three alternative variants require different *translations:* "of his son," "of Jesus Christ his son," and "of Jesus Christ." Though the translations differ, there is probably little exegetical difference among the options; we can safely ignore the problem for our purposes, unless we sense there is some special contextual significance in omitting reference to sonship or to Christ. The issue might reflect conflict with fledgling gnostic opinions that Jesus the earthly man and Christ the heavenly man are not the same person, and that God the Father relates to Jesus and to Christ—separately!

Textual problems whose alternate readings do imply an exegetical difference in the text's meaning but which have weak support. Textual variants which do make a *significant exegetical difference* (top tier of diagram) can be divided between those which have little to hardly any evidential support (top left), and those which have stronger claims to being the original reading (top right). A likely example of a weakly supported but exegetically significant alternate reading is the famous one at 1 John 5:7-8. Metzger tells the story[4] that around the year 1520, a zealous defender of the Latin Vulgate apparently manufactured to specifications a Greek manuscript supporting the Vulgate's reference at 1 John 5:7-8 to Father, Word and Holy Spirit (see the reading in the KJV). Confronted with this manuscript, and against his better judgment (but true to his promise), Erasmus of Rotterdam included the bogus Greek text in the third edition of his Greek New Testament (1522). Yet there is no clear evidence for the existence of this text *in Greek* dating from earlier than about 1520. Thus, even though the explicitly Trinitarian character of this reading has tremendous exegetical significance, the absence of support for the text in the ancient tradition makes it negligible here. As an unlikely "suspect," however fascinating, it needs no attention in an exegesis paper. It boasts a virtually ironclad alibi!

Textual problems with more than one well-supported and exegetically significant variant reading. Witnesses for the Greek text of 1 John 1:4c read either "that *our*

---

[4]Metzger and Ehrman, *Text of the New Testament*, pp. 146-47.

TRY IT OUT

Consulting your Greek testament, classify each of the following four textual problems, cited from NA[27] for Phil 3:12-13, into one of the three main categories listed above. In the pursuit of pastoral exegesis, which of them would deserve your further attention?

12a   Insert *or am already justified* (ἢ ἤδη δεδικαίωμαι) in front of *or have already reached the goal* (ἢ ἤδη τετελείωμαι).

12b   Omit *and/even* (καί) before *to make it my own.*
[Note: NRSV already does not reflect the presence of καί.]

12c   Read *Christ* instead of *Christ Jesus.*

13   Read *not yet* (οὔπω) instead of *not* (οὐ).

Check out your results below.

Comments:

NA[27] gives only a "negative apparatus" for the alternative reading in 12a, implying that the evidence in support of it is weak (see the NA[27] introduction, p. 50*). The exegetical implication would be considerable, however. We can classify this variant in the upper left quadrant of the diagram: interesting but not well supported. All three of the other alternative readings in vv. 12-13 boast "positive apparatuses"; textual support for them is stronger than that for 12a. In fact, the small superscript cross in the apparatus for v. 13 means that former editions of NA preferred this reading. The question then is whether any of these three makes enough exegetical difference to merit our attention. Certainly 13 might, but 12b and 12c may not. Individual judgment is called for. This puts 13 in the upper right quadrant (interesting and well supported) and the other two—possibly—in the lower right (well supported but not very interesting). In other words, only 13 would need to come up in an exegetical paper.

(ἡμῶν) joy may be full" or "that *your* (ὑμῶν) joy may be full." The exegetical difference between these two alternatives may not blow shingles off the roof, but there is indeed a difference. It involves the author's attitude: is he (or she?) adopting a slightly patronizing tone ("your joy"), an embracing tone ("our joy" [yours and ours]), or perhaps even a slightly exclusive tone ("our joy" [but not yours])? We could safely ignore the issue if one of these variant readings were poorly attested in the tradition, but the witnesses to them are fairly evenly balanced. If it truly matters to us what the author actually meant to say to his readers, we will have to make a decision, however tentative, between the two options, and take the consequences. This, too, is part of the exegetical task.

Textual problems which are otherwise negligible, but important for other reasons. We can discern on another level a fourth group of textual problems. Some weakly supported readings may be important simply because of their remarkable *history* (the trinitarian text in 1 Jn 5:7-8 is an example) or because they *cast light* on exegetically important issues. As an instance of the latter type, consider 1 John 2:20. The KJV for this passage reads, "But ye have an unction from the Holy One, *and ye know all things* (πάντα)." Modern translations render the passage differently; here is the NRSV: "But you have been anointed by the Holy One, *and all of you* (πάντες) *have knowledge*." The italicized portions of these two translations reflect optional Greek readings. There is little doubt that the text underlying the NRSV is more likely to be the original one (there is *some* doubt, nonetheless). Yet, the contrast between these two variants emphasizes the *gnosticizing* nature of the problem the author was dealing with. By saying, "you *all* have knowledge," he assures his readers that they need not feel inferior to those who claim to have special spiritual knowledge unavailable to less privileged believers. The poorly attested alternative reading misses this nuance. Noticing *that* helps *us* to catch the nuance!

2.2.4 Putting It All Together

The point to take home from all of this is that none of the many and complex considerations outlined here stands on its own. Solving a textual problem is a little like untying a complicated knot: carefully we trace this strand and that one, pulling first one free, then another. In this way, textual scholars gradually work backward through the stages of a textual problem's development, using as appropriate the various criteria summarized here. Each textual problem must be evaluated independently. For one problem, the issues may require that more weight be given to the evidence of intrinsic probability; for another problem, more weight will have to be given to, say, the testimony of the papyri. Occasionally several textual problems will be related to each other. Still, in the end, there is never a simple, formulaic solution for any of these "mysteries."

The role of a professional textual critic is to devote her career to solving New Testament textual problems and to refining the process for doing so. The text-critical role of a practitioner of "pastoral exegesis" is to have a working understanding of how professional critics go about the work of editing the New Testament Greek text. These are not the same roles! So I say again, *do not be afraid!* Do not be intimidated. The textual apparatus in our Greek Bibles is there for our use, but even so, many of us will remain mostly dependent on the wisdom of experts, as we are in all things. We must do our very best with what we have and otherwise be at peace.

2.3 THE TOOLS FOR THE JOB

Now that we have had a look at the state of the New Testament lawn, we can lay out a few of the more useful tools for mowing it, that is, for doing New Testament exegesis. Many of them will reappear in the following chapters, since their use is especially appropriate to various other tasks down the line.

Besides NA[27] and UBS[4] and their textual apparatuses, other tools useful in establishing the text of the New Testament include Bruce M. Metzger's *A Textual Commentary on the Greek New Testament.*[5] (This is a different book from his full-length introduction, *The Text of the New Testament,* already mentioned.) The introduction to *A Textual Commentary* (instructions for its use!) provides a concise and helpful orientation to the process of textual criticism (including a short classification of witnesses by text-type),[6] and the body of the commentary explains the decisions made by the UBS[4] editorial committee. For getting an over-the-shoulder look at the practice of this science/art, there is hardly a better experience than studying a number of the commentary's entries. Some of them, in fact, are rather entertaining.

Concordances. Because the Bible of the New Testament authors (and of the early church) was what we today call the Old Testament—in fact very often the Greek version of it, known as the Septuagint (LXX)—access to a copy of the LXX is extremely important for understanding many New Testament texts.[7] (Less often, the *Hebrew* Old Testament stands directly behind a New Testament passage.) Frequently a New Testament writer alludes to an Old Testament text without bothering to provide an explicit reference (as explicit as a New Testament reference to the Old Testament can be, anyway). We'll see some examples in later chapters. In cases such as these, a *concordance to the LXX*[8] can be indispensable for locating the source of an allusion, which in turn can illuminate an entire New Testament argument. We will see examples of this in later chapters.

---

[5]Bruce M. Metzger, *A Textual Commentary on the Greek New Testament,* 2nd ed. (Stuttgart: Deutsche Bibelgesellschaft, 1994).

[6]A somewhat fuller list of witnesses by text type appears in David Alan Black's useful booklet, *New Testament Textual Criticism: A Concise Guide* (Grand Rapids: Baker, 1994); see pp. 63-65.

[7]The standard edition is A. Rahlfs, ed., *Septuaginta: Id est Vetus Testamentum graece iuxta LXX interpretes,* 2 vols. (Stuttgart: Württembergische Bibelanstalt, 1935).

[8]The longtime standard printed version is E. Hatch and H. A. Redpath, *A Concordance to the Septuagint and the Other Greek Versions of the Old Testament (Including the Apocryphal Books),* 3 vols. in 2 (Grand Rapids: Baker, 1983; original: Oxford, 1897).

Concordances to the New Testament[9] provide the means of locating repeated patterns of speech, word usage, grammatical phenomena, correlated ideas and so on. They are available for the Greek New Testament as well as for various translations. Some of the latter type have links to the Greek (and Hebrew) Bibles. Since the advent of the personal computer, several software programs have appeared which function as biblical concordances; good ones are capable of highly complex searches of the entire Greek New Testament and LXX, as well as of the Hebrew Old Testament, numerous Bible versions, Josephus, Qumran literature, apostolic fathers and various other relevant material. If you can afford one of these, they are well worth the investment. The one offered by the Gramcord Institute (www.gramcord.com) is excellent in its Macintosh version, but there are others equally powerful, especially in the PC environment. Two in particular are BibleWorks and Logos (www.bibleworks.com and www.logos.com).

In fact, the evolving truth of the matter is that digitally based resources like these are fast becoming the tools of choice in this field. Not only biblical, and biblically related, texts (even with textual apparatus), but also entire dictionaries, encyclopedias, lexica, commentaries, language tutorials and much more are available in this lightning-fast format. Internet websites offer an astounding array of access to texts and information relevant to the subject, often free of charge to the user. I do not wish to believe that the age of the printed page, the multi-millennial era of the "book," is winding down; but certainly it is no longer necessary to juggle, shuffle and riffle through heavy tomes in order to obtain the information we want from them. Much of it is a mere set of keystrokes away, literally at our fingertips. The challenge in this is keeping up with what is continually coming out for our consumption. A good way to monitor it all, if that's what we want to do, is to visit regularly websites like the ones I listed above. They are not the only ones, either.

Meanwhile, back on the printed page, one exceptionally useful feature of NA^{27} and (to a lesser degree) of UBS^4 is the marginal reference system. (In UBS^4 it appears at the bottom of the page, the third of three sets of footnote material.) Properly used (read the introduction!), this set of cross-references provides extraordinarily helpful suggestions for making comparisons both intertextually (across texts) and intratextually (within texts). Some of these ref-

---

[9]H. Bachmann and H. Slaby, eds., *Computer-Konkordanz zum Novum Testamentum Graece von Nestle-Aland, 26. Auflage, und zum Greek New Testament*, 3rd ed. (Berlin: Walter de Gruyter, 1980). The old standby was W. F. Moulton and A. S. Geden, *A Concordance to the Greek New Testament According to the Texts of Westcott and Hort, Tischendorf and the English Revisers*, 5th rev. ed. (Edinburgh: T & T Clark, 2002).

erences focus on quotations and allusions, others on parallels in the use of vocabulary or even entire stories (especially in the Gospels). Still others trace
concepts treated elsewhere in the New Testament and beyond. If you already
own UBS[4], you might consider finding a copy of a recent edition of NA just for
the marginal references; they are worth the price of the book.

Dictionaries, encyclopedias and atlases. An absolute necessity for exegesis in
the Greek New Testament is a reliable *Greek-English lexicon.* Two in particular
are recommended: (a) the so-called Bauer (or BDAG[10]) and (b) the Louw-
Nida domain dictionary.[11] BDAG (published in 2000 and a significant improvement on its earlier editions, BAG [1957] and BAGD [1979]) covers the
vocabulary of the Greek New Testament and of the second-century apostolic
fathers. It is the absolute standard in New Testament lexicons and a *sine qua
non* for responsible exegesis. The Louw-Nida domain dictionary is primarily
intended for use by translators, alongside the UBS[4] text. Its chief distinction
and appeal is that it organizes the New Testament Greek vocabulary into semantic "domains," or fields, thereby listing in one place all the words pertinent to, say, the domain of "knowledge" or of "work." We will discuss these
tools in more detail later on.

For quick orientation to both highly specific and very general subjects in
New Testament study, a good *Bible dictionary* or encyclopedia is the way to go.
The New Testament (not to mention the Old Testament!) arose in a context
wholly unfamiliar to us. It was familiar to the authors and their first audiences,
however, and consequently they did not need explanations at every turn.
Reading Matthew 22:16, we might wonder who the Herodians were. It did not
occur to Matthew to explain, since his first audience likely knew. A check of
any good dictionary of the Bible will reveal what we have learned about these
people from sources other than Matthew (or Mark, where they are also mentioned). Book-sized introductions to the New Testament or to its theology (or
theolog*ies*) provide similar information, often arranged in a document-by-
document format. The extent today of easily accessible information of this
kind available through these tools (at least in North America and Europe) is
truly astounding. Dictionaries and encyclopedias range widely in scope and
depth. With access to everything from small handbooks on the entire Bible, to
hefty volumes devoted to selected Scripture portions or subject areas (Gospels,

---

[10]W. Bauer, *A Greek-English Lexicon of the New Testament and Other Early Christian Literature,* ed.
F. W. Danker, 3rd ed. (Chicago: University of Chicago Press, 2000). The initials "A" and "G"
in the abbreviation refer to earlier editors W. F. Arndt and F. W. Gingrich.

[11]J. Louw and E. A. Nida, eds., *Greek-English Lexicon of the New Testament Based on Semantic Domains,* 2 vols., 2nd ed. (New York: American Bible Society, 1989).

Paul, Pentateuch, New Testament backgrounds), and to massive multi-volume works, modern exegetes have never had it so good. Do yourself and your people an exegetical favor: invest in a good Bible dictionary. Two superb options are the InterVarsity Press series[12] and the *Anchor Bible Dictionary.*[13]

Likewise useful for exegesis is a *Bible atlas.* Most editions of the Bible, including NA[27] and UBS[4], provide a selection of maps relevant to biblical literature. A full-blown Bible atlas, however, provides a wealth of geographical, and sometimes archeological, data that can vastly illuminate the background circumstances of a New Testament document.[14] Why, for instance, does Jesus end up in Samaria in his journey back to Galilee in John 4? How does the geography of the Feeding of the Four Thousand (Mk 8:1-10) illuminate the meaning of the event in relation to the Feeding of the Five Thousand (Mk 6:32-44)? In this way, Bible atlases too provide access to part of the cultural understanding shared by biblical authors and their first readers.

Gospel synopses. As early as the second century, Christian readers were interested in the way the four Gospels interrelate with one other. Around A.D. 170, Syrian apologist Tatian compiled his famous *Diatessaron,* in which he harmonized all four Gospels into one. Today we make use of a Gospel synopsis as a tool for appreciating both the interrelationships among the four Gospels *and the separate, unharmonized integrity* of each one. A synopsis lays the text of each of the Gospels side by side in order to aid the reader in comparing them with each other. Making these comparisons is essential to understanding the particular message of each Gospel, as well as the way their authors may have compiled them.

Primary literature: Writings of the ancients. *Primary* literature is the material produced in closest association with whatever historical period or body of literature we may be studying. The corresponding *secondary* literature is the ma-

---

[12]There are four in the series for the New Testament: Joel B. Green et al., eds., *Dictionary of Jesus and the Gospels* (Downers Grove, Ill.: InterVarsity Press, 1992); Gerald F. Hawthorne et al., eds., *Dictionary of Paul and His Letters* (Downers Grove, Ill.: InterVarsity Press, 1993); Ralph P. Martin and Peter H. Davids, eds., *Dictionary of the Later New Testament and Its Developments* (Downers Grove, Ill.: InterVarsity Press, 1997); Craig A. Evans and Stanley E. Porter, eds., *Dictionary of New Testament Background* (Downers Grove, Ill.: InterVarsity Press, 2000). A fifth volume, selecting salient articles from the first three, is edited by Daniel G. Reid and titled *The IVP Dictionary of the New Testament: A One-Volume Compendium of Contemporary Biblical Scholarship* (Downers Grove, Ill.: InterVarsity Press, 2004). A similar series for the Old Testament is in the process of coming out.

[13] D. N. Freedman, ed., *Anchor Bible Dictionary,* 6 vols. (New York: Doubleday, 1992). This tool covers the entire Bible.

[14] E.g., H. G. May, ed., with assistance of G. N. S. Hunt and in consultation with R. W. Hamilton, *Oxford Bible Atlas,* 3rd ed. (New York: Oxford University Press, 1984).

terial written—usually much later—*about* that earlier period or material. If we are studying a passage of the New Testament, for example, the primary literature par excellence is the New Testament itself. Secondary literature on the subject is anything more or less contemporary to us, written *about* the New Testament and its world, as for example, the many commentaries and monographs written by Rudolf Bultmann. If we were to write a book about Bultmann's own life and career, however, rather than about the New Testament, his commentaries and monographs would now become our primary literature. Likewise, other scholars from Bultmann's day, especially those who interacted with him during his lifetime, would provide us in the form of their own writings further primary literature for the subject of his life. The same is true for the study of the New Testament: the ancient world has handed down to us a vast treasury of literature and other written material directly or indirectly relevant to the life and times of Jesus and his first followers. These many documents, like the New Testament, provide us additional primary sources for New Testament exegesis.

There is so much primary material available for the illumination of the New Testament documents that no one except the most dedicated scholars can master it all. Dictionary articles can help us here, of course, as can extensive secondary treatments by people like Craig Evans[15] or N. T. Wright.[16] However, for getting a hands-on feel for the first-century Mediterranean world there is scarcely anything more effective or, once we are "into" it, more fun than immersing ourselves in selected ancient non-biblical literature.

This material divides itself roughly into Jewish and non-Jewish categories, which is not to say there is no overlap or interrelationship between them. *Jewish literature* of the period[17] ranges from well before the birth of Jesus to well into the centuries following. The LXX, of course, including what we sometimes call the Old Testament Apocrypha (also called the deuterocanonical books), is extremely important in this category. The same is true of the Dead Sea Scrolls, the so-called Old Testament pseudepigrapha, the works of Josephus

---

[15]Craig A. Evans, *Noncanonical Writings and New Testament Interpretation* (Peabody, Mass.: Hendrickson, 1992).

[16]E.g., the first installment of Wright's massive, multivolume project on Christian origins and the question of God: *The New Testament and the People of God* (Minneapolis: Fortress, 1992). Two other volumes have since appeared: *Jesus and the Victory of God* (Minneapolis: Fortress, 1996) and *The Resurrection of the Son of God* (Minneapolis: Fortress, 2003). All three of these books make creative use of the primary literature of the second-temple period.

[17]A helpful map through this material is Larry R. Helyer's *Exploring Jewish Literature of the Second Temple Period: A Guide for New Testament Students* (Downers Grove, Ill.: InterVarsity Press, 2002).

and Philo (both of whom are examples of the overlap of the categories), and later rabbinic literature (Mishnah and Talmud). *Non-Jewish sources* include Greek and Roman historians (Tacitus, Suetonius, the two Plinys, as examples), philosophers (especially those from the Hellenistic period, such as Epictetus), cultic literature (Gnostic and Hermetic writings, and ancient discussions of mystery religions), as well as inscriptions and papyrus remains (including homey letters and documents from everyday life in Hellenistic Egypt). C. K. Barrett's *The New Testament Background* provides an excellent introduction to this wealth of material.[18] Craig Evans's *Noncanonical Writings and New Testament Interpretation* is a very useful book for becoming oriented to the whole range of the literature. An excellent place to begin reading in this material is the Old Testament Apocrypha, perhaps with the colorful stories of Judith, Susannah and Tobit, or with the exciting accounts of 1 and 2 Maccabees.

Again, the point is not that we master this literature (as if we could in the midst of ordinary life). Rather, the point is to be aware of its usefulness and its availability, and, as far as is practical, to be always reading in it. What we want is an ever-expanding sense of life among the ancients. We want an increased ability to hear the New Testament as its first readers heard it, to enlarge our understanding of their shared presuppositions about life. Reading in this literature is a bit like listening to tape recordings of their very voices, like watching an early newsreel of Kaiser Wilhelm strutting around in his plumed helmet and enormous moustache.

Secondary literature: Commentaries, journals and monographs. The bulk of *secondary literature* for New Testament study includes *commentaries, academic journals* and *monographs* (dictionary articles fall into this category, too). *Commentaries* come in various lengths and with varying ranges and purposes. Some are one-volume popular treatments of the entire Bible. Others cover individual books of Scripture, or even portions of them. Some serve a specialized purpose, such as helping preachers to prepare sermons, or explaining how the male-dominant literature of the New Testament sounds from a feminist perspective. Still others attempt to account for all current scholarly opinion on every aspect of the text, while others take a devotional line. In all cases, commentaries seek to illuminate the biblical text for the contemporary reader. *Journals*, too, range in purpose and scope, though most serve as a forum for scholarly discussion. Articles appearing in journals tend to represent "the latest think-

---

[18]C. K. Barrett, ed., *The New Testament Background: Writings from Ancient Greece and the Roman Empire That Illumine Christian Origins*, rev. ed. (New York: HarperSanFrancisco, 1987). The book is full of colorful excerpts.

ing" on a particular problem of biblical research; as such, they vary widely in plausibility and usefulness. Of course, the less recent a particular issue of a journal, the less likely an article in it will still represent the *latest* thinking! Journal articles by a particular scholar often represent stages in the development of a book, or monograph, by that scholar. *Monographs* represent extensive treatments of a particular subject, widely or narrowly defined. In the preparation of a sermon, you may not have time for reading an entire monograph on the subject of your text. Nevertheless, you might have time for a chapter. On the other hand, if you are pursuing a series on Galatians over a period of several months, you might consider reading a recent book on Paul and the law as part of your long-range preparation.

In the coming chapters we will return to these various tools in order to elaborate their usefulness in specific stages of the overall process of exegesis. For now, however, we will turn to the relation of the whole to its parts and the effect that dynamic has on a text's meaning.

3

TEXTS AND
THEIR STRUCTURE
Walls of Stones

For just as the body is one and has many members,
and all the members of the body, though many,
are one body, so it is with Christ.
1 CORINTHIANS 12:12

We saw in chapter one that, in a sense, the *text is all we have*. For this reason, understanding language structure and semantic structure, which give texts their communicative power, is an essential part of interpretive method. For our purposes, this issue takes two main forms. (1) It involves understanding how authors *synthesize, build up* or *construct* texts, that is, how they link smaller elements to one another to form larger units, and how they join those larger units together to form even larger units. (2) It also involves understanding how to *take a text apart*, how to *analyze* it into its constituent pieces, moving from the larger units to the smaller ones of which they are made. Even a modest grasp of this dynamic will enhance our skill in interpreting *anything* based in language. This chapter looks at biblical texts from these two perspectives of *synthesis* and *analysis*.

3.1 SYNTHESIS: STRUCTURE AND THE WHOLE
3.1.1 Coherence: Holding It Together
Before plunging into the subject of texts and their synthesis, we need to be clear about the notion of "coherence," since it plays an important part in the following discussion. If *Cold Case* detective Lily Rush says that the suspect's story lacks coherence, she means that some parts of it do not fit well with the

other parts. In court, non-coherence gives sufficient reason for discrediting a witness. If pieces of a broken vase do not cohere well, either we used the wrong glue or we were not careful enough about lining up the edges. Similarly, a text coheres if all its parts fit together, interlocking in one way or another to form a solid whole. Well-formed texts coordinate all their parts in order to convey a single, unified message. Coherence holds the parts together, and the result is a "coherent" message.

Texts employ an entire array of linguistic apparatus for forging coherence. Many of these devices come up for mention in this chapter, tools such as repetitions and other patterns, common vocabulary or subject matter, pronouns, verb tenses, logical connections, implied assumptions from (and links to) surrounding context and so on. The point to take with us into the following discussion is that coherence in texts is *recognizable;* we could analyze it, if we wished. We may seldom think about it, however, unless we encounter an incoherent text, and even then we may not take the effort to identify the source of the incoherence. It's easier to roll our eyes and walk away. For now, however, keep it in mind and think about stones.

3.1.2 Structured Texts and Stone Walls

In fact, visualize a stone wall. From a distance, the wall looks formidable, a solid barrier, a monolithic mass. Up close, we see that it is not just a stone wall; it is also a wall of stones, stones of various sizes, shapes and composition. The individual stones adhere together, perhaps with mortar, to form a single wall, but we can still see where one stone ends and its neighbor begins. The mortar not only holds the stones together but also marks the boundaries between them. Figure 3.1 illustrates a *brick* structure (the village church in Sloten, the Netherlands); bricks

Figure 3.1. Village church, Sloten, The Netherlands

are not as irregular as stones can be, but they operate in the same way.

If we move in close and chip away at one of the stones, we see that it is made up of smaller particles or maybe layers of sediment, which themselves have been cemented together in a particular pattern to form that single stone. We can even pick out various bits of mica or feldspar, all held together by some other substance just like the mortar that, *on another level,* holds the wall together, making it *cohere.* If we step back, we can see that the wall consists of large sections, each section made up of a *cluster* of stones in a particular pattern. These sections (north extension, gateway, south extension) adhere together with the help of steel tie rods and other internal strengthening and connecting devices. These devices keep the wall's various sections functioning together as one *coherent* unit and prevent the wall from toppling into discrete parts. The various patterns that organize the stones or bricks—herringbone, for example—give the wall its individual character. So does the wall's location, something we will return to a little later when we take up the topic of context.

Texts are no different from walls in this regard. Texts are "built up" from discrete parts put together in particular patterns to convey a particular message. These parts are synthesized into a single text through various grammatical and discursive means, such as conjunctions, pronouns, repetitions, themes, changes in cast or scene, and so on. Part of the task of exegesis—a very fundamental and important part—is to discern these discrete pieces and the patterns that arrange them into the form of a text. For *these coherent patterns* reveal a significant portion of the text's message. Likewise, the patterned texts themselves function within larger arrays, combining with other texts to build up an even larger stretch of patterned text, precisely as stones in a wall.

3.1.3 Assembling the Building Blocks of Texts

The most elementary level of complexity for the units constituting a printed biblical text is (for our purposes) that of individual alphabetic *letters.* In the stone wall analogy, the letters of a text might correspond to the grains of conglomerate material that form individual stones. In printed texts, letters adhere together to form a "stone in the wall" by standing immediately next to each other, without spaces between them (just like the ones you are looking at right now). These clustered groups of letters form the *next level* of complexity in units constituting a text. Units of this next level we call *words.*

This is true for all texts we deal with in biblical interpretation. Like stones in a wall, words (formed by clustered letters) cluster together themselves on yet a higher level to form *phrases* and *clauses.* Phrases (and/or clauses), then, though distinct from one another, combine at an even higher level to form *sen-*

tences. From there, sentences cluster to form *paragraphs*, and paragraphs cluster to form *sections*, and so on up to an *entire discourse.* This ability of language to reapply the same clustering rules on any level—from letters upward to paragraphs and beyond—is its *recursive power.* It allows meaningful, synthetic clustering to "recur," again and again, all the way up the ladder.

Besides its recursive powers, language also employs a kind of *reciprocity* in constructing texts. Like mortar in a stone wall, the techniques that languages use to mark the *divisions* between units of text, on any level, also serve to *connect those units to each other,* in order to hold the text together. These techniques (including modern punctuation) indicate both the location and the nature of these divisions and connections. They define the relationship between the units they divide, showing how they cohere to form a larger text. A comma can separate one clause from another, but in certain contexts that same comma indicates that the second clause actually restates the first one in different words. In a text, then, the very presence of one unit—the word *gray,* for example—determines in part the limits of another unit standing next to it—*skies,* perhaps. At the same time, however, it cooperates with that other unit in performing a larger task. The same is true about the word *skies* as has just been said about *gray.* The two words *gray* and *skies* serve to define each other reciprocally and then join cooperatively to say something larger than either of them could do alone. Each makes up a part of the *context* of the other—at least in this example (not everywhere, of course). We will come back to this idea in a moment.

3.1.4 Texts Function as Coherent Wholes, Like Communities

In the way it is built up, a text is like a stone wall. In the way it *functions,* the way its parts work together to express a coherent message, *a text is like a community.* A community is a group of people (or ants, bees, orcs, etc.) functioning as a single unit, as in "our church community worships together every Sunday evening." However, unless we can recognize the individuals making up a community, we cannot recognize the community itself *as a community.* Only by distinguishing among the individuals and groups within a community can we begin to define their mutual relationships, and these interrelationships are what give the community its shape and character as a community. We can apply this same principle up and down the scale of complexity within the idea of community. We can talk about the subcommunities in a church, for instance: Sunday school classes, families, small groups or committees. We can move further down the scale and analyze the physical body of an individual member: heart, lungs, skin and bones. We can move up the scale, too, analyzing whole denominations in terms of their constituent local churches and so on.

The same principle holds for communicative discourse. *A text is like a community.* We grasp the overall meaning of a discourse, its message, only if we can distinguish—consciously or unconsciously—its constituent parts and their interrelationships, that is, their *functions.* We might think that lines of delimitation destroy wholeness and unity, but without delimitation, we cannot define or grasp the nature of the wholeness. This unity, this *internal coherence* of a discourse, is what ordinarily carries its message. Coherent, interconnected wholeness also constitutes part of the *context* within which the individual constituent pieces of the whole have their various functions with respect to each other in producing the message. It can make a significant difference in the message of a discourse if we misinterpret or alter the function of a given part of the discourse. Try this example:

Flapping and fluttering birds made a mess of the kitchen.

Is this a description of how or of what sort? Who, in fact, flaps and flutters? Misconstruing the function of *flapping and fluttering* can make a significant difference. Does the sentence—as a whole—describe an invasion of sparrows, and were all of them responsible for the mess? Or does the sentence refer to the behavior of a deranged cook? We cannot begin to analyze this message and solve the puzzle until we identify the boundaries and functions of units within this statement. Additional punctuation would help a great deal in this, but so would a conjunction or two.

In terms of this community metaphor, the "community" at the top of the complexity scale for biblical exegesis, of course, is the entire Bible (however defined, and of course within its own larger literary and historical context). The Bible itself, with its parts and subparts, functions like a community. In preparing a sermon or a Bible discussion, or in personal study of the Word of God, we need to view any coherent scriptural passage as much as possible in terms of its function within the larger context of the biblical message as a whole. Naturally, by that larger context I mean our *current understanding* of the message of the whole Bible, something that undergoes constant refinement as we continually read and reread individual portions of the Scripture with new insight. How we *already* understand the Bible will determine in part how we understand Romans, for instance, or Ecclesiastes. Reciprocally, our study of Romans or Ecclesiastes may well *alter* our previous understanding of the Bible. But how do we study Romans? We study it piece by piece. We break up the letter into sections and subsections and *analyze* them one by one, gradually hearing them all within the larger context of the book and of the Bible as a whole. This is true whether we analyze each piece in careful exegetical style or we are simply reading through the book (or Bible) start to finish. It is a linear experience, but one that builds—and unceasingly rebuilds—a global perspective.

3.2 ANALYSIS: STRUCTURE AND THE PARTS

A coherent segment of the greater whole of a book like Romans is a *pericope*. (The word is pronounced *per-ICK-o-pee;* it does not rhyme with *periscope*, though your computer's spell-checker may replace it with *periscope* if you let it.) While the term *pericope* applies to any coherent portion of a book, whether large or small, the word normally refers to a paragraph or a small group of paragraphs, such as a passage for preaching. For responsible exegesis, the crucial thing about pericopes is the proper, fair and text-sensitive *identification of their boundaries,* their delimitations, both the external and the internal delineations. Where does a particular pericope legitimately begin and end? How is it internally structured, and how does it hang together as a coherent unit?

Saying there is a "proper, fair and text-sensitive" way to identify the outer boundaries and inner structure of a given pericope does not mean that there is only *one* proper, fair and text-sensitive way to do it. Sometimes these delimitations will be obvious: what could be more obvious than Matthew 1:1 as the beginning of a pericope? Much of the time, however, they will be open for discussion. We are dealing with an art, not a predictable chemical reaction. Practicing this art involves the issue of *context.*

3.2.1 Context and Meaning

A text's "context" partially determines its shape and function, *and* its meaning. *Context profoundly influences the meaning of anything.* The same "form" will change its meaning with every change in the context in which it occurs—at least in theory. Walking around the living room at night in your pajamas means one thing; walking around in your pajamas at noon, downtown, at the office, means something else. (This has less troubling implications for people who work at home.) The difference is *context.* The difference is *location.*

Any word or portion of a word, any phrase, clause, sentence, paragraph, section, chapter or main part of a literary work will have its meaning—*and* its shape—partially determined by its place within the *macrostructure* of the whole work. What larger unit does it belong to? What units of its own level follow and precede it, and how does it cooperate with them in developing the larger unit? How does the overall, unified message of the whole "book" determine just what role, and thus what meaning, this smaller unit has? In fact, *the meaning of the whole will help us in deciding what meaning the parts will have.* But what is the meaning of the whole? How do we learn the message of a New Testament letter if not by understanding the meaning of the smaller parts that make it up? We cannot! We need to know what the *parts* mean before we can know what the *whole* means.

In theory, then, we are stuck. We have neither the chicken nor the egg, but the family is seated at the table, waiting. This exaggerates the dilemma, of course. In reality, the task is more one of refining what we already know than one of figuring out from scratch what we have never known. It is a process of attacking text and context simultaneously, always letting the one lead to an improved grasp of the other, back and forth, back and forth. It works like a spiral: text illuminating context, context further illuminating text, and so on in an ever increasing understanding of each in terms of the other. Where do we begin, then, since we have to begin somewhere? Ordinarily, we will know the external boundaries of a "book": Philemon 1 and 25, for instance. But we need to determine the boundaries of the smaller (and still smaller) pieces of the book, before we can say what role those pieces play in the book's development. The question is how to identify the "proper" boundaries for those smaller units.

3.2.2 Marking Structure

Any good guide for writing a term paper provides instructions about organizing the paper and about what signals to use for pointing out the organization to readers (Roman numerals, Arabic numerals, indentation, headings and subheadings, bold-face and italic type, etc.). Ordinary language also provides means for *marking* various features in the organization of a text (written or not). The phrase "means for marking" refers to a system of textual signals that indicate whatever needs indicating (tense, mood, case, gender, function, relationship, etc.). Recognizing the markers commonly used for indicating the *structure* and *limits* of texts is essential for textual analysis. Consider a few of the more important markers.

The purpose of a book. Knowledge of a book's purpose and theme helps a good deal in determining the contextual boundaries for the book's smaller units. It provides us a direction in which to look. Sometimes authors are kind enough to state the purpose of the book in so many words. Examples of this appear at Luke 1:1-4 and John 20:30-31. If we are not so fortunate (which is normally the case), then we may try to determine the book's theme and purpose in a number of other ways. Here are three. (1) We can note what *commands* the author gives the readers (especially in the case of epistles), since the author will probably direct his readers along the lines of his overall intentions. (2) We can note the way in which an author *selects* and *arranges* narrated events. It is unmistakable that the Gospels intend to impress us with the resurrection of Jesus as the climax of his story, since every one of them (even Mark) places the resurrection and its aftermath at the climax of *their* stories. (3) We can also analyze the *topic or theme sentences* of the paragraphs and sections that constitute the book, since they will doubtlessly add up to its overall purpose. At least it is fair to think so.

Markers, or signals, for recognizing boundaries and seams. In typically recipro-cal fashion, these three methods for discerning a book's theme imply already recognizing the boundaries and seams between the component parts of the whole document. But how do we recognize these seams and divisions? Here is a list of signals ("markers") of textual boundaries suggested by John Beekman and John Callow.[1] It is by no means a complete list and provides only some of the more recognizable examples.

- repeated units (terms, phrases, clauses, sentences, syntactical structures)
- grammatical clues (conjunctions, changes in mood, tense, aspect)
- rhetorical questions (especially a series of them)
- changes in time, setting (scene), participants (cast)
- vocative forms (especially shifts from one person or group to another)
- changes in subject, object, topic
- announcement of a (new) theme at the head (or the end) of a para-graph or section

In combination with at least an initial sense of a book's overall purpose, rec-ognition of boundary markers like these provides solid ground on which to be-gin working out the book's message and the contribution to that message made by its individual parts.

Consulting your Greek New Testament or a translation, observe the follow-ing examples of boundary markers in their contexts. Avoid getting bogged down in this; I only want you to *see* these signals in the text, not to analyze them just now. Again, these examples are in no way exhaustive.

Repeated units.

- καὶ ἐγένετο ὅτε ἐτέλεσεν ὁ Ἰησοῦς . . ."And it happened, when Jesus had finished . . ." Matthew 7:28; 11:1; 13:53; 19:1; 26:1
- ἠκούσατε ὅτι ἐρρέθη . . . "You have heard that it was said . . ." Matthew 5:21, 27, 31, 33, 38, 43
- "I *saw* . . . there *appeared* . . . he *showed* me . . ." Revelation 12:1; 13:1, 11; 14:1, 6, 14; 15:1, etc.

It is worth noting, by the way, that the regularity in some of these patterns

---

[1] John Beekman and John Callow, *Translating the Word of God* (Grand Rapids: Zondervan, 1974), pp. 279-80.

can be lost in translation, if the translators are not fully aware of them or careful about preserving them. Of course, if they are "lost in translation," their purpose is defeated in the translation. This is another good reason to learn to read Greek.

Grammatical clues.

- Conjunctions: Romans 1:16 (γάρ "for"); 2:21 and 5:1 (οὖν "therefore"); 3:21 (νυνὶ δέ "but now"); 8:1 (ἄρα νῦν "therefore now").
- Changes in verb mood: note the shift from indicatives in Philemon 8-16 to imperatives in Philemon 17-22.

Rhetorical questions. See Romans 3:31 (end or beginning of a section?); 6:1, 15; 7:7 (Τί οὖν . . . "What then?").

Changes in setting, cast, time, etc. See Matthew 5:1; 8:1, 5, 14, 16; 17:1.

Changes in subject, object, topic. Note the shift from ice-breaker (Philem 4-7) to business at hand (Philem 8-22).

Vocative forms (direct address, like "Hey, Bob!"). See Ephesians 5:22, 25; 6:1, 4, 5, 9 (cf. Col 3:18—4:1).

Explicitly announced new theme. See 1 Corinthians 7:1, 25; 8:1; 12:1; 16:1.

Boundary markers as marks of coherence. It is important to recognize the way in which smaller units reciprocally interrelate with larger units to form coherent wholes. Boundary markers of the sort just listed, like mortar between stones in a wall, can help to hold the larger unit together even while dividing it up into its constituent smaller units. Take Matthew 5 as an example. Beginning with 5:21, Jesus repeatedly points out the difference between the tradition of the elders and his own teaching. Verses 21, 27, 31, 33, 38 and 43 open their respective "units" with the words "You have heard," or something similar, followed by the words "But I say." Observing this, we can distinguish each of these six units from its neighbor. However, *that very pattern,* the repetition of which divides one unit from another on one level, also functions at the next level to tie this entire string of units into one larger coherent whole. In fact, its coherence consists partly in that very pattern that internally divides the constituent units from one another. This larger unit is about Jesus' new approach to the law and consists of six examples. The interrelated rhetorical questions at Romans 6:1, 15 and 7:1, as well as the successive subject announcements throughout 1 Corinthians 7—16, work in exactly the same way.

Patterns of repeated items like these help to create synthesis, or unity, in texts. So do interrelated arrays of logical connectors, like conjunctions, for example. If a paragraph, coherent in itself, begins with the conjunction γάρ

SAMPLE BOUNDARY MARKERS AT WORK IN 1 JOHN

With your Greek New Testament and a translation open to the book of 1 John, work through the following partial list of boundary markers and other structural indicators culled from the book. Again, remember that there is seldom any way to avoid making your own value judgments in this process. Much of the skill in discerning literary structure comes with practice; you will have many opportunities to change your mind. God gives grace and space for this, too!

- *Stated purpose?* Note the use of the expressions ταῦτα γράφω / γράφομεν / ἔγραψα "I write / we write / I have written these things": 1 John 1:4; 2:1, [7, 8, 12, 13, 14, 21], 26; 5:13, suggesting the purpose(s) of the document.

- *Repeated "if . . . but if"* constructions: 1 John 1:6-7, 8-9; 1:10—2:2, 2:4-5, 9-11. Besides dividing 1:6-7 from 1:8-9, for instance, this sequence also suggests that 1:5—2:2 at least, and possibly 1:5—2:11, constitute a unit.

- *Repeated "tests"* ("By this we know . . ."): 1 John 2:3, 5, 18?, 29?; 3:10, 16, 19, 24; 4:2, 6, 9?, 10?, 13, 17?; 5:2. These "tests" can be analyzed in their immediate contexts to see if they give any clues to the structure of the book as a whole, as well as to its purpose.

- *The use of vocatives*
  - τεκνία / παιδία "little children": 1 John 2:1t, (12t, 14p), 18p, 28t; 3:7t, 18t; 4:4t; 5:21t
  - ἀγαπητοί "beloved": 1 John 2:7; 3:2, 21; 4:1, 7, 11
  - ἀδελφοί "brothers and sisters": 1 John 3:13
  - πατέρες / νεανίσκοι "fathers/young men": 1 John 2:13, 14

Robert Longacre bases his entire analysis of the structure of 1 John on the distribution of vocatives ("Towards an Exegesis of 1 John Based on the Discourse Analysis of the Greek Text," in *Linguistics and New Testament Interpretation: Essays on Discourse Analysis*, ed. D. A. Black et al. [Nashville: Broadman, 1992], pp. 271-86).

"for," it likely expresses a *reason* for the point made in the preceding text. If it begins with οὖν "therefore," it likely states the *conclusion* to be drawn from the preceding text. All languages appear to provide arsenals of such logical connectors, though they may not always look or work exactly as they do in Greek or English. For now, the important point is that not only do these connectors indicate where, say, a conclusion or a statement of rationale commences (and hence, where we should draw an "analytical" dividing line between units of text), but they also in fact *connect* those units of text. They provide the larger text some of its coherence, its unity, its synthesis. We will take this up further in chapter four. Other signs of coherence include concentrations of similar vocabulary, spans of verbal mood, characters in the cast of a narrative or coordinated sets of pronouns or "pro-verbs." (The English word *do* is a "pro-verb": *Who wants cheese? I do!*)

3.3 TOP-DOWN AND BOTTOM-UP: INDUCTIVE AND DEDUCTIVE DECISIONS

In the analysis of any book, even one with clear divisions and statements of purpose, it is sometimes necessary to decide for ourselves *inductively*—from the "bottom up"—the larger purpose of the book. Then from that we can *deduce*—from the "top down"—what the role (and therefore the meaning) of some smaller unit may be in carrying out that purpose. For example, from the many times in the book of Romans when Paul expresses his concern for *both* Jews *and* Gentiles (e.g., Rom 1:16), we might *induce* that the one of the main purposes of Romans is to argue the union of all humanity in Christ, both Jew and Gentile. If this is the right way to understand Romans, then we might *deduce* from it that the troublesome section covered by Romans 9—11, so often taken as a digression, actually functions as a stage in the case Paul is building for Christ-based "interracial" unity. The section serves as Paul's argument that even though the Gentiles, contrary to all expectation, now share equal privileges with the Jews in the economy of God, this does not mean that God has rejected the Jews. They remain God's people forever despite the addition of the Gentiles. On the other hand, if we assume that the *main* purpose of Romans is to argue justification by faith, then Romans 9—11 remains a puzzle and must be regarded as a digression. As a rule, if our top-down premise forces us to conclude that a significant segment of a document is a mere digression, then we should probably rethink our premise.

It is essential in exegesis to be able to *summarize in a sentence or two* the main thrust, the central burden and message of an entire book (assuming there is one!). For only then can we intelligently guess at how the parts fit into the whole. Only then can we begin to grasp what the author really wanted to say. Of course, from time to time we will need to adjust our summary statement and may do so any time we like. We should certainly do so if we come, bottom-up, to a position we think is better than our previous one.

3.4 COMING UP FOR AIR

Before we move on to consider the process of analyzing a text's structure (to analyze analysis, so to speak), we can take a moment to sum up this chapter. It provides a general orientation to the synthetic and analytic sides of understanding literary structure. It argues that just as any intelligible text is built up, synthesized, by a speaker-writer in order to convey a message, conversely, a reader-listener takes that text apart, analyzes it, in order to understand its message. The way a text is put together constitutes an essential clue to its message, its meaning. With some grasp of this perspective, we can turn next to applying it to the structure of actual sentences and discourses in the New Testament.[2]

---

[2]For further help on this extremely important and often neglected topic, I recommend the following among many others: Peter Cotterell and Max Turner, *Linguistics and Biblical Interpretation* (Downers Grove, Ill.: InterVarsity Press, 1989); Beekman and Callow, *Translating the Word of God*, chaps. 17-20; J. Beekman, J. Callow and M. Kopesec, *The Semantic Structure of Written Communication* (Dallas: SIL, 1981); and J. Louw, *Semantics of New Testament Greek* (Philadelphia: Fortress, 1982), chaps. 9-10. Much of the progress in this subject has come from the labors of Bible translators. Interesting and helpful essays on the theory of discourse analysis and on its application to specific texts are collected in J. T. Reed and S. E. Porter, eds., *Discourse Analysis and the New Testament: Approaches and Results* (Sheffield: Sheffield Academic, 1999), and in D. A. Black et al., eds., *Linguistics and New Testament Interpretation: Essays on Discourse Analysis* (Nashville: Broadman, 1992).

4

SYNTACTICAL AND DISCOURSE ANALYSIS
Some Dis-assembly Required

So they sat down in groups of hundreds and of fifties.
Taking the five loaves and the two fish, he looked up to heaven,
and blessed and broke the loaves, and gave them to his disciples to set before
the people; and he divided the two fish among them all.
And all ate and were filled.
MARK 6:40-42

If we can accept the fact that a meaningful text is meaningful in part because its author organizes it meaningfully, as chapter three attempts to demonstrate, then we should be able to expose some of a text's message by *analyzing* its organization, its structure. The linguistic signals a writer uses—even subconsciously—to create both coherence and organization in a text will provide us with some of the first keys we need for unlocking the writer's message. Two ways of talking about this analytical process are suggested in the title to this chapter: syntactical analysis and discourse analysis.

Frightening words, perhaps; but don't panic. Most of you, if not all of you, learned to drive and to tie your shoes. Some of you have learned to read Greek, repair a carburetor, and play bridge or the piano. Can you make quiche? Find your way around Boston? If your palms are sweating from the anxiety you feel over words like *discourse* and *analytical*, I want to reassure you now: all this you are about to read is nothing more than another way of looking at things. You learned to talk, right? You will be able to do this, too. It is far simpler than learning to talk. We can scarcely hope to plumb the depths of Holy Scripture without the sort of analysis discussed in this chapter, but God gives us a lifetime to master it, with ample room for trial and error. In fact, the more errors we make, the more opportunity we have to get it right the next time. Nothing keeps us from truly learning like getting it right accidentally, without knowing why. So be encouraged, plunge in, learn a new thing, and sin boldly.

4.1 DEFINING TERMS

It will help us later on in this chapter if we nail down a few things up front. For many readers, "English grammar" to this day remains a mysterious subject, even after a year of Beginning Greek. Although teachers over the last few decades have doubtless struggled valiantly, millions of students have emerged from secondary schools (and universities) woefully confused about the grammar of their own language and how it works. There is no way we can remedy that situation right now, but it will help to steer us in the right direction if we spell out some basics before we go on. Some of the following definitions of terms will be like "house rules" for a game of pinochle. Other "houses" may play by a slightly different set of rules. Other exegetes may prefer slightly different definitions of the following terms, but I use these definitions in my house. So, come in, close the door and take a seat.

4.1.1 Syntax

The term *syntax* is probably familiar to all students of a foreign language, including students of New Testament Greek. It has nothing to do with either sin or taxes. In the creation of a sentence, syntax has to do with the way a particular language clusters units together in meaningful ways (letters and words, for example), in order to form new units of a higher level. How do verb forms change to accommodate one grammatical subject rather than another or one time frame or "mood" rather than another? How do nouns alter their shape or position to show the function they perform in a sentence? How does an adjective indicate its relationship to one particular noun rather than to some other one? How do changes in the form of verbs enable a speaker to relate one clause of a sentence to another? The term *syntax* refers to the sum total of all the rules (and exceptions to the rules) governing these changes and accommodations. *Syntactical analysis*, then, is the process of unpacking the meaning of a sentence by noticing the syntactical signals an author has employed naturally, and often quite unconsciously, in creating it.

Be sure of this: *without a working knowledge of New Testament Greek syntax we cannot hope to understand the Greek New Testament.* For the same reason, without a working knowledge of English syntax, we will have trouble with the finer points of analyzing even an English translation of the New Testament. This is not to say, however, that we must be absolute masters of all the paradigms in our beginning Greek (or English) grammars before we can *begin* to study real texts from the New Testament. The ability to recognize syntactical forms and to interpret them correctly grows with practice. Only, make sure now that you know where to go for help, and go there when you need it. If you have already studied Greek, review your paradigms!

4.1.2 Discourse

We use the term *discourse* in a wide variety of ways, even within the discipline of biblical studies. In general, it applies to any complete, self-contained act of communication. Inarticulate groans or sighs (like the ones referred to in Rom 8:26) are discourses in this sense. So is a highly complex and lengthy book like Isaiah, or even collections of related works, such as the Pauline corpus. The discipline of *discourse analysis* has been developed fairly recently in order to account for the ways texts grow *beyond the boundaries of sentences*. How do sentences cluster together to form paragraphs, paragraphs to form larger sections, and so on? While the idea of syntax applies mostly within sentence boundaries, discourse analysis (sometimes also called "text-grammar") steps back to see the structure of larger and larger segments of text, all the way up to an entire book. (Some discourse analysts conceive of it as involving not only the text but also the historical-cultural context in which it arose, a completely legitimate perspective.[1] For present purposes, we will keep to the narrower definition.) As we saw in chapter three, the meaning of a larger portion of text is in part dependent on the meanings of its smaller constituent elements, and vice versa. Discourse analysis helps us to see how these reciprocal relationships are designed and marked for our attention, especially at levels above the sentence. Discourse analysis reveals textual coherence.

I can scarcely exaggerate the importance of grasping this exegetical principle: *The meaning of a text is in large measure determined by its internal structure and by its place within the structure of its broader context.* Analysis of the text's syntactical and discourse structure, both up the ladder and down, is indispensable to responsible and effective exegesis.

4.1.3 Phrase

The term *phrase* refers to a meaningful word-cluster that lacks a verb form. A *noun* phrase, for example, has at its core a noun (like *tractor* perhaps), together

---

[1]An excellent example of the broader application is Joel B. Green, "Discourse Analysis and New Testament Interpretation," in *Hearing the New Testament: Strategies for Interpretation*, ed. Joel B. Green (Grand Rapids: Eerdmans, 1995), pp. 175-221.

with any accompanying qualifiers: *the old rusty tractor*. A *prepositional* phrase combines a preposition (*in, with, under, beside, after, of, by*, etc.) with a noun or noun phrase: *under the tractor* or *beside the old rusty tractor*. Some prepositions can also function as subordinating conjunctions. *After the race* is a prepositional *phrase*, since it lacks a verb-form; *after the race was run* is a (subordinate, adverbial) *clause*—introduced by the "conjunction" *after*—because the addition of the verb form *was run* transforms the noun phrase *the race* into the clause *the race was run*. This means that (in English anyway) words like *after* can serve either as prepositions (introducing phrases) or as subordinating conjunctions (introducing clauses). It depends on what it "governs" (what comes after it). So then, in the parenthetical comment ending my last sentence, is the word *after* a preposition or a conjunction? (If you say, "It's a preposition," you are right, since the word *it* has no attached verb form and is therefore not a clause, just a one-word phrase.)

4.1.4 Clause

A *clause*, then, is any meaningful cluster of words that includes a verb form at its heart. These verb forms do not need to be "finite" forms, the sort that makes for "grammatically complete thoughts." For example, the clause *Gene is singing in the rain* is a grammatically complete thought. We are not left hanging in the air if someone says this to us out of the blue, even though we may not know who Gene is, or care whether he sings, or where. We would indeed be left hanging if someone simply said, "Singing in the rain" or "While Gene is singing in the rain." Hearing either of these last two utterances, we would be tempted to reply to the one, "What *about* singing in the rain?" and to the other, "Okay . . . and then what happens?" Grammatically *in*complete thoughts leave us gaping like baby birds, waiting for the rest of the worm. They are *dependent;* they need to be "completed."

We can also classify dependent clauses according to their function. A clause introduced by the conjunction *that* (ὅτι in Greek) is usually a "noun" clause, because it functions in the place of a noun (it acts like a noun). In the sentence *I know something*, we can specify the something known (the direct object of *know*) by using a noun clause: *that Gene is singing in the rain*. An adverb clause is one that functions as an adverb: "*While Gene is singing in the rain*, I'll just make a run to the store." The (italicized) adverb clause here tells when I will run to the store.

Grammarians usually refer to grammatically complete clauses as *independent* or *main* clauses. A "complete" sentence is an independent clause (or at least contains one). Grammatically *in*complete, or *dependent*, clauses are also called *subordinate* clauses. While they themselves do not qualify as sentences (as the last eight words I just typed do not), when they combine with independent clauses (like the next six words I'm about to type), they help to form complex sentences. We can turn now to the sentence itself.

4.1.5 Sentence

A *sentence* is any minimally complete thought, consisting of at least one independent clause. It can be *simple, compound* or *complex.* A simple sentence comprises at least a topic and a comment, also called subject and predicate. A sentence "predicates" something about its "subject"; it "comments" on its "topic." Even if one element or the other does not show up in the sentence as we hear it or read it, that missing element may be implied in the background nonetheless. (Consider "Gone!" as an answer to the question, "Where's Bob?" The topic [or subject], "Bob," is understood: "[Bob is] gone!"). Topics can be *simple* (a single noun or noun phrase, for example) or *compound* (multiple nouns or noun phrases, connected by "coordinating" conjunctions like *and* or *or*). Topics can also be *complex,* involving further refinement by adjectives, relative clauses, participles and so on. The same is true of the comment (or predicate) portion of a sentence: it can be simple, compound or complex. Here are some examples:

1. *Bob sings.* Simple topic *(Bob);* simple comment *(sings).*

2. *Bob and Vera sing.* The topic is *compounded* by the coordinating conjunction *and (Bob and Vera);* the comment remains simple *(sing).* Note, by the way, how English syntactical rules change *sings* to *sing* in the presence of a compound (and therefore plural) subject.

3. *Bob and Vera sing but do not dance.* Compound topic; compound comment (two "comments" connected by the coordinating conjunction *but*). Note that modern English resists saying *dance not* in this context, as English could do at earlier stages of its development; today, we have to say *do not dance.* That's just the way it is.

4. *The woman who is standing next to Bob sings badly.* Complex topic; simple comment. Note that the "complexity" of this topic is the result of an entire sentence having been reshaped as a "relative clause" *(who is standing next to Bob)* and plugged into the adjective position, in order to modify *the woman.* That is, it is not the "blue" woman or the "oval" woman, but that other woman, the one "who is standing next to Bob."

5. *Bob sings just fine when Vera does not join in.* Simple topic *(Bob);* complex comment. The comment's "complexity" results from an entire sentence having been reshaped into a dependent clause *(when Vera does not join in)* and subordinated (plugged) into the adverb slot (instead of, say, *usually*), in order to modify the verb phrase *sings just fine.* It tells us under what conditions Bob sings just fine.

Every language has its own set of tools for forming and connecting what we are calling phrases, clauses and sentences. Hebrew, for example, can condense an English prepositional phrase into one word, simply by prefixing the "preposition" to the front of the noun: *bĕrēʾšît* "in the beginning," where the prefix *bĕ* does in Hebrew more or less what the preposition *in* does in English. So-called agglutinative languages can put an entire sentence into one long and complex agglutinated "word." We have been providing examples from English for the most part, and in many respects New Testament Greek and English function similarly. Both, for instance, have separate words for prepositions, rather than prefixes; yet both can use prepositions as prefixes. Nevertheless, there will not always be a one-to-one correspondence between English and Greek in other respects. The way Greek uses participles and infinitives, for instance, differs noticeably from the way English does. I stress again, therefore, that it is essential for New Testament exegesis to master *eventually* the ways in which Greek expresses the message of the New Testament. Work at it over your lifetime as an exegete. Take your time, of course, but do work at it.

4.2 ANALYZING SENTENCES

With this much background, we can now turn to the syntactical analysis of sentences. Study the following sample New Testament sentences carefully. See if you can make sense of the way in which I have analyzed them, before you read the explanation below each one.

4.2.1 Analyzing John 3:16

Figure 4.1 (pp. 76-77) with its accompanying notes unpacks (analyzes) the syntactical structure of John 3:16 in the NRSV. It gets a little complicated, I know. Take each explanatory statement, one at a time, and be sure you understand it before you take the next one. If you plow through this material as if you were reading a novel, it will soon become slush in your head. When you are somewhat comfortable with the NRSV analysis, try the Greek (fig. 4.2).

1	οὕτως **γὰρ** ἠγάπησεν ὁ θεὸς τὸν κόσμον,
2	**ὥστε** τὸν υἱὸν τὸν μονογενῆ ἔδωκεν,
3	**ἵνα** πᾶς ὁ πιστεύων εἰς αὐτὸν
4	μὴ ἀπόληται
5	**ἀλλ'** ἔχῃ ζωὴν αἰώνιον

Figure 4.2. Syntactical Analysis of John 3:16 in Greek

Once again, as in the NRSV text, we have four conjunctions. One of them, ἀλλά "but" (line 5, shortened to ἀλλ᾿ before the initial vowel in the next word), is a coordinating conjunction, and the other two are subordinating. The Greek conjunction γάρ like its English counterpart "for" (line 1), operates on the discourse level, rather than on the sentence level. Overall, the chief difference between these two analyses is that the Greek conjunction ἵνα "in order that" (line 3) usually suggests *purpose* rather than *result*, contrary to English *so that* in line 4 of the NRSV analysis below. (But see 1 Jn 1:9 for an instance where ἵνα is used to signal result. We can't win!) Thus the Greek text appears to say that *because* God loved the world so much, he *intentionally* gave his only Son *for the purpose* of providing eternal life for mortal human beings, all of which assures us that the statements in John 3:14-15 are reliable.

Let's try another example.

4.2.2 Analyzing Romans 3:21-22

Do the same for Romans 3:21-22 NRSV in figure 4.3 (pp. 78-79) as you have done for John 3:16 in figure 4.1. Read it through carefully. The better you understand it, the better you will be able to deal with other texts of your own choosing. Then, when you are ready, try the Greek of Romans 3:21-22 (fig. 4.4).

The Greek prepositional phrases work in the same way as their English counterparts do. But the genitive noun θεοῦ (lines 2 and 5) appears instead of the English prepositional phrase *of God*. Another syntactical difference between English and Greek appears in line 3: the Greek participle μαρτυρουμένη "being attested" appears instead of the English finite verb phrase *and is attested*.

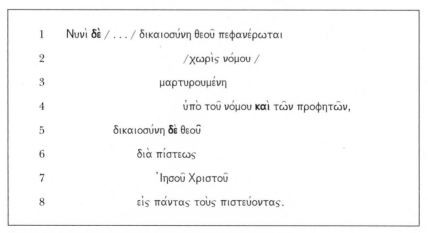

1	Νυνὶ δὲ / ... / δικαιοσύνη θεοῦ πεφανέρωται
2	/χωρὶς νόμου /
3	μαρτυρουμένη
4	ὑπὸ τοῦ νόμου καὶ τῶν προφητῶν,
5	δικαιοσύνη δὲ θεοῦ
6	διὰ πίστεως
7	᾿Ιησοῦ Χριστοῦ
8	εἰς πάντας τοὺς πιστεύοντας.

Figure 4.4. Syntactical Analysis of Romans 3:21-22 in Greek

1	**For**
2	God so loved the world
3	**that** he gave his only Son,
4	**so that** everyone who believes <u>in him</u>
5	may not perish
6	**but** may have eternal life

A. The four items in boldface type (one of them in two parts: *so that*) are conjunctions, the typical markers that connect clauses to one another. The underlined item is a prepositional phrase.

B. The only "main" (or independent) clause of this sentence (line 2) is "God [so] loved the world" (we will take up the *for* [line 1] and the *so* in comments L and H, below). The other two clauses (lines 3 and the cluster of lines 4-6) are each introduced with a subordinating conjunction, *that* and *so that*, and are therefore "dependent" (which is why, in the diagram, each one is indented under what it "depends on").

C. The second of these dependent clauses (clustered as lines 4-6) is actually a compound clause: the topic (line 4: *everyone who believes in him*) is followed by two coordinated comments: line 5 *may not perish* and line 6 *may have eternal life*, which are connected by the coordinating conjunction *but*.

D. We thus have three clauses in this sentence: (i) *God loved the world*, (ii) *[God] gave his only Son*, and (iii) *everyone who believes in him does not perish but has eternal life*. Clause (ii) is subordinate to the independent clause (i), and the compound-complex clause (iii) is subordinate to clause (ii).

E. The coordinating (as opposed to subordinating) conjunction *but* in line 6 indicates that both line 5 and line 6, which it connects in contrast to each other, are equally ("coordinatedly") true as comments on the complex topic *(everyone <u>who believes in him</u>)* expressed in line 4. This is why lines 5 and 6 are displayed vertically *parallel* to each other in the diagram. The conjunction *but* thus creates a compound clause, consisting of a complex topic (line 4) and a compound comment (lines 5-6).

F. The other two conjunctions (bold type, lines 3, 4) indicate *how* the three clauses interconnect or "conjoin." As conjunctions, they "mark" the logical relationships between clauses. Not only do they mark the point of separation between one clause and another, but they also serve to hold all three clauses together as a coherent, logically interconnected unit.

G. What do these markers tell us? The conjunction *so that* (line 4) tells us that lines 4-6 describe the *result* of line 3: the result of God's giving his only Son is that everyone who believes in that Son has eternal life.

H. Likewise, the conjunction *that* in line 3 tells us that lines 3-6 (that is, line 3 and everything dependent on it) are the *result* of the degree to which God (*so [much]*) loved the world. Putting this other way around, we can say that God gave his only son *because* he loved the world so much. For if lines 3-6 are the *result* of line 2, then line 2 is the *reason* for lines 3-6.

Figure 4.1. Syntactical Analysis of John 3:16 in NRSV

I. The two (bold type) conjunctions in lines 3 and 4 are both *subordinating* conjunctions. Line 3, together with its dependent material (lines 4-6), is thus subordinated to line 2, providing a statement of its result. Lines 4-6 (as a clustered unit) are similarly subordinated to line 3, providing in turn a statement of *its* result. We show this graphically by bringing the independent main clause (line 2 in this case) out to the left margin and by indenting subordinate (or dependent) material under whatever text it is subordinate to. Rephrasing the entire sentence after this analysis might produce the following: "God loved the world very much. As a result of that great love, he gave his only Son. The result of giving his Son, in turn, is that everyone who believes in the Son has eternal life." Cause-effect, cause-effect. Yet, is this right?

J. The problem with this analysis is that even though "proper" English uses the conjunction *so that* primarily to indicate a result, this same conjunction can also function in English to indicate *purpose*. The difference between purpose and result is important. The notion of purpose carries within it the elements of intention and uncertainty. On the one hand, purpose implies intention without guaranteeing the result (this is why Greek uses the subjunctive mood after ἵνα in such cases). Example: *Gene sang in the rain, in order to make money*. We could also say, *Gene sang in the rain, so that he could make money*. Did he make money? Hard to say, but he intended to. On the other hand, *result* implies certainty without necessarily implying purpose. Example: *Gene sang in the rain all day, so that he caught pneumonia*. He actually caught pneumonia, but not intentionally.

K. But the wording of lines 5 and 6 (in this analysis of Jn 3:16), with the English helping ("modal") verb *may* in both lines, introduces the element of uncertainty, which is inherent in "purpose" but foreign to "result." If lines 4-6 truly were meant to imply result, they would, like line 3, be framed in the indicative past tense: "so that everyone believing in him lived forever." As it turns out, then, lines 4-6 indicate purpose and intentionality, not necessarily an assured result. Will anyone believe in the Son and thus have eternal life? God knows.

L. This leaves us just the opening conjunction, *for* (line 1). It is obvious from the context that *for* is not functioning here as a preposition, as in *something for God*. Rather, it introduces this entire sentence in all its three-part complexity. As a conjunction, then, *for* functions to "conjoin" this entire complex sentence to what precedes it (Jn 3:15, at least). At this point, we move beyond sentence boundaries, passing outward from the internal syntactical analysis of a sentence to the analysis of the greater *discourse* surrounding it. Naturally, there is much more to the discourse structure of John's Gospel than the relation of 3:16 to what comes before it. Yet, the word *for* introducing 3:16 provides one piece of that larger structure. This particular conjunction typically indicates that what it introduces describes the reason for what precedes it. Thus, the fact that God loved the world enough to give his only Son, in order to provide eternal life for those who believe in him, explains why the statement in John 3:14-15 (at least) is reliable.

```
1    But now / . . . / the righteousness of God
2         has been disclosed,
3              / apart from law /
4         and is attested
5              by the law and the prophets
6                   the righteousness of God
7                        through faith
8                             in Jesus Christ
9                             for all who believe.
```

A. There are only three conjunctions (printed in bold) in this text, all of them the coordinating kind: *but* (line 1) as well as *and* twice (lines 4 and 5). There are also seven prepositional phrases (underlined).

B. The first occurrence of *and* conjoins the passive verbs in lines 2 and 4, whose shared topic (subject) is "the righteousness of God" (line 1). The other *and* (line 5) conjoins the two parts of a common expression for the Jewish Bible: *the law and the prophets*. Thus, lines 1, 2-3 and 4-5 form a single sentence with a compound comment, or predicate.

C. In the diagram, I displaced line 3 from its original place in line 1 in order to arrange it in a more helpful way. Placed where it is, we can easily see it as standing in contrast to line 5, a very important contrast for this text. The forward slash marks // indicate both the displaced text itself and the place where it belongs in line 1. This is only a trick of the trade, however, designed to keep us honest. At the end of everything, we must always return to the text as we find it. Remember, the text is all we have.

D. What about the prepositional phrases? Their shape is easy enough to identify: a preposition governing a noun or noun phrase, such as *of God, apart from the law* or *through faith*. What takes a bit more thought is deciding their function. In general, a preposition relates a noun to another noun (thus making it act like an adjective) or to an event (thus making it act like an adverb). In line 1, for example, the preposition *of* relates the word *God* to the word *righteousness*, telling us what sort of righteousness is in view here. It is the "God-sort-of" righteousness. In this case, the prepositional phrase *of God* functions as an adjective modifying the noun *righteousness*. In line 3, however, the prepositional phrase *apart from the law* does not tell us anything about righteousness itself; it tells us rather about how that righteousness has been revealed, or how it has *not* been revealed. As such, the prepositional phrase in line 3 functions as an adverb, telling us something about the verb *disclosed*. Similarly, the prepositional phrase in line 5 modifies the verb *is attested* in line 4, but this time the attestation is in accord with the Jewish scriptures ("by the law and the prophets") rather than "apart from" them.

E. So then, we have a compound sentence: "The righteousness of God has now been disclosed apart from the law, and [at the same time] it is attested by the law." Paul explores the irony of this statement in the following paragraphs, where he employs

Figure 4.3. Syntactical Analysis of Romans 3:21-22 in NRSV

the story of Abraham, drawn from the law (the Torah), in order to prove his point.

F. We are still not yet done with this passage. What do we do with lines 6-9? The only verb in this sequence of text is *believe* in line 9. However, it is isolated in a relative clause, *who believe*, and does not function as a comment on righteousness (line 6) in the same way as the verbs in lines 2 and 4 do. As a relative clause, the words *who believe* function as an adjective to restrict the reference of the term *all:* righteousness is "for all," but not *really* for "all"—just "all *who believe.*" Without its own accompanying verb, then, this second occurrence of the term "righteousness" in lines 6-9 does not form part of a new clause.

G. Instead, line 6 is a reiteration—repeated from line 1—apparently inserted here as a kind of disconnected hook on which to hang further qualifications on righteousness beyond the one provided in line 1: *of God*. It is thus additionally a righteousness of God [mediated?] *through faith* (line 7), but not through just any faith. It is mediated through faith *in Jesus Christ* particularly (line 8). And because (?) it is mediated through faith in Jesus Christ, it is available "for" all who believe [in Jesus Christ]. In this way, using a series of prepositional phrases as adjectives, Paul further defines the righteousness of God he has in mind.

H. We may now return to the conjunction *but* in line 1. In John 3:16 we saw this same logical marker conjoining in a paralleled contrast the two sides of the coin God minted in giving his only Son: believers would not die, *but* would live forever. In Romans 3:21, however, this conjunction joins two very high-level sections of the epistle. Here is what I mean.

I. Romans 1—8 argues the amazing fact that Gentiles and Jews are on equal footing before God. Both are completely condemned under the law and fully redeemed in Jesus Christ. The *but* in Romans 3:21 connects the two subsections making up this first main argument of the letter. Under the law, all humanity is completely condemned before God (Rom 1:18—3:20). *But now* God's righteousness has been revealed apart from the law (Rom 3:21—8:39). Thus, like *for* in John 3:16, the *but* in Romans 3:21 operates on the discourse level; in fact, it operates on a much higher discourse level than the *for* in John 3:16 does. The latter connects merely two or three sentences; the former connects two coordinated arguments spanning nearly eight chapters.

This means that in Greek we have a complex sentence rather than the English compound sentence. It also raises the question of how this subordinated participial clause in line 3 relates to the main clause in line 1. In fact, as you will recall from your introductory course in New Testament Greek (if you had one), Greek participles constitute one of the most confusing categories of Greek grammar.

Often it is necessary to infer from the context what the connection between a Greek participle and its main verb actually is. It helps in doing this to ask, "What question is being answered by the participle?" In this text, the implied contrast between being "revealed apart from the law" and being "attested by the law," might suggest that the connection between the clauses in lines 3-4 and lines 1-2 is one of "contra-expectation": *even though, in spite of.* This would give us something like "even though it is attested by the law and the prophets, the righteousness of God is nevertheless revealed apart from the law." However, when we take into account the continuation of Paul's argument in Romans 4, where he appeals to Abraham's story in support of his claim, we must assume that he himself sees no real contrast between these two ideas after all. We come back to the NRSV translation: "*and* is attested by the law and the prophets," that is, *in addition* to being revealed apart from the law. Based on this, in turn, we wonder whether Paul actually uses the term νόμος "law" in more than one sense here.

As we can see, the process of analyzing syntax helps us to grasp the structure of a sentence and to some degree its connection to the larger context. It also helps us (often forces us) to see and to deal with ambiguities inherent in the text, ambiguities like the meaning that Paul attaches to the word *law,* ambiguities we might otherwise miss because we are so familiar with the text.

4.3 ANALYZING DISCOURSE

Once we have grasped the "clustering" nature of literary structure at the level of sentences, it is a simple matter to transfer this same fundamental perspective to the levels of paragraphs, sections, parts and entire books. Just as individual alphabetic letters cluster together to form words, and words cluster to form phrases and clauses, and just as phrases and clauses cluster to form sentences, so now sentences cluster to form paragraphs, paragraphs cluster to form sections, and so on up the scale. Clustering at all these higher levels works in the same reciprocal, bi-directional way as it does with sentences. On the one hand, clustering makes units cohere to one another in order to form a larger unit. At the same time, on the other hand, by causing a unit to cohere more closely with other units in its own cluster, it automatically separates that unit from neighboring units belonging to a different cluster. In other words, clustering "sorts" units; it both gathers and separates them.

For example, I might "cluster" a pile of earth together in order to form a bed for a row of corn in my wife's garden. As I do that, I simultaneously separate that row of earth from a neighboring one that will serve as a bed for carrots. Nevertheless, both of these separately clustered beds belong to the same garden. It works in exactly the same way as I type this text. Each time I do or do not use the space bar, I am making decisions about clustering letters. When I type a period or a comma, I cluster phrases and clauses. Similarly now, in order to "create" a cluster of sentences called a paragraph, I am about to hit the return key.

A well-written book, whether a textbook or a novel, works in the same way. Each chapter can be reduced to a core sentence summarizing the central point. These brief summary statements can then be laid out side by side and connected to each other with "conjunctions." Doing so demonstrates their interrelationships, how one leads to the other and how they all combine to "argue" the main point of the entire book. Chapter one might provide the rationale for what happens or what is explained in chapter two. Together they might lead to a series of specific applications in chapters three to six. Chapters one to six might then constitute part one, which would be contrasted in part two (made up of chapters seven to ten) to a completely different way of looking at the book's fundamental point. The discourse-analyst could then sum up the entire book in a single sentence, highly generalized of course, or in a paragraph made up of summary sentences for each part or each chapter.

A warning here, however. The familiar chapter and verse divisions in the Bible, while often suggestive, are unreliable guides to the discourse structure of a biblical book. The same can be said about the paragraphing and the section titles provided in any modern edition of the Bible, Greek or otherwise. (Revisit fig. 2.2 to see section titles editorially added to the UBS[4] text.) In the end, it is up to us as exegetes to think about the way a book is put together. The question is always an open one. For this reason, if we desire to be as faithful as we can be to the text as its author first wrote it, then we should never set out to "preach through" a biblical book chapter by chapter (or worse, verse by verse). We have no guarantee that the later editors of Scripture who added the familiar chapter and verse divisions did so in the way the original authors would have done it. In fact, we have many reasons to suspect they did not! As far as you are able, let the book itself tell you where to make appropriate divisions in the run of its "argument" or its "plot." The next question is, how do we do that?

4.3.1 Coherence Within Units of Text

We may begin by watching for the kinds of boundary markers discussed above in 3.2.2: conjunctions, changes in tense, mood or voice, changes in time, cast and setting (in narrative), repeated units, rhetorical questions and so on. Co-ordinated with these, and working together with them, are signs of literary *coherence*. There are as many signs of coherence as there are imaginations to think them up, which is not to say that they are always *consciously* applied. Sometimes coherence will involve a concentration of vocabulary, perhaps the same word, or perhaps a group of semantically related words, over a given stretch of text. Sometimes the cast of characters, especially in a narrative, will indicate coherence; if a change in cast can mark the boundary between textual units, then the persistence of a particular cast of persons without change will suggest that there is no boundary. Pronouns create coherence by depending on previous references to their antecedents. If I say "Paul" in sentence 1 and refer to Paul again in sentence 3 by using the pronoun "him," then this can cause these two sentences (and sentence 2 between them) to cohere to each other. Shorthand references to time and space, such as "there," "here," "now," "then," "again" (operating as "pro-adverbs"), do more or less the same thing.

One of the interesting markers of coherence is the artful literary device called "chiasm" (pronounced *KAI-azm*). Chiasms are so named because, when analyzed schematically, they resemble the X-shape of the Greek letter *chi,* or the left half of it anyway. A five-part chiasm, for instance, "matches up" its first and fifth parts with each other and likewise its second and fourth parts; the third or middle part then forms the central hinge of the text. Here is an ex-ample, made up just to illustrate what I mean:

A   *He took his way*

   B   *Across the ice.*

      C   Hard, like iron.

   B'   *The frozen lake*

A'   *He made a road.*

Lines A and A', and B and B', respectively, match each other and bind all five lines together as a unit. The middle line C, *Hard, like iron,* is the central idea, the focus of the chiasm—like a picture in its frame. We are left to wonder whether that center line—*hard, like iron*—is talking about the ice or about the man on the ice. There is no limit on the size or number of a chiasm's mem-bers, nor on what shape they may take in a text. One result of a chiasm, never-theless, is that it creates a "coherent" text with a beginning, middle and end.

We can say the same about another literary device, the *inclusio* (that's right; no final *n*). This tool binds a text into a coherent unit by placing matching "bookends" around it. One of the more famous of New Testament inclusios places bookends around Matthew's entire Gospel with matching references to God's being "with us" (1:23 and 28:20). Inclusios not only bracket off a distinct, coherent unit, but they also give us a key to the nature of the coherence; the Gospel of Matthew apparently coheres around the theme of God's presence with his people in the person of Jesus. In fact, chiasms are complex inclusios.

Once again, however, it is important to keep in mind the fact that what is a distinct, coherent unit on one level combines with similar distinct units to form a larger coherent unit on the next higher level. Likewise, any unit is itself also analyzable into smaller distinct units of the next lower level. I might plant four distinct rows of corn in my wife's garden, but *together* these four rows constitute the corn section and would be set off *separate from* the section made up of two distinct rows of carrots. Let's look at some New Testament examples of coherence at work.

Concentrations. In a letter to his friend Philemon, Paul sets up a rapport with him by praising him for his faithfulness in the service of Christ (Philem 1-7). That done, he gets to the heart of the matter: what to do about Philemon's runaway slave, Onesimus, now that Onesimus has become a brother in the Lord. The next nine verses are framed mostly in the indicative mood and the past tense. At verse 17, however, the mood suddenly shifts to the imperative, as Paul begins to press his case and call for action. Even in verses 21-22, where he uses indicative verbs again, the tone remains imperative even if the verbs' grammatical mood is less often so. The internal coherence of verses 8-16 and of verses 17-22, respectively, is evident (in part) through concentrations of verbs of the same mood.

The coherence of the parable of the widow and the unjust judge (Lk 18:1-8) is in part recognizable from the persistent cast and setting. A concentration of vocabulary regarding vindication in an adversarial situation reinforces that coherence. The verb ἐκδικέω "avenge" occurs twice (Lk 18:3, 5), as does its cognate noun ἐκδίκησις "vengeance" (Lk 18:7, 8). The story is about vindication. (This concentration of vocabulary also sets up an interesting intratextual connection between this parable and Luke's text about the coming destruction of Jerusalem, the only other Lukan passage using the term ἐκδίκησις: "for these are days of vengeance, as a fulfillment of all that is written" [Lk 21:22].)

Chiasms. As preparation for proposing that Philemon do the unthinkable, Paul offers him some personal affirmation. According to a literal translation, the apostle says, "[I make] constant mention of you in my prayers, hearing of your love and faith, which you have toward the Lord Jesus and to all the saints" (Philem 4-5). This sounds to our ears as if Paul thinks Philemon not only has love for the Lord Jesus and faith in him, but that he has love for all the saints and *faith in them* as well. This is at least odd. However, by comparing a parallel text (Col 1:4: "for we have heard of your faith in Christ Jesus and of the love that you have for all the saints"), we see that Paul has actually shaped his words to Philemon as a chiasm:

A   love for

    B   faith in

    B'   Lord Jesus

A'   all the saints

Paul is chiefly concerned in this letter about Philemon's treatment of Onesimus, desiring that it conform to Philemon's reputed love for *all* the saints. Of course, that love finds its foundation in Philemon's faith in the Lord Jesus. By framing the relationship between love for the saints and faith in the Lord Jesus in the form of a chiasm, Paul forges an indissoluble link between the horizontal and vertical dimensions of Christian ethics: one's horizontal relationships with other people depend on one's vertical relationship with God. This chiastic clause (Philem 5) becomes thus an internally coherent unit, functioning as a part of Paul's opening appeal to Philemon's good judgment.

Similarly, Matthew's story of the magi (Mt 2:1-12) falls into five parts, divisible according to the central players in each. The opening two verses focus on the pagan magi who come to Jerusalem seeking to worship the newborn king of the Jews. Verses 3-4 relate the resultant paranoia of Herod and all Jerusalem. Herod's unnerved behavior is mirrored in verses 7-8, where he responds deceptively to the magi's query; this reveals to us the readers that Herod has not the slightest intention of worshiping the newborn king. The end of the story (Mt 2:9-12) matches the beginning (Mt 2:1-2), portraying the magi as finding the newborn king, carrying out their worship and returning to their own land without contacting Herod. At the center of the story, verses 5-6 treat us to the citation of Old Testament texts regarding the expected king's birthplace, cited ironically at Herod's request and by Herod's priests and scribes.

A   Magi, come to worship the newborn king, seek Herod's help (Mt 2:1-2).

    B   Herod and Jerusalem panic at the birth of the king (Mt 2:3-4).

        C   Biblical texts speak of the king's birth (Mt 2:5-6).

    B'   Herod plots and schemes his own form of "worship" (Mt 2:7-8).

A'   The magi carry out their worship and go away, eluding Herod (Mt 2:9-12).

Besides framing this story as a discrete and coherent part of Matthew's extended birth narrative, the chiastic structure highlights a profound irony. Herod "the king" and "all Jerusalem" (B, B') are contrasted with *pagan* stargazers (A, A') in their attitude toward the true king, one who would "shepherd" them (Mt 2:6) as Herod and those whom Matthew regards as Herod's religious sycophants would never do.

4.3.2 Connections Between Units of Text on the Discourse Level(s)

Once we identify discrete units of text at the level of sentences or above, both by observing boundary markers and by discerning evidence of internal coherence, we need to analyze how those units are interrelated. The principles for this that apply on one level will, for the most part, apply on all levels further up the scale, all the way up to the level of the entire book—Paul's letter to the Romans, for example. We will use Romans 6:15-23 for a sample analysis.

Figure 4.5 provides a syntactical analysis of Romans 6:15-23 NRSV. It represents one way of graphically relating the various elements of a series of sentences in a text. We could develop various other schemes for doing the same thing. In one sense it does not matter which technique we use, since the technique an exegete adopts is primarily adopted for his or her own use. The design used here brings main clauses out to the left margin, and indents subordinate material (as, e.g., at line 15.2). Parallel units fall into line with each other (as in 15.3-4). Arrows indicate which elements relate to each other, though they do not reveal *how* they relate.

Consult figure 4.5 carefully as you work through the following comments. Notice that material subordinated to another unit becomes *part of* that other unit, even if that other unit is itself subordinate to a yet "higher" unit. This is partly what we mean by clustering, and the arrows in the diagram show which items cluster with which other items. For example, lines 15.3-4 are subordinate to line 15.2, and all three lines 15.2-4 belong together, as a cluster, to 15.1. Paul is not asking whether we should sin because "we are" (which would be absurd); he is asking whether we should sin "because we are *not under law, but under grace.*"

Similarly, lines 17.2-5, as a single cluster, are subordinate to 17.1. Lines 18.1-2 are also subordinate to 17.1, parallel to but separate from 17.2-5. Likewise, within the cluster 17.2-5, lines 17.3-4 are separate from 17.5, even though *both* are (separately) subordinate to 17.2. The cluster 17.3-4 describes *in what two senses* "you" have become obedient, while 17.5 describes *what* "your" former circumstances were. Together these two clusters, 17.3-4 and 17.5 (one of them with only one "member"), qualify the sense in which Paul's readers have become obedient. Their obedience, then, qualified in this way, is one of two

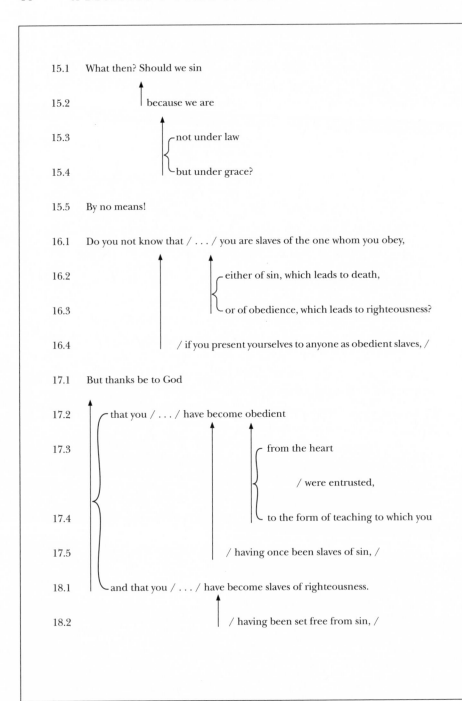

Figure 4.5. Syntactical Analysis of Romans 6:15-23 in NRSV

19.1   I am speaking in human terms because of your natural limitations.

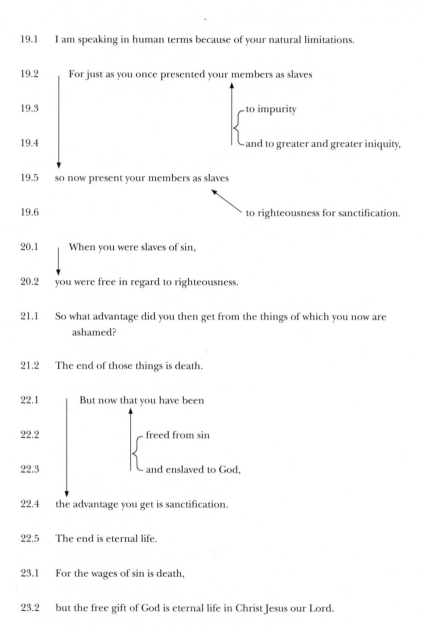

19.2   For just as you once presented your members as slaves

19.3   to impurity

19.4   and to greater and greater iniquity,

19.5   so now present your members as slaves

19.6   to righteousness for sanctification.

20.1   When you were slaves of sin,

20.2   you were free in regard to righteousness.

21.1   So what advantage did you then get from the things of which you now are
       ashamed?

21.2   The end of those things is death.

22.1   But now that you have been

22.2   freed from sin

22.3   and enslaved to God,

22.4   the advantage you get is sanctification.

22.5   The end is eternal life.

23.1   For the wages of sin is death,

23.2   but the free gift of God is eternal life in Christ Jesus our Lord.

(parallel) reasons Paul gives for thanking God (17.1). He expresses the other reason in 18.1-2: their present enslavement to righteousness.

We are now in a position to identify the next level of clusters, in which one or more "sentences" group together in the flow of Romans 6:15-23. After thinking it through from the display we have made, we might sum up the stages of Paul's argument there as follows.

A (15.1-5)   We should by no means sin simply because we are under grace.

B (16.1-4)   You are slaves of whatever you obey: whether sin (leading to death) or obedience (leading to righteousness).

C (17.1—18.2)   But thank God, you have become obedient, slaves of righteousness.

D (19.1)   I am speaking in human terms (using slavery metaphorically).

E (19.2-6)   Present your members now as slaves to righteousness, in order to be sanctified.

F (20.1—22.5)   As slaves to sin, your reward for obeying it was death; as slaves to God, your reward for sanctification is eternal life.

G (23.1-2)   What we earn by sinning is death; what God gives us is eternal life in Christ.

Some explanatory comments may help here. (1) In cluster A, the emphatic negative in 15.5 coordinates with Paul's rhetorical question in 15.1-4; the combination is equivalent to a simple statement that God's grace provides no excuse for sinning. (2) The "just as/so now" structure in lines 19.2-6 ties those lines together as cluster E. (3) In cluster F, the structural similarity between lines 20.1-21.2 on the one hand, and lines 22.1-5 on the other hand, together with the coordinating conjunction "but [now]" in line 22.1, justify taking the entire stretch as one internally contrastive cluster.

How then do these seven sentence-clusters work together to form a higher-level, coherent literary unit out of Romans 6:15-23? It would be helpful if each cluster in the sequence had a clear marker of the relationship it has with the whole. Some of them in fact do. "What then?" in 15.1 relates what follows it to what precedes it, asking whether what precedes Romans 6:15 justifies the conclusion implied in Paul's rhetorical question: "Should we sin because we are not under law but under grace?" Likewise, the conjunction *but* in 17.1 sets up a contrast between cluster B and cluster C, and the word *so* introducing the question posed in 21.1 invites readers to draw a conclusion from the preceding argument. Unfortunately (so to speak), line 21.1 comes in the midst of a cluster, and therefore probably does not relate its own cluster (F) to any of the others.

As is often the case, then, we exegetes are dependent partly on explicit signals in the text and partly on our own powers of inference. After considering everything up to now, we might propose the following discourse structure for Romans 6:15-21. Italicized type indicates the inferred connections between clusters.

A (15.1-5)   We should by no means sin simply because we are under grace.

The reason for this is as follows (clusters B-F):

B (16.1-4)   You are slaves of whatever you obey: whether sin (leading to death) or obedience (leading to righteousness).

Yet, in spite of this potential for bad news,

C (17.1—18.2) Thank God, you have become obedient and slaves of righteousness.

[Concession]

D (19.1)   I am speaking in human terms (using slavery metaphorically).

In accordance, then, with your new condition,

E (19.2-6)   Present your members now as slaves to righteousness, in order to be sanctified.

As further rationale for this demand, consider this:

F (20.1—22.5) As slaves to sin, your reward for obeying it was death; as slaves to God, your reward for sanctification is eternal life.

In other words, summing up clusters A-F:

G (23.1-2)   By sinning, we earn death; but God gives us eternal life in Christ.

Finally, we might sum up the message of Romans 6:15-23, as an entire text, like this: "God's grace is no excuse for sin, since sinning leads to death. But God's free grace is intended to provide life, not death."

We have operated entirely from the English text in producing this analysis. How does it look in Greek? In fact, it looks remarkably similar. There are some differences worth noting, nonetheless. Refer to figure 4.6 for understanding the following two comments.

1. In terms of Greek syntax, lines 18.1-2 relate to 17.1-3 differently from the way the corresponding text behaves in the English version. The NRSV inserts a second "that" (18.1) in parallel with the one in 17.2, creating a second dependent noun clause; the Greek, however, employs an independent clause in 18.1-2, connected with verse 17 by the conjunction δέ "but." Nonetheless, the content of the text leads us naturally to construe the Greek text just as we did the

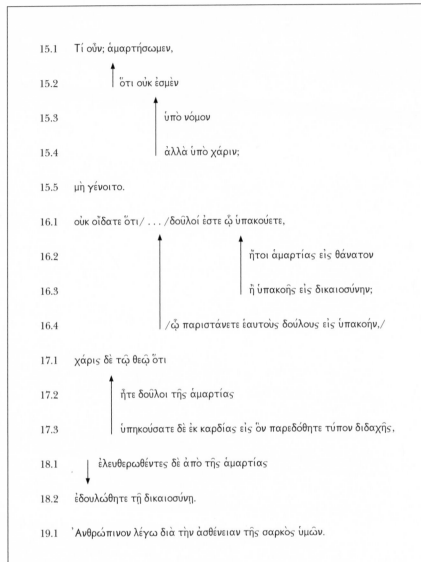

15.1   Τί οὖν; ἁμαρτήσωμεν,

15.2   ὅτι οὐκ ἐσμὲν

15.3   ὑπὸ νόμον

15.4   ἀλλὰ ὑπὸ χάριν;

15.5   μὴ γένοιτο.

16.1   οὐκ οἴδατε ὅτι/ . . . /δοῦλοί ἐστε ᾧ ὑπακούετε,

16.2   ἤτοι ἁμαρτίας εἰς θάνατον

16.3   ἢ ὑπακοῆς εἰς δικαιοσύνην;

16.4   /ᾧ παριστάνετε ἑαυτοὺς δούλους εἰς ὑπακοήν,/

17.1   χάρις δὲ τῷ θεῷ ὅτι

17.2   ἦτε δοῦλοι τῆς ἁμαρτίας

17.3   ὑπηκούσατε δὲ ἐκ καρδίας εἰς ὃν παρεδόθητε τύπον διδαχῆς,

18.1   ἐλευθερωθέντες δὲ ἀπὸ τῆς ἁμαρτίας

18.2   ἐδουλώθητε τῇ δικαιοσύνῃ.

19.1   Ἀνθρώπινον λέγω διὰ τὴν ἀσθένειαν τῆς σαρκὸς ὑμῶν.

Fig. 4.6 Syntactical Analysis of Romans 6:15-23 in Greek

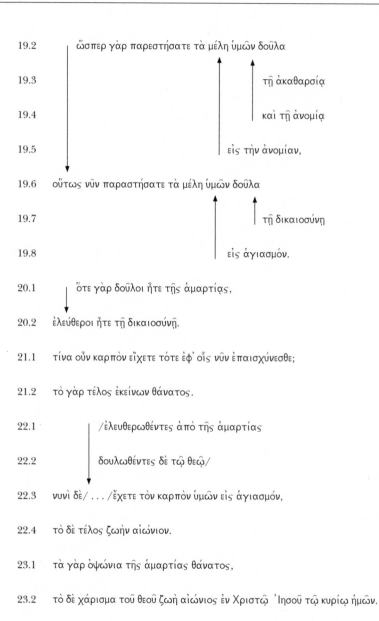

19.2   ὥσπερ γὰρ παρεστήσατε τὰ μέλη ὑμῶν δοῦλα

19.3   τῇ ἀκαθαρσίᾳ

19.4   καὶ τῇ ἀνομίᾳ

19.5   εἰς τὴν ἀνομίαν,

19.6   οὕτως νῦν παραστήσατε τὰ μέλη ὑμῶν δοῦλα

19.7   τῇ δικαιοσύνῃ

19.8   εἰς ἁγιασμόν.

20.1   ὅτε γὰρ δοῦλοι ἦτε τῆς ἁμαρτίας,

20.2   ἐλεύθεροι ἦτε τῇ δικαιοσύνῃ.

21.1   τίνα οὖν καρπὸν εἴχετε τότε ἐφ᾽ οἷς νῦν ἐπαισχύνεσθε;

21.2   τὸ γὰρ τέλος ἐκείνων θάνατος.

22.1   /ἐλευθερωθέντες ἀπὸ τῆς ἁμαρτίας

22.2   δουλωθέντες δὲ τῷ θεῷ/

22.3   νυνὶ δὲ/ . . . /ἔχετε τὸν καρπὸν ὑμῶν εἰς ἁγιασμόν,

22.4   τὸ δὲ τέλος ζωὴν αἰώνιον.

23.1   τὰ γὰρ ὀψώνια τῆς ἁμαρτίας θάνατος,

23.2   τὸ δὲ χάρισμα τοῦ θεοῦ ζωὴ αἰώνιος ἐν Χριστῷ Ἰησοῦ τῷ κυρίῳ ἡμῶν.

English: verse 18 provides a second reason to thank God (17.1), parallel to the (compound) one provided in lines 17.2-3 of the Greek analysis.

2. The Greek text in lines 19.4-5 falls into two parts, contrary to the English analysis at 19.4. This is because the NRSV takes the double occurrence of the noun ἀνομία "iniquity" in 19.4 and 19.5 as a single intensified expression ("to greater and greater iniquity" 19.4). Yet the Greek syntax parallels 19.4 with 19.3 (both nouns are datives) and parallels 19.5 in turn with 19.8 (both are prepositional phrases with εἰς). The contrasting parallel between 19.5 and 19.8, lost in English, is worth noting in Greek: presenting one's members as slaves to impurity and iniquity *leads to iniquity*; presenting them as slaves to righteousness *leads to sanctification*. While this difference has little bearing on the *discourse* analysis of Romans 6:15-23, it can have significance for how we understand Paul's view—here—of sanctification and iniquity.

We have now analyzed the discourse structure of Romans 6:15-23. How does this coherent argument against using God's grace as an excuse for sinning fit into the larger discourse of the entire epistle? If we compare the structures of Romans 6:1-3 and Romans 6:15-16, we can identify four elements they have in common: (a) What then? (b) Shall we sin? (c) Heavens no! (d) Do you not realize . . . ? The same structure is partially repeated at Romans 7:1 (Do you not know . . . ?). This may imply that Romans 7:1-6 belongs together with 6:1-14 and 6:15-23 as the third of three answers to the same issue. That issue, apparently, is this: does the absolute grace provided for humanity in Christ (Romans 5) imply the freedom to sin at will without fear of condemnation? Paul's three reasons for denying this potential objection to his gospel are (a) our identification with Christ in baptism (Rom 6:1-14), (b) our relationship to God as his slaves (Rom 6:15-23), and (c) the end of our relationship to the law (Rom 7:1-6). Romans 7:7, then, goes on to introduce a new question, different from the one treated in Romans 6:1—7:6. In Romans 6:1—7:6, the question is "Shall we keep on sinning?" In Romans 7:7-25, the question is "Is the law itself sinful?" Finally, Romans 8 describes the decisive influence of the Spirit on life in Christ. Thus, the arguments in Romans 6—8 demolish pious objections to Paul's gospel, objections based on fear of his doctrine of absolute condemnation and absolute grace (Rom 1—5) and on the desire to protect believers from indulging in sin because of it.

4.4 SUMMING UP

This chapter has tried to put analytical "feet" to the metaphor of the stone wall developed in chapter three. The process of analyzing texts into structured clusters depends on understanding the recursive nature of clustering, whereby textual clusters themselves cluster together to form larger and larger textual clusters. Part of the meaning of the two-word cluster (or sentence) found at Romans 6:15b (μὴ γένοιτο "By no means!") becomes evident from its relation to the immediate context (Rom 6:15a). And part of the meaning of Romans 6:15, as a three-sentence cluster, is to be found in its relation to Romans 6:15-23, and so on up the scale of structural complexity to the epistle as a whole.

Ideally, we do ourselves and our people a great service if we analyze the full discourse structure of any biblical book we wish to study, teach or preach. This is a long-range goal, however. Simply start wherever you are. Identify and analyze whatever paragraph you are currently working with. Use a commentary or dictionary article to get a sense of your paragraph's place in the larger work. At the same time, keep track of your own observations and conclusions. Begin to build up a living understanding of Colossians, or of Genesis, or of Mark's Gospel—whatever—as a whole. Make it your life's work, and take your time. Let yourself enjoy it.

We turn now in chapter five to a wider sense of discourse analysis, one that takes into account the *extra*textual context of history and culture.

5

HISTORY AND CULTURE IN EXEGESIS

You Can't Eat a Denarius

*For the Pharisees, and all the Jews, do not eat unless
they thoroughly wash their hands, thus observing the tradition of the elders;
and they do not eat anything from the market unless they wash it;
and there are also many other traditions that they observe,
the washing of cups, pots, and bronze kettles.*

MARK 7:3-4

We need to get one thing straight before we go any further. Gottfried Wilhelm von Leibniz (1646-1716) was the last man who knew *everything*. This means that no matter how compulsive we may be, no matter what expectations we think our professors or our congregations may have of us, no matter who we think we are, *we* can no longer hope to know everything. We cannot even know everything about some biblical book or pericope we might want to preach from. One important key to a lifetime of faithful, solid and productive exegesis is to remember that it truly does take a lifetime—and even then, it will not be finished! Go with what you have; build on what you gain. Listen, assimilate, absorb, but take your time.

We need to hear this word of reassurance (and probably more than once) for at least three reasons. First, since Leibniz's day, the world has seen such an explosion of information, not least in the field of ancient history, language and culture, that even fifty thousand Leibnizes could not contain it all. The temptation to feel responsible for buying a book (let alone reading it!) simply because it exists is an invitation to drop into the abyss. Second, a congregation does not need—or want—to hear everything we *do* learn about a text. I remember from my early days as a pastor, frantically trying to incorporate into sermons every last scrap of wisdom I had culled from reading commentaries. Each week I buried my people in so much information that no one, including me, could tell what the point of the sermon was. A third reason to emphasize this warning is that expecting perfection and thoroughness is the best way to become discouraged in the lifelong task of exegesis and to give it up in favor of lesser pursuits. Instead of that road, follow the road of realistic expectations: we need only do well what we have time for; we do not need to take on more than what we have time to do well. If the Lord can effectively use the "boy" Samuel (1 Sam 3:1-18), or Naaman's "little maid" (2 Kings 5:1-4), or a kid with bread sticks and sardines (Jn 6:9), he can use us too, even if we are "imperfectly" prepared. On the other hand, this "word of reassurance" is not a license to sloth! We have a job to do after all.

5.1 MEANING AS A FUNCTION OF PLACE IN CONTEXT

With that caveat, let's turn to the fascinating, if potentially intimidating, task of exegetically projecting ourselves backward in time and space. As a multiethnic, multigenerational, multimillennial community of Bible students, we work together in reconstructing for ourselves the ancient setting in which and for which the New Testament was first written. No one expects any one of us to do it alone. Leibniz is still dead. Yet, in a sense, even though none of us can "know everything" about this subject, the entire community working together can—sort of.

The importance of reconstructing the ancient biblical world rests on the same principle undergirding the point made above in chapter three: the significance of walking around in our pajamas depends on where we are when we do. The meaning of a word, a text, a "thing" or an event, is partly a function of its place in a context. This is just as true with regard to the historical-cultural context as it is with regard to the literary context discussed in chapter four.

5.1.1 An Example

Consider what Jesus' disruption of the temple strip mall would have meant (Mk 11:15-17 and parallels) if he had behaved this way in the market at Capernaum instead, or in Peter's house. We need to consider his "cleansing of the temple" within the context of the temple's cultural significance at the time. Throwing eggs at my neighbor's garage does not deliver the same message as throwing eggs at government buildings in Ottawa, London or Washington. Similarly, before we jump to conclusions about what the temple-cleansing episode means for us today, we need to understand first what it meant to Jesus and his contemporaries. It probably does *not* mean we should vandalize our local

Bible bookstores for selling "huggy-Jesus" dolls. Unfortunately, the Gospel writers who preserve the stories of Jesus' violent act in the temple do not bother to explain for us its cultural significance; they take it for granted. Today, we have to look elsewhere to find out about it. Where can we look?

5.1.2 Primary Texts and Secondary Texts

For this kind of background information, we are deeply indebted to generations of researchers who have combed and continue to comb the libraries, trash heaps and graveyards of biblical antiquity and who analyze thousands of relevant artifacts, documents and inscriptions surviving from the period. What they are looking for, usually, is exactly what we need: raw material for reconstructing the ancient historical-cultural setting. In terms of written materials, these researchers provide two types of data to help us understand that setting: primary and secondary sources, briefly discussed in chapter two.

Rarely will a primary text cast a direct light on some New Testament passage, though it can happen. For example, a stone inscription referring to Roman proconsul Gallio and dating his term of office helps us immensely in working out the chronology of Paul's missionary activities (cf. Acts 18:12-17). Likewise, the first-century ossuary (bone box) recently discovered in Jerusalem and bearing the inscription, "James son of Joseph brother of Jesus," is dramatic testimony to the historicity of James, Joseph and Jesus—unless it is a forgery, of course. On a somewhat broader scale, our understanding of a pivotal event in first-century Palestinian history, the destruction of Jerusalem and the temple in A.D. 70, is enormously enriched by the voluminous writings of first-century Jewish historian Flavius Josephus. Although this momentous event is nowhere unambiguously mentioned in the New Testament, both the anticipation of it and the memory of it underlie much of the New Testament text, Matthew 24:1-2, for example.

Most of the time, however, primary literature from the biblical period—including what Protestants have traditionally called the Old Testament Apocrypha and Roman Catholics know as the deuterocanonical books—provides us with indirect information, a big-picture backdrop to the New Testament. What we get from a firsthand acquaintance with this material is a gathering sense of "being there." The lively narratives in 1 and 2 Maccabees, for instance, bring us right into the midst of the passionate struggles for Jewish independence during the second century B.C. The revolutionary passion these books exhibit was just as rife during Jesus' day as it was nearly two centuries earlier. Reading through the nonbiblical material from Qumran (the so-called Dead Sea Scrolls) gives us some idea of how important the temple actually was to various streams of Judaism of the period, in spite of the fact that many Qumran sectarians regarded Herod's temple and its administration with abhorrence. Yet even this prejudiced perspective on the temple throws indirect light on Jesus' provocative act of "cleansing" it. Another example: I remember as a student picking up the old familiar Gospel of John shortly after completing a research paper on Gnosticism. Over several preceding months, I had read a large number of ancient Gnostic treatises, most of which were quite bizarre. With the smell of these documents still on my clothes, so to speak, the words of John's prologue (Jn 1:1-18) literally took my breath away; I gasped when I saw it. It was as if I had never read it before at all. Not that I suddenly became convinced that the author of John was a Gnostic; rather, I "heard" his message for the first time as he must have meant it to be heard in the context of first-century, "New Age," pseudoreligion. He spoke to what he knew.

Set yourself a goal of reading from these "original," primary documents over the remainder of your active life. (The Old Testament Apocrypha, or deuterocanonical books, provides a great place to begin.) Resist the false sense of obligation to master it all before your next sermon, but strive to read one or two of these texts each year, perhaps during Lent or Advent, or for your birthday. At a pace reasonable for you in the midst of life's other demands, gradually make yourself a "local" in the Judeo-Roman world.

Secondary literature in this field—in the shape of dictionary and journal articles, statistical tools, grammars, treatises, monographs and commentaries—forms the depository of results, and summaries of results, from centuries of study and reflection on the Bible. This vast material is profoundly valuable for a number of reasons. For one thing, it can help us in understanding the primary literature (including the New Testament itself), much as a tour guide at Carlsbad Caverns helps us to appreciate what we see there. Those who have gone before us pass on to us what they have learned, thereby enabling us to follow them and even to go beyond where they had to stop. Second, however, we can test their legacy, preserved in readable format, against what we ourselves now see. The significance of this is that secondary sources enable us to become involved in a colossal, slightly unorganized, universal conversation. Not one of us has the inside track on understanding all these things. Leibniz is dead, remember! We need each other and the various perspectives we represent in order to expand the scope of our view and to correct our misconceptions. In the third place, moreover, there is little point in perpetually reinventing the wheel. While we cannot possibly take as assured truth anything and everything we find in print, we can trust much of the consensus that our colleagues in this work, over many centuries and around the globe, have struggled to establish. We would be foolish to ignore it. If someone has hacked a pathway through the forest, why would we not tread it too, unless we thought it went in the wrong direction? If a Greek concordance tells me that there are eleven occurrences of the term ὁμοθυμαδόν "together" in the New Testament, I will not be likely to count them up myself by tediously reading through those twenty-seven books on my own—in Greek!

For our purposes here, though, among the foremost advantages of secondary literature is that it summarizes and digests centuries of collected wisdom and insight on the ancient biblical and relevant nonbiblical literature. In ministry, we seldom, if ever, have the necessary time or (yet) the accumulated experience for dealing adequately with this material. In such situations we can turn to an article on the temple in a Bible dictionary, or to a book on the first-century temple cult, or to a commentary on Matthew 21:12-13. Not only do these resources provide us a general orientation or a specific perspective on the subject at hand, they also give us suggestions for pursuing it further if we should want to. Once again, because the quantity of available information is overwhelming, we need to keep our wits about us. We must not let the utter impossibility of performing the task to perfection discourage us from doing anything at all. Do well what you can in the time you have, however short that time may be, and be content about it. Over the course of your life, engage the "big conversation" at some level; pick up "guide brochures" as you need them; get help wherever you require it. Three excellent guides to this material are worth mentioning here. One is C. K. Barrett's *New Testament Backgrounds*, another is C. A. Evans's *Noncanonical Writings and New Testament Interpretation*, and a third is L. R. Helyer, *Exploring Jewish Literature of the Second Temple*.[1] On the other hand, do not be satisfied with a mere guidebook when you can see Carlsbad for yourself. Have you ever actually read 1 Maccabees or Tobit or Qumran's *Manual of Discipline*? Or try the *Book of First Enoch*, which the Book of Jude quotes!

5.2 TWO TYPES OF HISTORICAL-CULTURAL SETTING

What we have been talking about until now in this chapter is one sort of historical-cultural setting. Jesus, Peter, Paul and all the other characters marching across the pages of the New Testament lived their lives in Roman-occupied Pal-

---

[1]C. K. Barrett, *New Testament Backgrounds: Writings from Ancient Greece and the Roman Empire That Illumine Christian Origins*, rev. ed. (New York: HarperSanFrancisco, 1987); Craig A. Evans, *Noncanonical Writings and New Testament Interpretation* (Peabody, Mass.: Hendrickson, 1992); Larry R. Helyer, *Exploring Jewish Literature of the Second Temple Period: A Guide for New Testament Students* (Downers Grove, Ill.: InterVarsity Press, 2002).

estine or in some other corner of the Roman Empire. All the varied political, religious, economic, linguistic, social and cultural features of that world, and of particular social pockets within that world, form the *general historical-cultural backdrop* to the action and the messages preserved for posterity in these documents. If we are to understand those documents, we need special information about much of what people living at that time simply took for granted. Real people composed, for other real people, all twenty-seven documents that make up our New Testament, and all these people were members of real cultural and social systems. Biblical authors and their audiences held a great deal of information in common, information that for them needed no explicit mention in the text. In fact, it would have been obnoxious to an audience to have each detail explained; it would be a bit like a sportswriter for the *Seattle Times* telling his local readers that "the Mariners, *a Seattle-based professional baseball club,* lost their fifteenth consecutive home game last night." That italicized piece of insultingly gratuitous information, however, would be extremely useful (in the year 3535) to the archaeologist who finds the Dead Puget Sound Scrolls in the ruins of the ancient city of Seattle illustration (inspired by Moises Silva). The more we understand about that general first-century cultural backdrop, the better able we will be to read any New Testament text intelligently.

The other type of historical-cultural setting, equally important for understanding these texts, represents the more *specific historical "occasion"* lying behind each of them. Consider the Gettysburg Address, for example. President Abraham Lincoln wrote that speech for the dedication of a cemetery at the site of one of the bloodiest and most decisive battles of the American Civil War. He delivered it in November 1863, within the mostly agrarian world of the mid-nineteenth-century United States. The American "union" was not yet a century old; some of its living citizens could still remember its infancy. The great open lands to the west of the Mississippi River were as yet "unsettled," at least in the minds of the expansionists in the east. Railroads were just coming into their stride. Apart from the horrific war currently underway, it was an age of cultural optimism and innovative energy. That was the world Lincoln knew. The event, however—the specific *occasion*—that gave rise to the address was the dedication of that particular cemetery on that particular Pennsylvania battlefield. The message of the Gettysburg Address speaks to the solemn occasion and to the war itself, and its meaning is inextricably connected to both. Nevertheless, Lincoln's address, together with the event that inspired it, is only understood against the larger, general backdrop of life in the United States in the 1860s.

In the same way, Paul's letter to Rome stands out against the general backdrop of the first-century Roman Empire. The *pax Romana*, still in effect since

Augustus' day, ensured a degree of public security hardly known in the western world before this era. Christianity, from the perspective of official Roman policy, had not fully distinguished itself from Judaism, a permitted religion. Yet, seeds of change were evident even at the highest levels. According to the Roman historian Suetonius (*Life of Claudius* 25.4), the emperor Claudius had expelled all Jews from the city of Rome somewhere between the years 49 and 52, because of disturbances regarding someone named "Chrestus" (cf. Acts 18:2). Additionally, Jewish communities existed all over the Roman world, not least in Rome itself, and many of these provided beachheads for the proclamation of the Gospel in far-flung places. These features of Judeo-Greco-Roman society, and many others, constitute the historical-cultural backdrop to the book of Romans and, with some adjustments, to virtually all New Testament documents.

The specific *occasion* behind Paul's penning the letter to Rome, on the other hand, is peculiar to Romans alone. Sitting out the winter in Corinth, awaiting favorable weather for traveling to Jerusalem with an offering from the Gentile churches, Paul casts his eyes westward to Spain, where he wants to go next. He visualizes the church at Rome, which he has never visited, as a support base for his projected western operations, much as Syrian Antioch has been the base of his eastern mission. Yet, he is also aware of dissension in the Roman congregations, running along Jewish-Gentile lines. It has apparently resulted from the recent return of Jewish Christians to Rome following Nero's rescinding of Claudius's edict (compare Acts 18:1-3 with Rom 16:3). All this makes for a complex situation, a multilayered *occasion* for Paul's letter. Understanding that situation enables us to grasp Paul's primary concern in writing what he writes, and understanding that primary concern helps us to understand Paul's message.

We will return to the specific occasion for a document in chapter six. The present chapter is principally about the larger, more general picture. Still, it is important to be aware of the difference between the two types of historical context.

5.3 BIBLICAL TEXTS AS CULTURALLY DETERMINED

It surprised me the first time I understood that we have to reckon with the cultural differences between the original situation presupposed by a biblical text and the situation we ourselves occupy today, a situation to which we might want to "apply" the Bible's teachings. Yet it surprised me far more profoundly when I realized that the Bible documents themselves, the Bible's teachings, are also culturally determined. I had somehow inconsistently assumed a level of absolute, universal relevance to the very wording of Holy Scripture. I apparently visualized the Bible as two-dimensional, flat: God from within his dimension speaks to us human beings in our dimension. I most assuredly do subscribe to the universal authority of God's will for humanity, but I now see that the expression of that divine will takes on manifestations appropriate to whatever society it addresses.

A biblical text in this sense is *three*-dimensional, rounded: it represents the God-dimension, the "original" human-dimension and (third) the later, secondary human-dimension—ours, for example. The message tailored to the Corinthian church will be somewhat different from the message delivered to the Galatian churches, or to Presbyterians in Seoul or Atlanta, or to Pentecostals in Chelmsford. The reason of course is that the cultures in these various settings differ from one another. Like Alice, we exegetes must step through the seemingly flat surface of the looking glass and into the three-dimensional world of the Bible. The miracle embodied in this fact is that God willingly stoops to meet *particular* human beings and particular groups of human beings, wherever he finds them. It has always been this way. What we hear Moses telling his new nation in the desert speaks to them on their own familiar ground. He addresses them in terms appropriate to the political climate of the Near East in the mid-second millennium. By the time Jesus appears in Galilee, hundreds of years later, much has transpired. Jesus now reinterprets Moses' message for a new cultural situation, and we have this reinterpretation in the Sermon on the Mount (Matthew 5—7). As cultures change, so does the shape of the message. God meets human beings where he finds them, and we can see this process in the very pages of the Bible itself. Let's consider some ways this dynamic plays itself out in the exegesis of the New Testament.

5.3.1 The Septuagint as a Cultural Context

The wording of 2 Peter 3:16 suggests that by the time 2 Peter was written, Paul's letters, or some of them, had already begun to take on the dignity of Scripture. Otherwise, the Bible used by the New Testament authors is what Christians today call the "Old" Testament. The New Testament message is drenched in Old Testament literature. More specifically, the Bible as the New Testament authors knew it was usually the Old Testament in Greek translation, much of it completed in the third century B.C. and called the Septuagint (abbreviated LXX; *septuaginta* is Latin for "seventy"). The legend that seventy translators produced it survives in the pseudepigraphical *Letter of Aristeas*. The importance of the LXX for the New Testament authors can hardly be exaggerated and constitutes one of the most important elements in the contextualization of New Testament documents. From start to finish, the New Testament simply assumes the biblical story of God and his people, Israel. Allusions to that story abound in its pages, and quotations from it are almost always in their LXX form. (Surprisingly perhaps, this implies that for New Testament exegesis the LXX is even more important than the Hebrew Old Testament.) Some examples will illustrate this.

Matthew's Gospel, as is well known, makes frequent appeal to the fulfillment of Old Testament prophecy as a way of demonstrating Jesus' significance (cf., e.g., Mt 1:22; 2:15; 8:17; 12:17). This fact implies that such a tactic would impress Matthew's intended readers, that they would be familiar with and venerate the source of these quotations. However, Matthew does not restrict himself to quotations alone. In chapter one, following his highly stylized version of Jesus' genealogy, Matthew narrates the strange circumstances of Jesus' birth (Mt 1:18-25). Woven into his account are several deft literary allusions to the Genesis story of Abraham and the birth of Isaac. These allusions culminate at Matthew 1:21 with a nearly verbatim appropriation of Genesis 17:9 LXX to Joseph, Mary's betrothed; in the Genesis passage, the Lord tells Abraham that Sarah, his wife, will bear him a son. Implied in Matthew's subtle allusions and in his application of this Old Testament passage to Joseph is the expectation that the original readers will "get" the allusion and see Jesus as, among other things, the son of Abraham par excellence (cf. Mt 1:1). They will understand Jesus as the ultimate "seed" of Abraham, through whom all the nations of the world will be blessed by Abraham's God (as promised in Gen 22:18; 26:4, etc.).

Simply because it comprises three-quarters of the Christian Bible, the Old Testament has its own legitimate claim on our attention, demanding to be understood as God's contextualized word in its own right. But in a treatment of New Testament exegetical method like this one, the Old Testament becomes one (or thirty-nine!) of the primary texts for the study of New Testament historical-cultural background, perhaps the most significant of all primary texts. Many of us who feel called to the exegetical task but have not grown up in a biblically literate social context will need tools and helps for the job. Besides reading the Old Testament, one of the most productive things we can do is to acquire the habit of consulting an Old Testament concordance, one for the LXX in fact, whenever we study the New Testament. This process becomes infinitely more do-able with various electronic, computer-based programs dedicated to biblical and related texts. Elaborate searches can be designed to find specific places in the Old Testament that provide immediate or general background to some remark of Paul's or to an allusion in Luke.[2]

---

[2]Three of the more popular programs are available from GRAMCORD, BibleWorks and Logos. URLs for their respective websites are as follows: <www.gramcord.com>; <www.bibleworks.com>; <www.logos.com>.

Consider Matthew 3:1, which begins with the words ἐν δὲ ταῖς ἡμέραις ἐκείναις "and in those days." Since these words immediately follow Matthew's account of Jesus' infancy, we might naturally think that the expression "those days" refers to that early period of Jesus' life, when Joseph took the boy and his mother to live in Nazareth (Mt 2:19-23). The phrase, however, introduces the appearance of John the Baptist in the desert, some twenty years or more after the events narrated in Matthew 2. What, then, does the phrase mean here? An electronic concordance search of the LXX for this Greek phrase (minus the δέ "and") turns up a long list of texts. Many of them come from the prophetic books, and all of these prophetic occurrences use the phrase to refer to the dawn of the long-expected messianic age. Here's just one example, Jeremiah 50:20 (= Jer 27:20 in the LXX): "*In those days* and at that time, says the LORD, the iniquity of Israel shall be sought, and there shall be none; and the sins of Judah, and none shall be found; for I will pardon the remnant that I have spared." As an opener to the story of just how Jesus does "save his people from their sins" (Mt 1:21), these three words (five in Greek) could hardly have been better chosen. Matthew's first readers would likely have recognized them and their significance in much the same way as we might recognize the allusion and significance of the words, "A horse! A horse! My kingdom for a horse!" Nevertheless, the introduction to Matthew 3 is lost on us today unless we take the extra effort to acquaint ourselves with the LXX context. We get the same results, more or less, from searching an NRSV concordance[3] for Old Testament occurrences of the phrase "in those days."

5.3.2 Paganism as a Cultural Context

Many Gentiles in antiquity were familiar with Jewish Scripture, whether through exposure to it in the synagogues of the Diaspora or through becoming members of the early church. Nevertheless, literary maneuvers like the ones in Matthew 1:21 and 3:1 would probably have made little sense to the originally intended readers of certain other New Testament documents. As I mentioned above, the prologue to the Gospel of John reads like a corrective to gnosticizing interpretations of Jesus and his work. Today we sometimes follow John in speaking of Jesus as the *Logos*, or the "Word," and that epithet may ring deeply theological in our ears, even though most of our audiences will not really know what we are talking about when we speak this way, any more perhaps than we do ourselves. Yet John's first readers—mostly Gentile Christians—were enormously

---

[3]E.g., John R. Kohlenberger III, *The NRSV Concordance Unabridged: Including Apocryphal/Deuterocanonical Books* (Grand Rapids: Zondervan, 1991).

concerned with what they understood the universe to be like and their place in it. In their minds, the Logos—a sort of divine emanation charged with running the universe—played a profound role in the outworking of their personal destinies. (The ancient "hermetic" book *Poimandres* gives some light on this.) To hear now that the Logos had become a human being and lived among them would have had far-reaching implications for them.[4]

The point, again, is that the more we understand about the various ways ancient Jewish and Greco-Roman people thought about the world and interacted with each other within and across cultural lines, the better we will understand the New Testament. And the better we understand the New Testament, the more adequately we as teachers of the church will be able to proclaim God's ancient message appropriately to contemporary cultures. We are not in this alone, of course, but the responsibility does lie with us to be always informing ourselves. Our role as faithful shepherds of God's flock demands it. And one of the most exciting and illuminating techniques for becoming further acquainted with the New Testament's cultural background involves access to and the ability to study the LXX, or at least the Old Testament.

5.3.3 Vocabulary as a Cultural Context

If the Old Testament, especially the LXX, is an obvious cultural backdrop to the New Testament, even more obvious in this regard is the language in which the New Testament is written. A very significant element in New Testament language is the vocabulary its writers had to work with. Ironically, however, the vocabulary of the Greek New Testament has been simultaneously one of the most eagerly investigated fields of its historical-cultural background and one of the most abused.

Preachers and teachers of the Bible frequently appeal to "what it says in the Greek," in order to add authority and interest to their presentations. Now I am firmly committed to the value of using the Greek text of the New Testament in carrying out exegesis. Nonetheless, there are dangers to avoid. Chief among these is the temptation to impress the uninitiated with our prowess (or apparent prowess) in using Greek. For many people in the pews, hearing the pastor preface a pronouncement with the words, "In the Greek it says," is tantamount to hearing Moses proclaim, "Thus says the Lord!" While we do indeed want to

---

[4]"Word"-theology was also known in Jewish circles. Philo of Alexandria and certain Aramaic paraphrases of the Old Testament (targums, perhaps dating to the first century or earlier) speak of the "Word of God" as an agent of creation. Evans cites these sources as examples of the value primary literature has for New Testament exegesis (*Noncanonical Writings*, p. 5).

hear what the Lord says (that *is* the point of exegesis, after all), we need to remember that exegesis is a community project, not the sole responsibility of
one person. By silencing all discussion through an appeal to "the Greek," even
without intending to do so, we effectively short-circuit the community's active
participation in the process. Add to that the very strong possibility that our
solo reading of "the Greek" may simply be wrong.

One common reason for misusing Greek in exegesis is the fascination students, pastors and scholars often feel for the way in which Greek vocabulary
"reveals" hidden meanings. Many preachers have told their people that the
Greek word for "church," ἐκκλησία, means the "called-out ones." They have
this impression because they can identify two parts to the word: ἐκ "out" and
-κλησια, a derivative of the verb καλέω "to call." Yet, nowhere in Greek literature does the term ever mean "the called-out ones." Again, we may marvel over
the four separate Greek words for "love," or assume that the plethora of Greek
prepositions implies minutely exact nuances of meaning, discernible only by
the trained exegete. I have heard a pastor insist that the preposition εἰς "into,"
when used in the phrase πιστεύω εἰς Χριστόν "I believe in *[to]* Christ," implies
the mystical union between the believer and Christ. Somehow, by believing, we
enter *into* Christ. This relationship between believers and Christ may in fact be
justifiably supported on other grounds, but this use of the preposition by no
means implies it, as another occurrence of πιστεύω εἰς can show (1 Jn 5:10b).

Following a summer trip my wife and I took to Sweden, one of my cousins
there wrote to us in English to say that he hoped we would soon return and
"take a bath" with him again. Even if we allow for certain elements of Sweden's
national reputation, this is *not* what he meant. The Swedish verb *bada*, etymologically related to English *bath* and *bathe*, is a common word for "swim,"
though it can also refer to taking a bath, contrary to the English *swim*. The vocabulary stocks of Swedish and English, while somewhat related, do not neatly
overlap. My cousin's invitation might have made more sense to a British
speaker, especially if he had said, "go bathing with me." This is because even
British and American English do not perfectly correspond in the distribution
of vocabulary. "Knickers" went out of fashion in America in the 1930s, whereas
half of all Britons still wear them, or something else by that name.

Realizing this simple fact about languages helps us to overcome the impression that somehow New Testament Greek words are full of special, hidden
meanings. What we do need to recognize about Greek vocabulary is not its hidden mysteries, but its historical-cultural relevance to the message of the New
Testament. Translating or reading a selection of the Greek New Testament is
no more mysterious than translating or reading a text in Swedish, Spanish,

DANGERS LURKING IN WORD STUDY

James Barr's epoch-ending book *The Semantics of Biblical Language* (Oxford: Oxford University Press, 1961) made biblical scholars painfully aware of the many linguistic pitfalls surrounding the study of biblical words. Various authors since then have based their advice on Barr's work. Particularly helpful are the following: D. A. Carson, *Exegetical Fallacies,* 2nd ed. (Grand Rapids: Baker, 1996), chap. 1; D. A. Black, *Linguistics for Students of New Testament Greek: A Survey of Basic Concepts and Applications,* 2nd ed. (Grand Rapids: Baker, 2000), chap. 5; and M. Silva, *Biblical Words and Their Meaning: An Introduction to Lexical Semantics,* rev. and exp. ed. (Grand Rapids: Zondervan, 1995). Here are Barr's main warnings (consider this a side-Barr):

1. Avoid the dangers of etymologizing.

Etymology is the study of words from the perspective of their root forms and their historical usage.

- Avoid searching for the "basic," "root," or "original" meaning of a word—as if it were discoverable or as if it were relevant even if discovered.

- Avoid dividing words into their component parts and then adding them up again to arrive at the "real" meaning.

- Do not assume that only etymologically related words are relevant to each other. Louw and Nida's "domain" dictionary goes a great way toward rectifying this error in traditional dictionaries and word studies.

2. Avoid getting language structure confused with thought structure.

- *With respect to a language's stock of vocabulary:* The fact that the Greeks had two terms for flesh and body, σάρξ and σῶμα, while Hebrew had only one, *bāśār*, does not imply that the Hebrews saw no distinction between the body and its constitutive material.

- *With respect to a language's grammatical structure:* God is not feminine simply because the Hebrew term *rûaḥ* "spirit" is grammatically feminine; nor is he masculine because he is referred to with a masculine pronoun.

3. Avoid getting concepts confused with the words that refer to them.

Words *refer* to concepts; they do not *contain* them. The word θεός "god" in the New Testament *means* the same thing there as it does in Plato, "supernatural, divine being." Its *reference,* however—what (or whom) it refers to—is different in the New Testament from what it is in Plato. Paul and Jesus use the word to refer to the God of Israel; Plato presumably did not. *Reference* and *meaning* are two different things.

Special dangers in this category include

- The *"illegitimate totality transfer."* This happens when we look up every occurrence of, say, "flesh" and assume that the sum total of all its possible meanings is present in its every occurrence.

- The *"illegitimate identity transfer."* This happens when we assume that because two items are referred to by the same word, they are essentially the same concept. Or we may assume the reverse, that because one item is referred to by several words, those words all have essentially the same meaning, or that they always refer to the same concept.

4. Avoid ignoring context.

- In general, the meaning of a given word in a given context will be *the simplest meaning—the least full meaning*—necessary for the word to make sense in that context, except in the case of a pun. That is, we can use the context to eliminate all possible senses but one for a potentially ambiguous item.

- That is, from the range of a word's possible meanings, a single context will select the one it requires and eliminate all the others.

- To sum up: Context eliminates possible meanings.

French, German or Japanese, and often a lot *less* mysterious than translating a play by Euripides or one of Plato's dialogues. If we have not learned the relevant language adequately, however, we will need to use special tools for the job, one of the most useful being a lexicon. The word *lexicon* is a technical term for the list of vocabulary items available to speakers of a particular language, together with a description of their typical (conventional) use. Native speakers of a language carry theirs around in their heads; non-native speakers gradually acquire additional "mental" lexica to varying degrees of fullness, but they often use a printed version of the lexicon (sometimes calling it a "dictionary"). This is where all students of New Testament Greek find themselves, since there are no surviving native speakers of that language.

So then, because the authors of the New Testament documents needed to write their messages in the common Greek (called *koine*) of the first century, they had to express what they wanted to say through the vocabulary available to them in that language. If they wished their readers to understand the messages they sent, they were under an obligation to use words familiar to their readers and to use them in ways recognizable to those readers. This does not mean they could not be creative in their use of those words, or even perhaps coin new words for their specific purposes. It does mean, however, that their creativity in this regard could not exceed the limits of ordinary intelligibility if they wished their messages to remain intelligible. (Some modern theologians and philosophers have apparently not grasped this principle!)

A good lexicon is designed to assist the non-native speaker in understanding texts. For our purposes, we need a good lexicon for the New Testament, and for English speakers none today surpasses the third edition of W. Bauer's *A Greek-English Lexicon of the New Testament and Other Early Christian Literature*.[5] This tool, commonly referred to as BDAG (standing for editors Bauer, Danker, Arndt and Gingrich), packs a staggering amount of information on every term appearing in the New Testament and on many others besides. As with any tool, it behooves the user to study the instructions before use; it is also worth reviewing them from time to time as the years go by. BDAG's design is typical for a dictionary; it organizes the vocabulary alphabetically, and within the article on a particular vocabulary item it arranges all the data in a logical way. We can see at a glance how a word was used and what it meant in various contexts; some words, like σάρξ "flesh," occur in several different senses. References to New Testament passages in which a word occurs appear in bold print for easy identification (a big improvement over early editions of the book). See figure 5.1 for sample entries from BDAG illustrating these features.

Another sort of lexicon is the semantic domain dictionary edited by Johannes Louw and Eugene A. Nida.[6] In this work the Greek vocabulary of the New Testament is organized into "semantic domains," or fields of meaning, rather than alphabetically. For example, instead of listing together in one article the several different senses of σάρξ, the domain dictionary gathers together all of the vocabulary items appropriate to a particular field of meaning, for example, "flesh," or "human being." These vocabulary items can be verbs, nouns, adjectives, synonyms or antonyms, general terms or specific. The various domain-centered articles then discuss how the words collected under a

---

[5]W. Bauer, *A Greek-English Lexicon of the New Testament and Other Early Christina Literature*, ed. F. Danker, 3rd ed. (Chicago: University of Chicago Press, 2000).

[6]J. P. Louw and E. A. Nida, *Greek-English Lexicon of the New Testament Based on Semantic Domains*, 2nd ed., 2 vols. (New York: UBS, 1989).

ἱλάσκομαι (s. two next entries) mid. dep.; fut. ἱλάσομαι LXX; 1 aor. pass. impv. ἱλάσθητι (in mid. mng. ἱλάσθην LXX) (Hom. et al.; ins; LXX [Thackeray 270f]; s. also Dodd and Hill, below).

❶ **to cause to be favorably inclined or disposed,** *propitiate, conciliate* (Il. 1, 100 Apollo; Hdt. 5, 47, 2 an offended Olympic victor; 8, 112, 3 Themistocles; Strabo 4, 4, 6 τὸν θεόν; Cornutus 34 p. 73, 5; Heraclit. Sto. 16 p. 24, 9 τὸν Ἥλιον; Appian, Samn. 12 §6, Hann. 27 §115 θυσίαις κ. εὐχαῖς ἱ. τ. θεούς; Herm. Wr. 1, 22; Philo, Spec. Leg. 1, 116; Jos., Ant. 6, 124 τὸν θεὸν ἱ.; 8, 112, C. Ap. 1, 308 ἱ. τοὺς θεούς; SibOr 3, 625; 628). Pass.: of one addressed in prayer, to act as one who has been conciliated, but with focus on the initiative of the one who functions thus: *be propitiated, be merciful* or *gracious* (4 Km 24:4; La 3:42; Da 9:19 Theod.) w. dat. (of advantage, Esth 4:17h ἱλάσθητι τ. κλήρῳ σου; cp. also Ps 78:9) ἱλάσθητί μοι τῷ ἁμαρτωλῷ (dat. of advantage) *have mercy on me, sinner that I am* **Lk 18:13** (Sb 8511, 7 [ins, imperial times] ἵλαθί μοι, Μανδοῦλι [a divinity]; GJs 5:1 (twice; in the first instance perh. with inf. foll., s. deStrycker 289 n. 2).—B-D-F §314.

❷ **to eliminate impediments that alienate the deity,** *expiate, wipe out,* of Christ as high priest εἰς τὸ ἱλάσκεσθαι τὰς ἁμαρτίας τοῦ λαοῦ *to expiate the sins of the people* **Hb 2:17** (so Mft. [NRSV 'make a sacrifice of atonement'] cp. SIG 1042, 15f [=IG II², 1366; II/III AD] ἁμαρτίαν ὀφιλέτω Μηνὶ Τυράννῳ ἣν οὐ μὴ δύνηται ἐξειλάσασθαι 'let him be liable to Men Tyrannos for a sin he can have no hope of expiating' [cp. 1Km 3:14; on this ins s. New Docs 3, no. 6]; Ps 64:4 τὰς ἀσεβείας ἱ.; Dssm., NB 52 [BS 225]; Breytenbach 98).—CDodd, JTS 32, '31, 352–60; also Dodd 82–95 on ἱ. and related words (against Dodd: LMorris, ET 62, '51, 227–33; RNicole, WTJ 17, '55, 117–57; in support: NYoung, EvQ 55, '83, 169–76); SLyonnet, Verbum Domini 37, '59, 336–52, Sin, Redemption and Sacrifice, '70, 120–66, 256–61; DHill, Gk. Words and Hebrew Mngs. '67, 23–48; KGraystone, Ἱλάσκεσθαι and Related Words in the LXX: NTS 27, '81, 640–56; GHorsley, New Docs, 3, 25 (on Graystone and Hill); JFitzmyer, 'Reconciliation' in Pauline Theology, in: No Famine in the Land (McKenzie Festschr.) '75, 155–77; JLunceford, An Historical and Exegetical Inquiry into the NT Meaning of the ἹΛΑΣΚΟΜΑΙ Cognates, diss. Baylor '79; CBreytenbach, Versöhnung '89.—DELG. M-M. TW. Sv.

ἱλασμός, οῦ, ὁ (s. prec. and next entry)—❶ *appeasement* necessitated by sin, *expiation* (τῶν θεῶν Orph., Arg. 39; Plut., Fab. 18, 3; cp. Plut., Sol. 12, 5. In these cases we have the pl.,

prob. referring to the individual actions to be expiated. But also sg.: Plut., Mor. 560d, Camill. 7, 5; Lev 25:9; Ps 129:4; Philo, Leg. All. 3, 174) εἰς ἱ. ἐμοί *for my expiation* GJs 1:1; so perh. abstr. for concr. of Jesus as the ἱ. περὶ τ. ἁμαρτιῶν ἡμῶν **1J 2:2; 4:10.** But mng. 2 has been popular.

❷ *instrument for appeasing, sacrifice to atone, sin-offering* (Ezk 44:27 προσοίσουσιν ἱ. cp. Num 5:8; 2 Macc 3:33) s. above.—S. also lit. cited s.v. ἱλάσκομαι. DELG s.v. ἱλάσκομαι 1. M-M. TW.

ἱλαστήριον, ου, τό (subst. neut. of ἱλαστήριος, ον [PFay 337 I, 3ff—II AD; 4 Macc 17:22; Jos., Ant. 16, 182]; s. prec. two entries). In Gr-Rom. lit. that which serves as an instrument for regaining the goodwill of a deity; concr. a 'means of propitiation or expiation, gift to procure expiation' (IKosPH, 81, 347 ὁ δᾶμος ὑπὲρ τὰς Αὐτοκράτορος Καίσαρος θεοῦ υἱοῦ Σεβαστοῦ σωτηρίας θεοῖς ἱλαστήριον; ChronLind B 49 Ἀθάναι ἱλατήριου; Dio Chrys. 10 [11], 121. The mng. is uncertain in POxy 1985, 11).

❶ *means of expiation,* of Christ, ὃν προέθετο ὁ θεὸς ἱλαστήριον *whom God set forth as a means of expiation* **Ro 3:25** (so REB; cp. CBreytenbach, Versöhnung, '89, 168 [s. below]; difft. GFitzer, TZ 22, '66, 161–83 and NRSV 'sacrifice of atonement'). The unique feature relative to Gr-Rom. usage is the initiative taken by God to effect removal of impediments to a relationship with God's self. In this pass. ἱ. has also been taken to mean

❷ *place of propitiation* (as Ezk 43:14, 17, 20; cp. also Luther's 'Gnadenstuhl', and s. on Hb 9:5 below) that of ἱ. **Ro 3:25** s. TManson, JTS 46, '45, 1–10 (against him Breytenbach 167f.)—S. also Dssm., ZNW 4, 1903, 193–212 (s. EncBibl III, 3027–35); PFiebig and GKlein ibid. 341–44; SFraenkel, ibid. 5, 1904, 257f; CBruston, ibid. 7, 1906, 77–81; GottfKittel, StKr 80, 1907, 217–33; EdaSMarco, Il piano divino della salute in Ro 3:21–26: diss. Rome '37; VTaylor, ET 50, '39, 295–300; GBarton, ATR 21, '39, 91f. WDavies, Paul and Rabbinic Judaism² '55, 227–42; ELohse, Märtyrer u. Gottesknecht '55; LMorris, NTS 2, '55/56, 33–43; DWhiteley, JTS n.s. 8, '57, 240–55; DBailey, Jesus the Mercy Seat: diss. Cambridge '99 (ins).—The LXX uses ἱ. of the lid on the ark of the covenant, כַּפֹּרֶת, which was sprinkled w. the blood of the sin-offering on the Day of Atonement (Ex 25:16ff al. Likew. TestSol 21:2; Philo, Cher. 25, Fuga 100, Mos. 2, 95.—JStelma, Christus' offer bij Pls [w. Philo] '38). So **Hb 9:5,** transl. *mercy-seat;* for the history of this word s. OED s.v.—DELG s.v. ἱλάσκομαι 1. M-M s.v. ἱλαστήριος. EDNT. TW. Sv.

Figure 5.1. Entries for ἱλάσκομαι and related words in BDAG

Some things to notice: (1) Individual lexical entries (these are taken from pp. 473-74) and the common definitions for each entry are set in bold type. (2) Each definition is followed by italicized "glosses," i.e., English words that might be substituted for the Greek term in a translation. Of course, this implies that definitions and glosses, though related, are not the same thing. Note as well that some entries have only glosses (e.g., ἱλαστήριον). (3) The densely packed paragraphs for each entry contain information on the history of the word in Greek literature, whether from the grammatical (morphological) point of view (usually in the first paragraph), or from the semantic point of view (under each separate definition). Usage in New Testament texts is indicated with bold references to specific passages, which makes them easy to spot. (4) In addition, most paragraphs refer to a wealth of secondary literature on the term in question. For the purposes of "pastoral exegesis," much of this information will not be needed, but for scholarly exegesis, it is of enormous help. It is something like the untapped potential available to you in your garden rototiller; you may never get around to using it to thatch your lawn, but the special attachments are there if you ever need them. (5) Just be sure you read the instructions before you use the machine. For BDAG, the instructions and abbreviation lists appear in the front of the book.

B   Forgiveness (40.8-40.13)

40.8 ἀφίημι[f]; ἄφεσις[a], εως f; ἀπολύω[c]: to remove the guilt resulting from wrongdoing – 'to pardon, to forgive, forgiveness.'

ἀφίημι[f]: ἄφες ἡμῖν τὰ ὀφειλήματα ἡμῶν 'forgive us the wrongs that we have done' Mt 6.12.

ἄφεσις[a]: τὸ αἷμά μου . . . τὸ περὶ πολλῶν ἐκχυννόμενον εἰς ἄφεσιν ἁμαρτιῶν 'my blood . . . which is poured out for many for the forgiveness of sins' Mt 26.28.

ἀπολύω[c]: ἀπολύετε, καὶ ἀπολυθήσεσθε 'forgive and you will be forgiven (by God)' Lk 6.37.

It is extremely important to note that the focus in the meanings of ἀφίημι[f], ἄφεσις[a], and ἀπολύω[c] is upon the guilt of the wrongdoer and not upon the wrongdoing itself. The event of wrongdoing is not undone, but the guilt resulting from such an event is pardoned. To forgive, therefore, means essentially to remove the guilt resulting from wrongdoing.

Some languages make a clear distinction between guilt and sin, and terms for forgiveness are therefore related to guilt and not to the wrongdoing. Therefore, 'to forgive sins' is literally 'to forgive guilt.' Since terms for 'forgiveness' are often literally 'to wipe out,' 'to blot out,' or 'to do away with,' it is obviously not possible to blot out or to wipe out an event, but it is possible to remove or obliterate the guilt.

40.9 ἱλάσκομαι[a]: to forgive, with the focus upon the instrumentality or the means by which forgiveness is accomplished – 'to forgive.' εἰς τὸ ἱλάσκεσθαι τὰς ἁμαρτίας τοῦ λαοῦ 'so that the people's sins would be forgiven' or 'so that God would forgive the people's sins' He 2.17.

40.10 χαρίζομαι[b]: to forgive, on the basis of one's gracious attitude toward an individual – 'to forgive.' χαρίσασθέ μοι τὴν ἀδικίαν ταύτην

'forgive me for being so unfair' 2 Cor 12.13. It may be useful in some instances to translate χαρίζομαι in 2 Cor 12.13 as 'be so kind as to forgive me.'

40.11 ἐπικαλύπτω: (a figurative extension of meaning of ἐπικαλύπτω 'to cover over, to put a covering on,' not occurring in the NT) to cause sin to be forgiven – 'to forgive, to cause forgiveness.' μακάριοι . . . ὧν ἐπεκαλύφθησαν αἱ ἁμαρτίαι 'how happy are . . . those whose sins are forgiven' Ro 4.7.

40.12 ἱλασμός, οῦ m; ἱλαστήριον[a], ου n: the means by which sins are forgiven – 'the means of forgiveness, expiation.'

ἱλασμός: αὐτὸς ἱλασμός ἐστιν περὶ τῶν ἁμαρτιῶν ἡμῶν '(Christ) himself is the means by which our sins are forgiven' 1 Jn 2.2.

ἱλαστήριον[a]: ὃν προέθετο ὁ θεὸς ἱλαστήριον διὰ τῆς πίστεως 'God offered him as a means by which sins are forgiven through faith (in him)' Ro 3.25.

Though some traditional translations render ἱλαστήριον as 'propitiation,' this involves a wrong interpretation of the term in question. Propitiation is essentially a process by which one does a favor to a person in order to make him or her favorably disposed, but in the NT God is never the object of propitiation since he is already on the side of people. ἱλασμός and ἱλαστήριον[a] denote the means of forgiveness and not propitiation.

40.13 ἱλαστήριον[b], ου n: the location or place where sins are forgiven (in traditional translations rendered 'mercy seat') – 'place of forgiveness, place where sins are forgiven.' ὑπεράνω δὲ αὐτῆς Χερουβὶν δόξης κατασκιάζοντα τὸ ἱλαστήριον 'above the box were the glorious winged creatures spreading their wings over the place where sins are forgiven' He 9.5.

Figure 5.2. The New Testament semantic domain of "forgiveness," according to Louw-Nida. (Used by permission.) Some things to notice: (1) Louw-Nida primarily serves those who translate the New Testament into the languages of remote people groups. Much of the discussion in the domain dictionary reflects this (notice the second and third paragraphs under 40.8). (2) The example shown here (from Louw-Nida, pp. 1.503-4) represents the nine New Testament Greek terms that the editors regard as belonging to the semantic sub-domain of "forgiveness." That sub-domain itself belongs to the larger domain of "reconciliation and forgiveness" (numbered 40 in the overall scheme of the dictionary). (3) Entries 40.12 and 40.13 represent the same lexical items featured in fig. 5.1 for BDAG, but here they are related to the other terms listed among words relevant to "forgiveness." One of them, ἱλάσκομαι also appears elsewhere, in connection with the semantic domain of "mercy/merciless" (88.75), since the editors analyze the notion of "showing mercy" as somewhat different from that of "offering forgiveness." (4) This figure illustrates the way Louw-Nida helps us to see what other terms a New Testament writer might have used, in a particular context, in place of the ones he actually uses. It also helps us to see how Louw-Nida can highlight the components of meaning peculiar to a word actually used, components that may be significant for the context in question.

domain interrelate with one another. Thus the word σάρξ, because it has so
many different meanings, appears in nine different places throughout the dictionary. (Greek and English indexes guide users in finding their way around.)
This approach to "lexicography" stands on the conviction that the meaning of
a term occurring in a given context is partly defined by the other words that
were available for that context but were rejected (consciously or not) by the
speaker or writer. It can often be profoundly illuminating to know what Paul
might have said, but did not say, what words he might have used but did not
use. Louw and Nida help us to see what those alternative words might have
been. Figure 5.2 reproduces the semantic domain of "forgiveness," as defined
by the Louw-Nida dictionary.

5.4 CULTURAL "RELEVANCE" AND CULTURAL TRANSFERENCE

How we impart the fruits of our labors to the people among whom we live and
work takes us beyond the pale of exegesis and into the realm of hermeneutics.
We will touch on this matter in a later chapter, though only briefly, since this
book is primarily about exegesis. Still, at this stage of things it is worth empha-
sizing something that lies implicit in the preceding discussion. If the ancient
biblical documents themselves are culturally conditioned, and if an important
element of the exegetical task involves reading those documents as completely
as possible from the perspective of the relevant ancient cultures, what exegetes
end up with are messages appropriate *to those ancient settings.* How, then, are
those ancient messages to be made relevant to another time and place—our
own, for example? We will often need to carry out a kind of cultural transfer-
ence, whereby the "transcultural" core of a message is recloaked in the garb of
some new cultural setting. (Return to fig. 1.1, which diagrams this process.)

Paul's instruction to women in Corinth to cover their heads led to centuries
of Christian women wearing scarves, veils and other headgear in church services. It is not a universal practice today, however, and probably was not in
Paul's day either. It made sense, apparently, in first-century Corinthian culture, and we can investigate why (since Paul is not exactly clear about it in
1 Corinthians 11). Yet, even for those contemporary Western churches where
women still do cover their heads, it may not be obvious just how *this practice* addresses anything transcending all time and all cultures. Even those who insist
on a hierarchy of genders (itself a culturally debatable question) would, I suspect, be hard pressed to explain what scarves have to do with it. The point is
this: keep the big picture in mind. Do not let yourself be distracted unduly by
isolated factors, however fascinating, without trying to understand them in the
context of that bigger picture. When you bring the results of your exegesis

back to your own people, remember to re-clothe them in the categories your people understand, all without losing the "word" of the Lord. This is what he has called us to do.

We encounter a similar problem when we read the New Testament through the lenses of previous culturally influenced exegesis. One of the more important of these current problems is the one addressed by the "new perspective" on Judaism, Paul, and the law. This new perspective comprises two main issues. First, it has become clear that traditional Christian views of second-temple Judaism have been sorely mistaken.[7] The dramatic events of the sixteenth-century Reformation convinced the church for hundreds of years to come that Pharisaic Judaism of the New Testament period virtually mirrored the worst features of medieval Roman Catholicism. In recent decades, however, Jewish and Christian scholars alike have demonstrated that this is simply not so and that Jewish theology in the first century had a profound appreciation of God's grace and mercy.

Second, if this reassessment of second-temple Judaism is well founded, it means that the typically Protestant understanding of Paul and his view of the Law is in need of revision as well, at least in so far as it depends on that mistaken perception of second-temple Judaism. The resulting debate[8] has led to a growing realization that what Paul rejected as illegitimate "works of the law" were those features of Judaism that tended to support distinguishing the covenant people of God on the basis of ethnicity and cultural practices. In other words, Paul's concern was not one of arguing against the sort of "works righteousness" that occupied the Lutheran Reformation (legitimate as that Reformation surely was). Rather what concerned him in this regard was an illegitimate restriction of the covenant people to those who subscribed to the Jewish practices of circumcision, sabbath laws and holy days, and dietary observances. The "new perspective" has not involved as dramatic a "revision" as the Reformation itself did perhaps, but it has been dramatic nonetheless.

5.5 PROBABILITIES, AMBIGUITIES AND ALTERNATIVES

What we cannot avoid in this process, any more than in the process of analyz-

---

[7]"Second-temple Judaism" refers to the various strands of Judaism characterizing the postexilic period from Ezra and Nehemiah in the sixth century B.C. to the Roman destruction of Jerusalem in A.D. 70.

[8]Sporadic since around 1900, but especially vigorous since the late 1970s. Among other articles on the subject, see F. Thielman's summary of the history and substance of the discussion in "Law II: Paul," in *The IVP Dictionary of the New Testament*, ed. Daniel G. Reid (Downers Grove, Ill.: InterVarsity Press, 2004), pp. 687-702.

ing grammatical structure, is the fact that we are always dealing with probabilities. All of historical research and reconstruction seeks the *most probable* solution to some question. What philosophers used to refer to as "absolute certainty" forever eludes us here. We will always be weighing alternative proposals and considering the effect of ambiguity. That is the nature of the beast, and until and unless we come to grips with it, we will always be in danger of taking the law into our own hands, so to speak. We will be tempted to insist that God has revealed to *us* that there can be no further discussion of some issue or other, whatever it may be.

This does not mean that we should avoid proclaiming anything at all with deep conviction, even perhaps with something approaching absolute certainty on an emotional level. Nor does *this* mean that we establish our faith on our emotions, though it does indeed involve them. I am personally convinced that Jesus' physical resurrection, from death to life again, was a genuine, historical event. I am convinced of it enough to die for it if I have to. Yet, simultaneously, I recognize that many people from all walks of life, no less sincere than I am, are unable to commit themselves to such a fantastic notion. We may hope for them that someday they can. But the point is that there is no way to prove absolutely, as with mathematics or logic, that Jesus rose from the dead. We find our historical assurance of the event from weighing other explanations that would account for the amazing sequel. There are plenty of available options (as witnessed in Mt 28:11-15). For me, nothing explains the big picture quite so well as exactly what the New Testament tells us—that God raised the crucified Jesus to life. To that we can add the ever ambiguous, ever elusive testimony of the Spirit, who comes to us in times of trouble, speaking words of wisdom: *It is true, it is true.*

Our confidence lies somewhere in the midst of these many factors. In Scripture, we read the story and its interpretations. The Spirit opens the eyes of our hearts to believe. As a community we immerse ourselves in the cultures and history of that ancient day in order to understand the old, old story more perfectly, testing and weighing the possibilities, talking them over with colleagues from across the centuries. We read, listen and speak from within the contexts we ourselves inhabit, recognizing how deeply rooted we are in our own cultures and allowing the same dignity to the writers of the biblical documents. We are in this *together!* We believe the voice of Jesus, echoed from deep within us by the voice of his indwelling Spirit: "Remember, I am with you always, to the end of the age" (Mt 28:20). We have no reason to fear the process. We may engage in it, together, in peace.

6

LETTERS

Reading Someone Else's Mail

And when this letter has been read among you,
have it read also in the church of the Laodiceans;
and see that you read also the letter from Laodicea.

COLOSSIANS 4:16

We turn now from topics more or less applicable across the scope of New Testament literature to topics pertinent to particular literary subgroups. The particular subgroup we will discuss in this chapter is that of the New Testament letters or epistles. (There is little practical value in distinguishing between "letters" and "epistles," as some have done; we can use the words interchangeably here.) The various subgroups of New Testament documents are defined in terms of *genre*, something worth being clear about before we continue (6.1). Once we settle that issue, we will consider the matter of reading letters as historical documents (6.2) and reading them as arguments (6.3).

6.1 GENRES AND SUBGENRES

Literature comes in many genres, and this affects its interpretation. As used in English, the French word *genre* could logically be applied to types of anything: animals, music, paintings, occupations, people and even vehicles. But it is actually used to refer almost exclusively to categories of art, especially literature. Literature comes in many types and subtypes, distinguished by style, content, purpose and so on. We are familiar in our culture with such literary forms as letters, newspaper articles, treaties and other legal documents, as well as poetry, short stories, novels and comic strips. Scholarly essays, moral discourses, jokes, sermons, advertising slogans, campaign speeches and many other kinds of writing constitute some of the vast array of literary genres and subgenres we use.

The exegetical implication is that in order to be fair to a pericope, we exegetes must consider the kind of literature to which it belongs. That is, we must take into consideration its function, which is closely related to its genre. Consider this little ditty from the late 1950s, advertising a product for styling men's hair:

Brylcreme, a little dab'll do ya!
Use more only if you dare!
Watch out! The girls'll all pursue ya!
They love to run their fingers through your hair!

We cannot approach this "dab" of literary elegance with the same interpretive attitude we would assume in approaching a farewell letter that a Civil War soldier writes to his wife a week before he is killed in battle at Manassas. The approach we would take to the online help for our new Bible software would be different still.

It is equally important for biblical interpretation to know what particular type of material we are dealing with. Traditionally, scholars identify four main genres in New Testament literature: *epistles, Gospels, Acts* and *apocalypse.* We might even wish to say there are only *three* main genres, grouping Gospels and Acts together under the rubric of "narrative." However that may be, within these main genres there are many other subgenres (sometimes called "registers"), each with its peculiar character and interpretive restrictions. Parables, for example, and household codes (also known by the German term *Haustafeln*), speeches, hymns, summary statements, aphorisms and many others give the three main genres variety and color. They also require specialized attention from exegetes.

Texts belonging to the genre of epistle appear only here and there in Old Testament books (e.g., in Jeremiah, Ezra, Nehemiah and the deuterocanonical 2 Maccabees), but the New Testament is full of letters. As many as twenty or twenty-one of the twenty-seven *books* in the New Testament are letters or compilations of letters. Acts 15, 23, and Revelation 2—3 contain more. Most of these biblical documents have the basic shape typical of letters from Mediterranean antiquity, hundreds of which have turned up in the garbage dumps of ancient Egypt (see the two examples provided in the sidebar on page 116):

Opening:	Sender, to receiver. Greeting.
Ice Breaker:	Thanksgiving or prayer for . . .
Body:	The main business
Closing:	Greetings, blessing.

Various subgenres (subtypes or "registers") are represented even among the New Testament letters. Philemon and Philippians function as personal recommendations; Philippians also contains a thank-you note. First Corinthians

TWO ANCIENT LETTERS FROM EGYPT

The following two letters, the first written around the middle of the third century B.C. and the second sometime during the first century A.D., were both recovered toward the end of the nineteenth century. The first is from a young man to his father, Cleon, an architect in the Fayum district of Egypt. The second, likewise from a son to his father, lacks an icebreaker, quite fitting for the spoiled-brat tone of the message. The openings and closings of the letters are printed in bold, the one *icebreaker* in italics, and the body of both letters in plain type. Brackets [ ] insert explanatory information. Translations (slightly adjusted) are from George Milligan, *Selections from the Greek Papyri* (Cambridge: University Press, 1927), pp. 7-8, 102-3.

LETTER 1

Polycrates to his father, greeting. *I am glad if you are in good health, and every thing else is to your mind. We ourselves are in good health.* I have often written to you to come and introduce me, in order that I may be relieved from my present occupation. And now if it is possible, and none of your work hinders you, do try and come to the Arsinoe festival [in honor of the late, deified Queen Arsinoe]; for if you come, I am sure that I shall easily be introduced to the king [Ptolemy II]. Know that I have received 70 drachmas from Philonides [the writer's brother]. Half of this I have kept by me for necessaries, but the rest I have paid as an installment of interest. This happens because we do not get our money in a lump sum but in small installments. **Write to us yourself, that we may know how you are circumstanced and not be anxious. Take care of yourself that you may be well, and come to us in good health. Farewell.**

LETTER 2

Theon to Theon his father, greeting. [No *icebreaker.*] You did a fine thing! You have not taken me away along with you to the city! If you refuse to take me along with you to Alexandria, I won't write you a letter, or speak to you, or wish you health. And if you do go to Alexandria, I won't take your hand, or greet you again henceforth. If you refuse to take me, that's what's up! And my mother said to Archelaus, "He upsets me: away with him!" But you did a fine thing! You sent me gifts—great ones, husks! They deceived us there, on the 12th, when you sailed [down the Nile River, presumably]. Send for me then, I beseech you. If you do not, I won't eat, I won't drink! So there! **I pray for your health. [Date: month and day] Tubi 18.**

7—14 responds to questions, and Romans reads like a didactic treatise, as does 1 John. Apologies (in the sense of defenses) characterize Galatians 1—2, 2 Corinthians and perhaps 1 John, and ethical instruction (called "parenesis") can be found in many epistles, including 1 Thessalonians, Ephesians 4—6, and James. Galatians and 1 Corinthians 7 give advice. More formal instruction can be found in the "church orders" recommended in the Pastoral Epistles and in the household codes *(Haustafeln)* preserved in Colossians 3—4, Ephesians 5—6 and 1 Peter 2—3. Some epistles actually look like sermons or homilies, once preached to a particular constituency; 1 John, James and Hebrews fall into this category.

All New Testament letters, even the most personal (e.g., Philemon, 2 and 3 John), appear to be either semiconsciously or fully consciously intended by their writers for *public* consumption. They are "public" either in regard to a local congregation (Philem 1-4) or in regard to several congregations (Col 4:16; Rev 2—3). This is true even though all of them are "occasional" in nature. Whether any of them was *never* actually intended to function as a public document (3 John?) is moot, since they have all been public now for nearly two millennia. We do need to realize, however, that being intended for "public consumption" does not necessarily imply "consciously written as Holy Scripture," valid for all time on a par with what we now call the Old Testament. Very likely Paul would be shocked, and perhaps embarrassed, to find generations of Christians diligently studying his brief note to Philemon, especially if he were to recall how forceful, almost to the point of pushy, he becomes in it. The fact that this little gem *has* been canonized as Scripture is a testimony to the earthiness of the incarnation: God is not ashamed to use us as we are, even to become one of us.

6.2 HISTORICAL CONTEXT: WHO IS ON THE OTHER END?

This point brings us back to the issue of historical context, introduced in chapter five. A very important point to grasp about New Testament letters is in fact their *occasional* nature. They were each written, like Lincoln's Gettysburg Address, with respect to a very specific occasion, not as a general treatise on some theological topic, good for all time. They may indeed be good for all time, but that presumably was not their writers' original intention. Therefore, in order to interpret New Testament letters properly, we must work at understanding what the original occasion was for each of them and treat them accordingly. We can consider their historical context from three perspectives: (1) the tasks they were intended to accomplish, (2) the other side of the conversation conducted in them, and (3) the cultural assumptions the author tacitly made as he wrote.

6.2.1 Task-Oriented Theology: Sent on a Mission

The "task-oriented" theology of the epistles, resulting as it does from their occasional nature, from their authors' sense of mission, is actually not all that different from the purpose of sermons and counseling in the local church today. Unfortunately, the dates, origins and sometimes even the authors of New Testament documents are unspecified—or inadequately specified—and the letters are often (for us) plagued with vagueness arising from cultural and situational assumptions shared by writers and readers, to which we have no immediate access today. What, for example, does Paul mean by accusing his Jewish readers of hypocritically robbing temples, even though they abhor idols (Rom 2:22)? As Krister Stendahl has said, "Even the divinely right answer is not heard aright if it is applied to the wrong question. . . . Our vision is often more obstructed by what we think we know than by our lack of knowledge."[1] Let's take this up in more detail.

We have in mind the identification of the specific problem a document seeks to solve, the mission it hopes to accomplish, the occasion *to which* it speaks—the cemetery dedication at Gettysburg, for example—rather than the broader historical backdrop *within which* it speaks. That specific situation is often referred to with the German phrase *Sitz im Leben* ("situation in life"). All Scripture is occasional in this sense; each piece has its own *Sitz im Leben*. (Actually, this term is more common in the study of Gospel material, which we will take up in the next chapters, but it works here as well.) All of the Bible's individual books (and even separate parts of some books) originated in response to concrete historical situations or occasions. In the New Testament, epistles most readily demonstrate this characteristic (just as prophetic books do in the Old Testament). Knowledge of those situations is helpful, often indispensable, to an accurate exegesis of a given passage. This is not to say, however, that we always have that knowledge.

Some New Testament epistles give clear and helpful clues to their historical situation and the task at hand. First Corinthians, for example, sketches the outlines of the problems of schism and power struggle in the Corinthian body, things Paul has heard about from Chloe's people (1 Cor 1:10-12). In fact, the entire letter reflects various aspects of the Corinthian "situation." Second Thessalonians 2:1-12, on the other hand, provides a classic example of insufficient information, referring as it does to "the" coming rebellion, to "the lawless one," and to something which "now restrains him." Not wishing to waste his ink, Paul

---

[1]Krister Stendahl, *Paul Among Jews and Gentiles and Other Essays* (Philadelphia: Fortress, 1976), p. 6.

slips into shorthand: "Do you not remember that I told you these things when I was still with you?" (2 Thess 2:5). We can see that he wished to rectify a problem in Thessalonica, and what he says about it here may have been enough for the first readers. But two millennia later, we are left wondering what it was all about and how it might affect us. There has been no shortage of suggestions.

Today the irony of our situation is that while we need to reconstruct the historical contexts lying behind various New Testament passages in order to understand their original messages, the majority of our reconstructions are hypothetical. The commentaries and professional journals are filled with conflicting theories and alternative scenarios. But as we saw at the end of the last chapter, that is precisely the nature of the discipline, and we must do our best with what we have. (This problem is compounded in the Gospels, where there are at least three possible life-situations: (a) that of Jesus himself in the days of his earthly ministry, (b) that of the post-Easter communities, and (c) that of the Evangelists as they write to particular churches later in the first century.) Still, no matter how frustrating it may be not to know what we would like to know, the principle remains that we understand biblical documents (and therefore biblical teaching) best when we allow for and try to account for the "tasks" they were first meant to carry out.

6.2.2 The Other Side of the Conversation

Part of our problem in this is that what we overhear in a New Testament letter is just one side of the conversation. It would be enormously useful (not to mention exciting) if we were to find Paul's personal correspondence files, including any disturbing letters he had received from Corinth, or possible communiqués from Priscilla and Aquila telling him about the situation in Rome. Lacking these resources, scholars have done their best to reconstruct the other side of the conversations represented in the New Testament correspondence. They do this believing with good reason that the more we understand about those conversations, the better we will understand what Paul or James or any of the other letter-writers is saying.

One technique for reconstructing the "full" conversation is a kind of "mirrored" reading of an epistle. Consider 1 John 1:5—2:2 as a test case. Careful analysis of that text reveals a series of six if-then constructions. Take 1 John 1:6, for example: "*If* we say we have fellowship with [God] while we are walking in darkness, *[then]* we lie and do not do what is true." Further analysis reveals that these six if-then constructions pair off into three sets. In this way verse 6 is answered by verse 7: "but if we walk in the light as he himself is in the light, [then] we have fellowship with one another, and the blood of Jesus his Son cleanses us from all sin." Verses 8 and 9 form the next pair and 1:10—2:2 covers the third pair.

What appears to be happening here is that the author (we can call him John) first quotes the sort of thing he has heard his theological opponents teaching (1 Jn 1:6, 8, 10) and then replies to it with what he considers to be sound teaching (1 Jn 1:7, 9 and 2:1-2). His opponents, then, were apparently insisting that their fellowship with God was unaffected by what John regarded as walking in darkness (1 Jn 1:6), and that they were neither sinful (1 Jn 1:8) nor guilty of having committed sins (1 Jn 1:10). Combined with other hints from throughout 1 John (e.g., 1 Jn 4:2), these "mirrored" claims strongly suggest that John was dealing with people of a gnostic stripe, people who sharply distinguished between the reality of the spiritual world and the irrelevance of the material world. In their view apparently, the way they lived out their physical existence had no connection to the realities of their spiritual existence. Thus they even denied that the divine Christ had come as a human person of flesh and blood, and insisted therefore that they themselves as members of that divine Christ had no further need to be concerned with the constraints of their own fleshly existence. These are the notions John confronts in 1:5—2:2, and reading 1 John with these late-first-century issues in mind brings a depth of exegetical understanding otherwise not possible. "Mirrored reading" is an effective method for recovering those issues, if it is used with discretion and with the realization that it is open to circular reasoning and thus no less subject to abuse than any other procedure in historical studies.

6.2.3 Cultural Assumptions

Reading widely in the primary literature of the period is especially helpful with regard to reconstructing such situations. It provides the "gathering sense of being there" discussed in chapter five. (Again, a sampling of that literature, such as that provided by C. K. Barrett,[2] gives us a tantalizing taste of it.) Contemporary gnosticizing philosophies, for example, provide clues to the issues 1 John addresses with its insistence on the "fleshly" Christ, or to those that Colossians has in view when it speaks of the cosmic Christ. Knowledge of first-century Roman laws relating to slavery and slave ownership illuminates what Paul says in his letter to Philemon, helping us to guess intelligently at what he really wants Philemon to do. Information of this kind helps to fill in the gaps left for us by the fact that epistolary "tasks" are often implied but not defined. It does the same thing for other gaps, such as those left by the "inaudibility" of the conver-

---

[2] C. K. Barrett, ed., *The New Testament Background: Writings from Ancient Greece and the Roman Empire That Illumine Christian Origins,* rev. ed. (New York: HarperSanFrancisco, 1987).

sation partners or by unspoken cultural assumptions. A person near and dear to me used to point out the brake pedal and other familiar vehicular controls every time I used his car. We call such unnecessary information pedantic; we shun it if we can. There is no reason to believe that the ancients felt any differently about it. The New Testament writers and their readers shared an enormous wealth of cultural assumptions, common information needing no reiteration, but much of this information has gone lost with the passing of time and the cultural migration of the church. Providing it is no longer pedantic.

One of the more obvious of these cultural assumptions is embodied in the choice of *koine* Greek as the language the authors used. No New Testament writer bothers to explain Greek grammar and vocabulary to his readers; he assumes they will understand. Evidently the original addressees did. We never catch Paul saying something like, "You do understand what I mean by the future tense, don't you? It means it hasn't happened yet. And the word *evidently?* It means 'as far as we know,' right?" Today, however, we spend thousands of dollars and hundreds of hours just learning the rudiments of that language so that we can get in on the biblical conversation.

On another level, 1 Corinthians 11 presupposes an entire complex of cultural practice foreign to modern readers, at least to readers in much of the English-speaking world. What is all this fuss about demanding head coverings for women and regarding long hair on men as degrading (1 Cor 11:14-15)? In the mid-1960s, my father certainly thought he understood the problem with long hair on men (or on teenage boys anyway), since I was letting mine grow out in order to imitate the Beatles. But I suspect that the issues involved for my dad were different from the ones Paul dealt with. Consider what Paul means when he says (in 1 Cor 11:10), "For this reason a woman ought to have a symbol of authority on her head, *because of the angels.*" Angels? What angels? Paul's Corinthian readers apparently understood what he meant without needing it explained to them. For us it is a "gap." The point once again is that without access to this information about the historical setting of a biblical text, our understanding of that text is impaired; but our need for this sort of information does not guarantee that we will always have it. Conveniently for us, much of what we do need—as far as it can plausibly be reconstructed—is available in a good Bible dictionary or commentary. For quick help with 1 Corinthians 11:10, for instance, we might consult articles on angels or head coverings in the *Dictionary of Paul and His Letters.*[3]

---

[3]E.g., Daniel G. Reid, "Angels, Archangels," and Craig S. Keener, "Man and Woman," in *Dictionary of Paul and His Letters*, ed. Gerald F. Hawthorne et al. (Downers Grove, Ill.: InterVarsity Press, 1993), pp. 20-23, 375-77, and 583-92 (esp. pp. 585-86).

THROUGH THE LOOKING GLASS INTO 2 JOHN

Using the sorts of questions suggested just above in section 6.2.2 and nothing but the text of 2 John, try your own hand at reconstructing the situation behind that letter. Then compare your results with those provided here.

The raw data

v. 1a   "Lady": an individual (cf. 3 Jn 1) or a congregation? If the latter, why so designated here? Need for a code?

v. 1b   "the elder": description or position? If the latter, what sort of leadership structure implied?

v. 1c   "I love in truth": veiled allusion to others who do not love (note the emphatic ἐγώ "I"), or who claim to love but do not do so "truly"?

v. 1d   "all those who know the truth": veiled allusion to members of some other group who do not know it?

v. 3a   "Jesus Christ, the Father's Son": possible emphasis on the relation of Jesus to the Christ and to the Father?

v. 3b   "in truth and love": characteristic of John. Seems almost added here to "Johannize" the standard greeting "grace, mercy, and peace." Is there some special Johannine reference for "truth"/"love," that is, some particular behavior in mind?

v. 4a   "*some* of your children": an allusion to a faction within the congregation?

v. 4b   "from the Father": any special reason for not saying "from the Son"?

v. 5a   "new commandment": reminiscent of John 13:34. Here, however, it is not a new commandment anymore, but an old one (cf. 1 Jn 2:7; 5:3).

v. 5b   "not a new commandment": allusion to the opposition's having invented a "new" one? (cf. v. 9)

v. 5c   "from the beginning": if the "old" commandment is that recorded in John 13:34, then does the "beginning" refer to the earthly ministry of Jesus?

v. 5d   "love each other": reference to perceived flaw in the opposition's ethic?

v. 7   "many deceivers . . . world": a clear reference to one aspect of the situation

v. 8   "look to yourselves": another aspect of the situation: the elder's anx-

	iety for the spiritual welfare of the "lady," which he sees threatened by the schismatic, heretical traveling teachers
v. 9a	"goes ahead": likely an ironic reference to the "advanced" new teaching (cf. new commandment in v. 5, and the content of the advanced teaching in v. 7)
v. 9b	"does not have God": denial of the opponents' claims
v. 9c	"both the Father and the Son": corrective to opponents' division of Father from (human) Son?
v. 10a	"comes to you": allusion to the traveling-missionary or itinerant-teacher style of leadership? See also 2 John 12: "I hope to come to you."
vv. 10b-11	"receive . . . give greeting": reference to means by which early teachers had their base of operation, dependent on local hospitality (like traveling Christian singing groups today). Contrast 3 John 5-8.
v. 12	"much to write to you": possible reference to what is now known as 1 John? Any historical relationship to 3 John 13-14?
v. 13	"elect sister": testifies to a system of churches or local congregations, under the elder's leadership. How might this be related to the congregation of 3 John?

Summary of results, based on raw data taken right from the text

a. Several locally meeting congregations associated with each other under the leadership of (at least) "the Elder."

b. Congregations nourished by traveling, itinerant teachers, perhaps administered by and including the Elder.

c. Some of these traveling teachers, or perhaps, "strangers" from elsewhere, have begun teaching a "new," self-claimed "advanced" doctrine, at the core of which is the denial of real humanity to the divine Christ; Jesus the man is not the Christ, and vice versa. Perhaps implies Jesus is no longer needed as a means of access to God.

d. Further characteristic of this "advanced" doctrine is that it encourages (if not outright teaches) a de-emphasis on loving behavior.

e. Some members of the group have been swayed by this teaching, and others, while not swayed yet, are nonetheless (innocently, perhaps) supporting the heresy by giving hospitality to its traveling teachers.

f. The Elder is alarmed enough about the spiritual welfare of his flocks that he himself plans to visit them and announces his intention in this letter.

One other area of research worth mentioning here is that of sociological analysis of the biblical world. Although exegetes and historians have long been attentive to the social aspects of first-century Judeo-Greco-Roman culture, recent decades have seen remarkable efforts to bring scientific rigor to this subject. Scholars specially trained in sociological theory have turned their talents and their science to analyzing the biblical cultures, with an eye to illuminating the biblical text.[4] Issues such as family structure, weddings and giving in marriage, divorce, politics and economics, the overlapping of politics and religion, power and authority, shame and honor, class distinctions and social mobility (or the lack of it)—all these factors play silent but significant roles in the background of a text. People growing up immersed in those cultures had no particular need to hear their socio-cultural assumptions spelled out to them in a communication from Paul or James; those assumptions could be taken for granted no less than Westerners take free-market trade and trial-by-jury for granted. Yet for Western exegetes, a knowledge of the privileges, authority and responsibility of the first-century Greco-Roman *paterfamilias* (the ruling patriarch) in his household throws much light on a passage like Ephesians 5:21—6:9. The exegete sees how counter-cultural the message of "mutual submission" (Eph 5:21) is for the Christian husband-father-master. Christ remains "head" of the church, his body, and thus provides a rationale for a first-century man to act the role of "head" of his own household. However, the actual way in which Christ *functions* as head of the church, sacrificing himself for her sake, radically revolutionizes the socially acceptable—in fact, legal—way a Christian ought to "rule" over his family. Thus, original readers of the letter to the Ephesians would have caught the implications without having the sociological backdrop spelled out, but modern Western readers will not. Sociological analysis helps to fill in this gap.[5]

6.3 ARGUMENT

It is an oversimplification to say that what we have just been discussing is the *why* and the *how* of an epistolary communiqué, and that turning to the "argument" of an epistle involves the *what*. Still, there is some logic in putting it that way. We do indeed need to understand the historically determined (occasional) theological-missional task addressed by a biblical writer, as well as the

---

[4]A useful survey of this area of study for Pauline literature is S. C. Barton, "Social-Scientific Approaches to Paul," *Dictionary of Paul and His Letters*, pp. 892-900; note the literature he cites.

[5]The same principle applies to Gospel study. See, e.g., K. C. Hanson and Douglas Oakman, *Palestine in the Time of Jesus: Social Structures and Social Conflicts* (Philadephia: Fortress, 1998).

particular form his writing takes and the cultural accommodations he makes in order to communicate with his audience. But we also need to understand the content of his message. What in fact is he saying on this "occasion" and in this format? What is his argument? We can take this up under three headings: rhetorical criticism, syntactical structure and logical development.

6.3.1 Rhetorical Criticism

Among the many fascinating approaches taken to biblical literature in recent decades, one particularly appropriate to New Testament letters is rhetorical criticism. Working from the theories of famous rhetoricians of antiquity (Aristotle, Cicero, Quintilian), some scholars have analyzed Paul's letters as if Paul himself were a student of Greco-Roman rhetoric and as if he crafted his letters more or less in strict accordance with the "rules" of the masters. Many of these analyses are probably exaggerated, but they are helpful nevertheless. They make us aware that Paul was, after all, a man of his time, one who was eminently capable of adapting himself, even as a Jewish scholar, to the conventions of his Gentile audiences.

Critics recognize three main "orientations" for ancient Greco-Roman rhetoric: *forensic, epideictic* and *deliberative*.[6] Forensic rhetoric is oriented toward the past; it defends or accuses someone regarding actual past actions ("But when Cephas came to Antioch, I opposed him to his face, because he stood self-condemned"; Gal 2:11, where Paul defends himself). Epideictic rhetoric is oriented to the present; it praises or blames (evaluates) a person regarding present values or behavior ("For, to begin with, when you come together as a church, I hear that there are divisions among you; and to some extent I believe it"; 1 Cor 11:18). Deliberative rhetoric is oriented toward the future, encouraging or dissuading someone regarding a possible future action ("We who are strong ought to put up with the failings of the weak"; Rom 15:1).

Likewise, there are three grounds from which an ancient author or orator can motivate the audience or make an appeal to them: *ethos, logos* and *pathos*. An appeal from *ethos* is made on the basis of the communicator's moral authority. Mothers use this one: "Because *I* said so; that's why!" If the basis of the appeal is a demonstration of the rightness or logic of the proposal, it is made on the ground of *logos*. Husbands use this one: "Well, it just makes sense; that's why!" And if the argument is driven home on the basis of personal affection

---

[6]E.g., G. A. Kennedy, *New Testament Interpretation Through Rhetorical Criticism* (Chapel Hill: University of North Carolina Press, 1986), and a classic application, H. D. Betz, *Galatians,* Hermeneia (Philadelphia: Fortress, 1979).

or obligation, it is founded on *pathos*. Marlon Brando, as the Godfather, used this one: "You owe me this; that's why!"

In addition to orientation and grounds of appeal, modern rhetorical critics also recognize ancient schemes for organizing a communication. For example, a typical scheme of this sort lists the following elements in the body of a formal letter (or a speech):

Opening: identifying writer and addressees

Exordium: establishing a rapport with addressees

Propositio: stating the main burden of the letter, its thesis

Confirmatio: describing what makes the *propositio* necessary

Refutatio: silencing any anticipated objection to the *propositio*

Peroratio: summing up the matter and possibly laying out for the addressees once again the expectations that the writer has for them, based on the *propositio*

Closing: greetings and good wishes to addressees

Other rhetorical features of a text include tricks of the trade, such as some of those we discussed above in chapter four: chiasms, inclusios, repetitions, contrasts and the like.

Paul's short letter to Philemon provides a handy example for illustrating these things. If you can, take a moment to read it before going on (it takes less than two minutes). We can quickly see that Paul is asking Philemon to perform some deed regarding the runaway slave Onesimus. This deed is not explicitly specified in the letter, but it is not something Philemon has already done, nor is it something he is presently doing (at least from Paul's perspective); it is something as yet undone, future. Thus, from a rhetorical point of view, the letter to Philemon betrays a "deliberative" orientation. Paul is not trying to accuse, defend or evaluate; he is trying to persuade Philemon to act.

The letter is heavy with issues of motivation. Paul admits, for instance, that he has the "ethical" authority (rhetorical *ethos*) to command Philemon to do this thing (whatever it is), but he prefers instead to appeal to Philemon's regard for Paul and his obligation to Paul (Philem 8-9; rhetorical *pathos*). Logic *(logos)* appears to play no significant role in the matter, except perhaps in verse 17, where Philemon's love for Paul should perhaps "logically" be transferable to someone Paul himself loves (note the if-then construction). Yet the overall tone of the letter echoes Paul's sense of what Philemon owes him, a Brando-like calling-in of debts. We might not want to call it a "pathetic" letter, but if we did, rhetorical critics would know what we meant.

We can also analyze the letter's rhetorical structure. If you took two minutes to read the letter a moment ago, you may have already observed some of what now follows. The opening three verses provide exactly that—the *opening*. Paul, in the company of Timothy, addresses himself to his friend Philemon, to Philemon's family (apparently), and to the church meeting in Philemon's house. Next, with the *exordium* (Philem 4-7), Paul attempts to reestablish rapport with Philemon, praising him for his good record among the saints. He hopes this will prepare Philemon to hear what he really has on his mind. This request Paul sets out now in verses 8-10 as the *propositio*, making his basic (if vague) appeal on behalf of (or perhaps "for") Onesimus. The following section, as the *confirmatio* (Philem 11-16), outlines Onesimus's new state of affairs justifying Paul's request: the formerly useless boy has now become a brother in Christ. In verse 17, Paul begins the *peroratio* to sum up his case. But he breaks off for a moment in a *refutatio* in order to acknowledge some of the objections Philemon may legitimately raise and to "refute" them (Philem 18-19). He then resumes his *peroratio* (Philem 20-21). Just before the *closing* greetings in verses 23-25, Paul inserts one last motivational twist, based more on *ethos* than on the *pathos* he has operated from for the most part up to this point. Paul evidently intends to come and personally check up on how Philemon and Onesimus are getting along (Philem 22).

It is unlikely that Paul consciously imitated the rhetoricians of his day as he composed his letters. He probably did not pause to say to himself, pen in hand, "Now for the *refutatio!*" But he may well have had an educated sense of the proper way to write to a wealthy and respected "gentleman" about one of his runaway slaves. Either way, our own awareness of the typical Greco-Roman method of arguing an issue brings us a good distance down the road toward seeing how Paul, or some other biblical writer, might have pursued the crafting of such an epistle. And that can help us hear that epistle as the first readers must have heard it.

6.3.2 Syntactical Structure

None of these rhetorically motivated structures would have affected the readers at all if what was said in them made no sense. The phrases and sentences making up the stages of Paul's letter must also be well designed, as we argued above in chapter four. If communication is to take place, the syntax of a text needs to be meaningful to writer and readers alike, ideally meaning the same thing to each. The very fact that we have been able to identify the rhetorical stages of Paul's argument in the letter to Philemon shows that Paul the writer has adequately conformed to the "rules" of *koine* Greek syntax (and that his

English translators have conformed to the rules of English syntax). Analyzing the structure of that syntax, consciously or not, helps readers to grasp the writer's message. (To review what we mean by the syntactic structural analysis of a text, refer again to figures 4.1-6.)

6.3.3 Logical Development of Discourse

Laying out a graphic representation of the syntactical relationships existing within and between sentences of a text, even though it is an essential stage of exegesis, can only take us so far. Knowing *that* two clauses are related to each other does not necessarily tell us *how* they are related—that is, the meaning or logic of their relationship. In which one of the many possible ways, for example, is clause B logically subordinate to clause A? Is B the reason for A, the result of A, the condition for A, the purpose of A, the conclusion to be drawn from A, or is A its "contra-expectation" *(even though B is true, nevertheless [and contrary to all expectation] A is also true)?* Is the relationship chronological *(when, after, before, during)?* If A and B are *coordinated* clauses (rather than one of them being *sub*ordinated to the other), does B expand on A, contradict A, restate A or provide a specific example or examples for the more general A?

What these possibilities represent is the logic of communication, the discourse logic. This is not the same thing as the *logos*-based rhetorical motivation (alternative to *ethos* and *pathos*) mentioned above under 6.3.1. That kind of logic is the sort where one might write *q.e.d.* at the end (*quod erat demonstrandum*: "What we set out to prove has now been demonstrated!"). Here, however, we are referring to the way language juggles ideas and puts them into various relationships. Even an illogical argument (in the *q.e.d.* sense) needs to be expressed "logically," in order to be recognized as illogical.

Let's apply this to the letter to Philemon. The opening word of the section in which Paul introduces the main order of business is the high-level conjunction διό "therefore" (Philem 8). This is a "high-level" conjunction because it functions here to connect ("conjoin") two paragraphs, rather than two sentences or two clauses within a sentence. We have already seen that in verses 4-7 (the *exordium*) Paul establishes rapport with Philemon by letting him know how much he appreciates Philemon's excellent testimony and good-hearted treatment of the saints. We now see from this little word διό that Paul strokes Philemon's ego in this fashion not simply in order to reconnect with him pleasantly but in order to put Philemon in a kind of dilemma. Philemon is presumably listening to the letter being read aloud (by Tychicus?) in the presence of his family and the church in his living room. If he has been nodding in a pleased (but modest) way as he listens to the text of verses 4-7, he will now find it very awkward to refuse Paul's request regarding Onesimus, expressed in the *propositio* (Philem 8-10). For with διό Paul has tied the two paragraphs together "logically" as grounds-to-exhortation: "A is true about you, *therefore* do B." Philemon cannot refuse Paul's request now without simultaneously demonstrating that Paul is wrong in his good opinion, an opinion Philemon has already assented to (so we gather). Whether strictly "logical" or not (in the *q.e.d.* sense), this analysis represents the "discourse logic" of what Paul says here.

At a "lower" level, even between clauses within a single sentence, the same logical relationships exist. Some of these are only implicitly "marked," particularly those formed with participial constructions. Consider Philemon 4-5a (which constitutes only part of a sentence stretching from Philem 4 through Philem 6):

Εὐχαριστῶ τῷ θεῷ μου πάντοτε
μνείαν σου *ποιούμενος* ἐπὶ τῶν προσευχῶν μου,
ἀκούων σου τὴν ἀγάπην καὶ τὴν πίστιν . . .

In the main clause, pulled out to the left margin, Paul claims, "I always thank my God." This statement is supported by two subordinated participial clauses (note the italicized participles ποιούμενος "making" and ἀκούων "hearing"), but supported how? Participial clauses do *not* explicitly define the "logical" relationship between themselves and their "governing" main clause; readers must infer the relationship on their own. This is in contrast to the clause at the end of Philemon 7, which is explicitly marked by the causal conjunction ὅτι "because." The absence of an explicit marking of the logical relationships between clauses in verses 4-5a does not mean those relationships do not matter, much less that they do not exist. But what are they? Consider how the NRSV makes the relationships explicit by supplying English conjunctions (italicized here):

When I remember you in my prayers,
I always thank my God
because I hear of your love . . . and your faith.

Of course, whether the NRSV has correctly understood the connections between the main clause and its two subordinates is another question (I suspect it has). Correct or not, this way of reading Philemon 4-5a represents Paul as thankful to God *because* he keeps hearing what a fine, faithful Christian brother Philemon is, and as expressing his thanks to God for that fact *every time* he prays. The two participial clauses answer the "logical" questions *when* and *why* Paul thanks God so much.

To understand the implications that a biblical epistle may have for contemporary readers, we must faithfully analyze its textual content—its argument, paragraph by paragraph, no less than reading it within its historical, cultural and literary contexts. It is the solemn and holy duty of ministers of the Word of God to devote themselves to this task for the health of the flocks entrusted to them. To neglect this calling in the name of management and organizational administration, or for any other good and wholesome aspect of pastoral ministry, is to foster a weak and shallow congregation, no matter how large it gets.

6.4 A SIMPLIFIED PROCEDURE FOR EPISTLE EXEGESIS

We can close this chapter with a series of "steps" providing a shorthand method for getting a good grounding in the text of an epistle. Presupposed are all the issues we have dealt with so far in this book (textual criticism, translation, boundaries, etc.).

A. Acquaint yourself with the structure of the book as a whole, the "macro-structure" for your pericope.

1. Do *not* simply plunge into a passage or a pericope without taking account of its book as a whole. Ideally, if you can do so, work out the book's structure yourself before you consult other opinions.

2. If you do not have enough time to work out your own analysis, at least get an orientation in the book from commentaries or dictionary articles, preferably more than one.

3. Long-range, always be working with *some* biblical book. Use perhaps six months or a year to develop a working grasp of, say, Galatians or Jeremiah (the Old Testament is ours, too).

4. It is immensely useful to do an "annotated outline" for an entire book, in order to see the flow of the argument and the place occupied by individual pericopes in the scheme of the whole. An annotated outline provides short, pithy summaries of each section and subsection, enabling the user to skim intelligently over the surface of a book's argument before plunging into the details. It also helps in "placing" a particular pericope within its literary context.

B. Analyze the pericope's "microstructure." Do a syntactical analysis and a discourse analysis of the pericope itself. Base these analyses on your own translation, of course. If you have not studied Greek yet, then at least consult several translations and compare how they treat the syntactical and discourse relationships.

C. Summarize results so far. From steps A and B, write out, in your own words, short preliminary summaries for both (1) the internal logic and content of the pericope and (2) the way the pericope fits into the logic of its larger

ANNOTATED OUTLINE OF ROMANS 6:1—8:30

Below is an outline and annotation of the subsections of the third major portion of Paul's letter to Rome. Having demonstrated absolute condemnation (Rom 1:18—3:20) and absolute grace (Rom 3:21—5:21) in the previous two sections, Paul now refutes the false conclusion that we are free to be as sinful as we please.

Grace, law and libertinism (Rom 6:1—8:30)

How does this doctrine of righteousness by faith square with the obvious necessity of being obedient to the law of God?

1. Grace is not an excuse to sin. (Rom 6:1—7:6)

   a. Can those identified with Christ continue in sin? (Rom 6:1-14)
   Once baptized into union with Christ, we share in all that is his, including his having died to this world and his having been raised to a new life free from the power of sin.

   b. Must the liberated still be enslaved? (Rom 6:15-23)
   It is not possible simply to be free from sin; we must submit to righteousness as our new master or be enslaved to sin again. Christ has made it possible to be enslaved to righteousness.

   c. Are the widowed still married? (Rom 7:1-6)
   In Christ, our fatal marriage to the law, which provokes our sin, is over. The worst the law can inflict upon us is death; once dead we are out of reach of the authority of law. But Christ has died under the law, and we are in Christ; consequently we too have died under (and therefore to) the law.

2. The law is not sinful. (Rom 7:7-25)

   a. Sin, not the law, is the culprit. (Rom 7:7-12)
   While not itself sinful, the law has been used by sin to produce sin and death.

   b. The law is powerless against sin. (Rom 7:13-25)
   The law is holy, just and good, yet helpless to keep the Christian from sinning. However, although in one respect the Christian does sin, in another all-important sense it is no longer the believer that does it but his or her sinful old nature, which of course has already been condemned. The Christian's new nature is not subject to the law.

3. The Spirit changes everything. (Rom 8:1-30)

   a. The mind of the Spirit—the mind of the "flesh." (Rom 8:1-11)
Paul contrasts the disobedient old nature and the obedient new nature in terms of the "flesh" and the Spirit. The believer, renewed in the Spirit, abides by the law of the Spirit.

   b. Death to the "flesh" by the power of the Spirit. (Rom 8:12-17)
The flesh is both dead and in the process of (daily) being put to death. The suffering associated with this process is the same suffering endured by Christ and is the lot of the Christian who is obedient to Christ, as God's child, in this present life.

   c. The Spirit aids us in our suffering. (Rom 8:18-30)
Being led by the Spirit means suffering in this world, as it did for Christ. But the Spirit supports us in this suffering by his perfect prayers for us and by encouraging us with the hope, a secure knowledge, of future glory.

context and of the book itself. Remember the image of the stone wall from chapter three, in which sections of the wall are both joined to other sections to make up the whole wall and are likewise themselves formed from the joining together of smaller pieces. Summarize these results in short statements, each in one sentence if possible. These summaries should be considered working statements, subject to revision as your research continues, but functioning as a kind of guide for the time being.

D. Take into account any significant cultural issue that would illuminate the ancient text. Consider such cultural factors as the social role of the *paterfamilias,* or the imperial laws governing slavery, or the possible reasons Corinthian Christian women were expected to cover their heads when the church gathered for corporate worship. All of these (and many more) significantly determine how we ought to read the texts affected by them.

E. Determine the historical "occasion" for the book and your pericope. Analyze the historical occasion for the book and passage and feed that data back into your considerations in step C. Make any necessary adjustments in the statements you composed for that step.

F. Formulate a text-based plan for teaching or preaching your text. Use the resultant statements from step D to assist you in formulating the theme and subpoints of a Bible study, or the theme (not necessarily the subpoints) of a sermon. Think through how the cultural context represented in the original situation relates to the cultural context in which the people you serve are living. Those two cultural contexts will seldom be in a one-to-one relationship; that is, wearing hats and scarves will not likely bear the same cultural value in today's Vancouver as they once did in Corinth.

We turn now in the next two chapters to the genre of New Testament narratives: the four Gospels and the Acts of the Apostles.

7

NARRATIVES I

Telling the Old, Old Story

The passageway of the side chambers widened from story to story;
for the structure was supplied with a stairway all around the temple.
For this reason the structure became wider from story to story.
One ascended from the bottom story to the
uppermost story by way of the middle one.

EZEKIEL 41:7

Stories, or narratives, sort themselves into a variety of categories—heroic action, mysteries, romances, tragedies and comedies, biographies and adventures, fables and fairy tales, to name only a few. Yet, they all differ from letters in the same basic way. Letters argue; stories plot. That grossly oversimplifies the matter, I admit, since some stories contain letters (or consist of nothing but letters) and some letters incorporate stories (as Galatians does at 1:13—2:14). For that matter, a plot is nothing but an argument in the form of a sequence of events (a good story always has a point to make), and an argument is something like an abstracted plot—a sequence of ideas. Nevertheless, it works for the moment to paint this broad-stroke distinction between the two categories: letters argue and stories plot.

On the other hand, what a good story has in common with a well-formed letter, indeed with a well-formed communication of any sort, is *coherence.* Like a good argument, an effective story has a beginning, a middle and an ending, all identifiable and all related to each other in some meaningful way. The coherent relationship between the parts and the whole is the subject of chapter three. There the point is made that coherence operates on many levels, holding words together to form clauses and phrases, joining sentences into paragraphs, and similarly on "up" to sections, parts and whole documents. Each "brick"—or cluster of bricks—in a "wall" is identifiable partly by virtue of its in-

ternal coherence, as well as partly by its boundaries. Each finds a part of its significance within the context of some larger whole it helps to build. (Internal
content, of course, also contributes to significance.) The idea of coherence on
various levels underlies what we now have to say about interpreting the stories
of the New Testament. In order to be fair to these ancient documents, we must
keep in mind that their authors worked very hard to shape them into self-
contained, coherent wholes, and we must read them that way.

7.1 THE GOSPELS AND THE ACTS OF THE APOSTLES AS SELF-CONTAINED, COHERENT STORIES

The variety of means writers can use for creating and sustaining coherence in
a literary piece is probably limited only by the imagination of the writer. Yet,
every culture and age—not to mention the very nature of language and the
human mind—offers a ready-made set of tools for the job. We discussed a
number of these in chapter three: inclusios, chiasms, themes, pronouns, consistency of players in the cast (perhaps in a series of related stories), repetitions
and patterns of various kinds, and many others. Here are two examples.

7.1.1 The Gospel of Matthew as a Whole

Several features of Matthew's Gospel are famous for their power to create coherence. Some of them operate at a very high level, stitching the entire book
together; others operate at various lower levels, giving smaller units their dis-
tinctly identifiable character. This is similar to the difference in "levels" we saw
in chapter six between the higher-level function of διό "therefore" in
Philemon 8 and the lower-level function of ὅτι "because" in Philemon 7: one
connects whole paragraphs, while the other connects clauses within a single
sentence. In chapter three, we noted Matthew's patterned repetition of Jesus'
words, "you have heard . . . but I say to you," which (at a lower level) marks off
Matthew 5:21-48 as a separate but coherent unit within the Sermon on the
Mount. At a much higher level, however, Matthew 1:23 and Matthew 28:20
function like bookends around the entire Gospel (they form an inclusio), reflecting each other with the shared theme of God's presence with his people.
This literary technique serves not only to tie together the beginning and the
end of Matthew's Gospel, but to give the overall Gospel account a particular
slant as well: the story of Jesus, according to Matthew, is about God's return to
be "with us." This suggests to the exegete that in some fashion everything
about Matthew's Gospel story contributes to this theme. In his first public appearance, for example (Mt 3:13-17), Jesus comes *with the people* to receive
John's baptism of repentance (see also Mt 18:20).

Simultaneously, another Matthean repetition helps us to see the shape of the whole story as Matthew apparently saw it. Matthew 4:17 and 16:21 display the same wording: ἀπὸ τότε ἤρξατο ὁ Ἰησοῦς . . . "From that time on, Jesus began to . . ." In the first case Jesus *began to proclaim* the Gospel message, and in the second he *began to show* the disciples that the other side of Messiahship involves suffering and death. This repetition (found only at these two places in the book) suggests that Matthew presents Jesus' story in three parts: his birth, baptism and temptation (Mt 1:1—4:16); his preaching, teaching and healing ministry in Galilee (Mt 4:17—16:20); and his ministry of suffering and death, chiefly in Judea (Mt 16:21 and on). Taking this clue in combination with the "God-with-us" theme announced in the bookends, we begin to get an idea of Matthew's theological message. God has come once more to his sinful people, to be with them, identifying himself with them in their suffering, and through his own suffering setting them free to bless all the nations of the earth.

Thus every portion of the Gospel of Matthew, every pericope, every parable, every healing story, every speech, needs to be read in the context of his larger, overriding theme. In the Sermon, when Jesus contrasts the inherited tradition with his own spin on things (Mt 5:21-48), we are to hear the *voice of God among us*, helping us to understand more perfectly his perfect will. When Jesus unnecessarily touches the untouchables (Mt 8:1-15), we get a bold look at what *God's presence among us* sets us free to do. Each piece of the story contributes to portraying God as having returned to us as a God—a king—who suffers with us in order to make us his instrument of redemption for the entire world. It does not take a rocket-scientist or a seminary professor to figure this out. It simply requires paying attention to the big picture and the signals an author provides for recognizing it. Using tools like a Bible dictionary, a concordance and a Gospel synopsis (which we will look at in a moment), even reading entirely through a Gospel in a single sitting, make it possible to see some of these signals in relatively short order. What we have said here about Matthew goes double—so to speak—for Luke.

7.1.2 Volume 1 and Volume 2

We need to recognize one very important thing about Luke's Gospel that sets it off from the other two Synoptic Gospels, as well as from John. That major distinction is that the Gospel of Luke is only the first part of a two-volume work. Each of the other three Gospels stands alone, but Luke does not. The canonical positioning of John's Gospel between Luke and Acts obscures this fact; Luke is grouped with the other two Synoptics (Mark and Matthew), and John is grouped with the other three Gospels, leaving Acts chopped off from its Gospel base. This probably explains why many of us preachers and teachers fail to factor in the presence of Acts when we do exegesis in Luke, or for that matter fail to factor in Luke when we do exegesis in Acts. This common failure is unfair to both books. The story told in the Gospel of Luke provides the prelude to a much larger story, and we need to read it in that larger context. Conversely, the story of Acts arises out of the earlier story told in Luke and cannot be understood apart from it. Obviously, we cannot understand the early church without knowing the story of Jesus; that is not the point here. What I mean instead is that we cannot understand the story of Jesus *as it is told in Luke* without understanding the subsequent story of the early church *as it is told in Acts* and vice versa. There are clear literary relationships between the books of Luke and Acts that bind them together as an organic, coherent literary unity. Every time we preach or teach from Luke, we need to keep in mind the sequel in Acts, for they work together, the one rising out of and fulfilling the other.

Set Luke and Acts end-to-end (pulling John's Gospel out of the way for the moment), and step back for a better view. Notice how they are introduced with matching prefaces addressed to someone named Theophilus, possibly a Roman official giving financial sponsorship to Luke's project (unless his name is merely a symbol for any "God-loving" reader). Note too, that in the early stages of the Gospel, Luke goes to exaggerated efforts to coordinate the story with Roman political history (Lk 2:1-2; 3:1-2). The final scenes of Acts are correspondingly set in Rome, making Rome an inclusio around the two-part work (operating something like the God-with-us theme in Matthew). Meanwhile, the actual story in Luke begins in Jerusalem, in the temple, and contrary to the version in Mark and Matthew, it culminates not in Galilee, but again in Jerusalem. This causes Jerusalem to function as an inclusio for the first volume, the Gospel. Acts then (as volume two) begins in Jerusalem (where volume one leaves off), and in accordance with the programmatic statement in Acts 1:8, the story traces the expansion of the church from Jerusalem, by various geographic intervals, all the way to Rome. Directly in the center of this two-part story, acting as the hinge, the fulcrum, the pivot point of it all, is the complex event of the death, resurrection and ascension of Jesus. Figure 7.1 graphically represents this structure.

Understood in this way, Luke-Acts presents us with the story of how God has intervened in *world* affairs, not just in Jewish affairs. He has done so through the Jewish Messiah, Jesus of Nazareth, bringing about not only the resolution of Israel's long exile but also the resolution of the entire world's predicament. Everything in *both* Luke and Acts needs to be understood in this larger perspective, for that is how the author Luke designed his project. In fact, the very

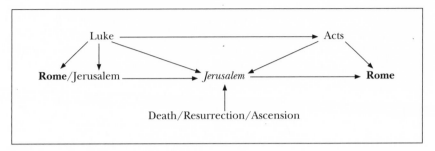

Figure 7.1. Luke-Acts: Geographical Structure

structure of Luke-Acts speaks in this way to the disturbing question raised by many liberation and contextual theologians: how can the *particular* nature of Jesus, as a male Jew, be of significance to females and males of all cultures? We honor Luke, and Scripture, when we pay attention to this question, because Luke himself does so through the "universal" way in which he presents the story of Jesus, the male Jew.

7.2 HISTORY OR LITERATURE?

There is, however, an elephant in the room. Although we have too little space in a book like this to deal with it in any adequate way, we should at least acknowledge its presence (and we will return to it in a bit more detail in chapter eight). Many of us grew up with no clear sense of the differences among the four Gospels, nor, really, of their various similarities. For me at least, the Gospels merged into one confused and undifferentiated account of Jesus' life. It never occurred to me that they represented anything other than straightforward records of Jesus' actual words and deeds. At some point I began to realize that there were *four* Gospels for a reason and that each one had its own particular way of telling Jesus' story. And with that, the elephant entered the room. Simply put, the elephant is this: What is the relationship between (a) what actually happened day-to-day during Jesus' earthly life in ancient Palestine, on the one hand, and (b) what these four documents separately report about that life, on the other? Are the Gospels "histories," or are they "literature"?

Of course, putting it this way assumes that history and literature are mutually exclusive: an account of an event can be either one or the other, but not both. This is an unnecessary assumption; in fact, it presupposes the impossible, for there is no way to record an event without recording it *from a particular perspective*. Even if we had a videotape of Jesus healing the leper, the point of view from which the camera was aimed would have been a *particular* point of view. Even if we had a holographic video recording of it, we ourselves, the "readers," could "read" it from only one angle at a time. Any account of any event engages in the processes of selection, arrangement and adaptation, and these three story-telling activities are only do-able from one perspective at a time. The sum total of these processes applied to creating a particular account represents the storyteller's own point of view. The fully orbed context of any event is far too complex to allow a complete description in an account of that event, let alone the full comprehension of it by some hapless listener. Perspective is inescapable.

This, I believe, is why we have four Gospels, not just one. No single retelling of any event can capture it in all its profundity and complexity, and certainly not an event of such cosmic magnitude. We know only a very little about Jesus' entire life (as Jn 21:25 suggests), but we do hear about it from four different angles. The exegetical question, given this state of affairs, is this: what are these four Gospel witnesses actually like (including the fact that one of them comes in two volumes), and how does knowing this help us to understand their respective messages?

7.3 HISTORICAL-, FORM- AND SOURCE-CRITICAL APPROACHES TO THE GOSPELS

Gospel analysis has developed elaborately over the last two or three centuries, and with increasing speed since the mid-twentieth century. The history of this development to some degree follows the shifts in the philosophical and political climate, especially in the industrial West. Today, however, these mostly Western trends find themselves challenged by outspoken theologians, male and female, from Latin America, Africa, and Asia, and even from within the West—and none too soon in many respects. Still, with regard to the nature of the Gospels as documents—especially in connection with the attempt to recover their original message—much of the result of Western scholarship provides us a platform from which to work. For the present purposes, we can make several assumptions about the Gospels.

7.3.1 Historical Frameworks

Chapters five and six emphasize the importance of studying a biblical document within the context of its historical and cultural setting. This perspective applies no less to the Gospel materials than to others. To appreciate Luke 18:9-14, for example, we need to know how a Pharisee and a tax collector were each regarded by the respectable populace of first-century Jerusalem ("respectable," because Luke has Jesus telling this parable to a respectable audience). Getting this wrong spoils our grasp of Jesus' point, as well as any benefit we might hope to derive from it. We do not need to review this principle here. We do need to notice, however, that the historical setting of the Gospels is more complicated than that of, say, Paul's letter to Philemon.

There are in fact three historical settings relevant to Gospel exegesis (four, if we count our own as exegetes, but we do this for epistles, too). Most obvious is probably the *historical setting of Jesus himself* as he walked the dusty roads (and stormy lakes) and talked with the people of Palestine. (Scholars often refer to this with the German phrase *Sitz im Leben Jesu,* "Jesus' life situation.") We can legitimately ask where he was and what happened in such and such a situation to prompt him to tell the parable of the Good Samaritan (Lk 10:29-37). Sometimes the Evangelists spell out these circumstances for us (as Luke actually does in Lk 10:25-29), and other times they leave them unstated, or only vaguely indicate them (note ἐν ἐκείνῳ τῷ καιρῷ "at that time" as a vague setting-marker: Mt 11:25; 12:1, etc.).

A second historical setting represented by the Gospels is the *situation of each Evangelist* as he wrote his Gospel. Just as it is unlikely that Paul wrote the epistle to Philemon with all of *us* in mind, it is almost certain that the authors of Mark, Matthew, Luke and John had their own respective congregations or patron(s) foremost in mind as they wrote. It is also fair to assume that part of what motivated each Evangelist to tell his own version of Jesus' story would have been the issues plaguing the people to whom an Evangelist originally wrote. Mark, for example, emphasizes the secrecy of Jesus' Messiahship, and Matthew is especially interested in the fatherhood of God. In John's mind apparently, the "signs" (σημεῖα) that Jesus performed were particularly effective for convincing John's readers of Jesus' identity as Son of God. We can reasonably infer that these features appear because of needs the Evangelists saw in their respective audiences.

A third historical setting relevant to the Gospels sits between the other two: the *period of the early church.* It is again fair to assume that in the days, years and decades following the Resurrection and Pentecost, Christians nourished themselves with what they remembered from the ministry of Jesus. Some of this "memory" would have been written down, but much of it doubtless survived for a long time in oral form before being committed to writing (and probably for a long time after). This interim setting, though difficult to document, is important nevertheless, because it was during this time that many of the Gospel pericopes acquired their present form. At least, that is the theory of *form critics.*

7.3.2 Form Criticism

Scholars who speculate about the effect of this freelance usage of oral tradition in the period of the early church conclude that particular types (forms) of Gospel pericopes were used in particular ministry situations. Some pericopes focus on a pithy remark of Jesus and frame it within a description of the circumstance leading up to it. Others recount an exorcism or a healing story, or an altercation between Jesus and antagonistic religious leaders, in which Jesus successfully outwits his enemies. Form critics have identified numerous "forms" and assigned them to typical settings, forms such as parables, nature-miracles and so-called legends like the transfiguration or the temptation. (The somewhat incendiary word *legend* refers to events that do not lend themselves to historically verifiable investigation. Except to some people, it does not imply that they did not or could not have happened.) It is entirely reasonable to imagine typical situations in which such stories and sayings would have been used in that early period. Then, in a somewhat circular way of course, form critics use these hypothesized settings to interpret the forms in question and the particular pericopes classified under them.

Take, for example, the temple conversation Jesus has with the Pharisees about "David's son" (Mt 22:41-46; Mk 12:35-37; Lk 20:41-44; "If David thus calls him Lord, how can he be his son?"). If we abstract the story from its several Gospel contexts and look at it as an independent piece of floating Jesus-tradition in the middle of the first century, we can easily conjecture how it might have functioned as a handy little weapon in apologetic or evangelistic circumstances. As a brilliant stroke of Jesus' exegesis, effectively silencing his critics (Mt 22:46), this brief story could quite reasonably have been handed down orally for years before someone, Mark perhaps, took the trouble to write it up. These hypothetical but entirely plausible "oral" circumstances "contextualize" the speech in the life of the early church and provide a basis for understanding its significance to the earliest believers. That significance will not necessarily match the significance it had for Jesus in the original conversation. Nor will it necessarily match the significance it later has for Mark (or Matthew or Luke).

Many form critics have cynically assumed that the oral tradition about Jesus was subject to so much informal and uncontrolled adaptation in the period of the early church that we can now have very little confidence in the historical reliability of its results for the life of Jesus; they believe that it mostly testifies to the evolving state of the early church. By the same token, for many other students of the Gospels, there is just a bit too much speculation in the form-critical program to inspire great confidence in its results at all. There is in fact good reason to believe that the tradition was far more controlled, though in many respects "informally," than Western form-critics have confidently affirmed.[1] Still, one of the most useful fruits of form criticism is the awareness that many stories of Jesus' words and deeds doubtless survived for some time as discrete units, unconnected with one another in a literary way. On the other hand, a good deal of what the early church "remembered" during this time had almost certainly been written down, some of it in the form of extended narratives (the trial and crucifixion, perhaps), others in the form of sayings-collections or extended speeches. This leads us to *source criticism.*

7.3.3 Source Criticism

Luke 1:1-4 makes it abundantly clear that in the compilation of his Gospel the author made use of various sources, some of them *written* sources. In other words, Luke's story of Jesus was not composed from Luke's own first-hand memories of Jesus' life and ministry. He had other resources to work with. Some of these may have been live interviews he conducted with persons in Palestine who had been on hand to see Jesus in the flesh, or who had been specially charged with "remembering" the stories. (This role of keeping the tradition may be what Luke means by "servants of the word" ὑπηρέται τοῦ λόγου, Lk 1:2.) By his own testimony, he was with Paul during the latter's two-year imprisonment in Caesarea on the Palestinian seacoast (Acts 21—27), which would have provided Luke with ample opportunity for research. Luke's admission to using sources (Lk 1:1-4) opens the door for asking how much any of the four Evangelists relies on his own personal, eyewitness experience in writing his Gospel. In answering this question, source criticism takes us in another direction of immense importance.

After centuries of studying and debating the issue, New Testament scholars now recognize that there probably exists some sort of direct literary interrelationship among at least the first three Gospels, the so-called Synoptic Gospels, Matthew, Mark and Luke. John's Gospel stands in a category all its own in this respect. We cannot afford the space in this book to discuss the matter in any detail, but we do need to present the two most common explanations for the way the Synoptic Gospels resemble one another in the order in which they present Jesus' story and in their frequently verbatim agreement with one another.

---

[1]Kenneth E. Bailey, "Informal Controlled Oral Tradition and the Synoptic Gospels," *Asia Journal of Theology* 5 (1991): 34-54. Though I intend to keep footnotes to a minimum in this book, Bailey's article is so fascinating and "satisfying," that I feel it is worth mentioning. Bailey has spent most of his life and long career among the peasant cultures of the Middle East and has a thing or two to say about the reliability of peasant oral traditions. The article is hard to find, but it is well worth tracking down. A reprint of it appeared in the journal *Themelios* 20, no. 2 (1995): 4-11.

The facts, greatly simplified, are these. For one thing, some accounts of Jesus' words and deeds show up in all three Synoptic Gospels, often in the same order and often in verbatim agreement. Scholars call this material the *triple tradition*. The transfiguration (Mk 9:2-10 and parallels) is an example of this triple tradition. Second, sometimes Matthew and Mark preserve material missing from Luke (like the story of the Syrophoenician woman, Mk 7:24-30; Mt 15:21-28), and sometimes Luke and Mark preserve material missing from Matthew (the healing of the demoniac in the synagogue, Mk 1:23-28; Lk 4:33-37). But more intriguing for Gospel source-theorists is, third, the fact that Matthew and Luke preserve in common a very large selection of material not found in Mark. Much of it consists of Jesus' words and much of it exhibits verbatim or nearly verbatim agreement between these two Gospels. This material common to Matthew and Luke, but lacking in Mark, is known as the *double tradition*. The Lord's Prayer provides one of the more famous examples of the double tradition (Mt 6:9-13; Lk 11:1-4). Fourth—besides the triple and double traditions and the overlaps between Mark and either Matthew or Luke (but not both)—each of the three Synoptic Gospels also has *material peculiar to itself*. Only Luke, for instance, reports the visit of the shepherds to the manger (Lk 2), and only Matthew preserves the account of the magi and of Joseph's taking the holy family to Egypt in order to escape the Slaughter of the Innocents (Mt 2). Mark contains the least amount of peculiar material, but his account of Jesus' family regarding him as out of his mind (Mk 3:19-21) provides an example. Gospel source criticism attempts to explain these various interrelationships.

The most commonly accepted source-critical explanation assumes that Mark's Gospel was written first, that is, it assumes "Markan priority." According to this theory, both Matthew and Luke later made use of Mark's work as they wrote their own Gospels, but they did so *independently of one another.* We could call this explanation the *"one-Gospel* hypothesis," since only Mark serves as a source for each of the other two. However, treating Mark as the sole source for Matthew and Luke does not account for the double tradition—that very large portion of the astonishing agreements between Matthew's Gospel and Luke's Gospel that the common use of Mark cannot explain, since it is not found in Mark. This is a serious problem. How do we solve it? Viewing the data in this way (that is, assuming Markan priority) encourages us to postulate a *second written source,* which, like Mark's Gospel, Matthew and Luke both used (though, again, independently). Scholars use the German word *Quelle* "source" to refer to this otherwise unknown document used independently by both Matthew and Luke. They call it "Q" for short. Thus, there are two source *documents* in this scenario: the Gospel of Mark and Q, a hypothetical collection of (mostly) Jesus' sayings. This gives us the designation, "*two-document* hypothesis" (or, sometimes, the "two-*source* hypothesis"). Taking into consideration the presumed (also hypothetical) sources of material peculiar to Matthew and Luke ("M" and "L," respectively), some people speak of this solution to the Synoptic problem as the "*four*-document hypothesis."

In place of Markan priority, however, a less widely accepted solution to the synoptic problem assumes instead that Matthew's Gospel appeared first (therefore "Matthean priority"). People call this approach the "two-*Gospel* hypothesis." This can become confusing, since the other solution is known as the "two-*document/source* hypothesis." So be careful! According to this alternative theory, Luke made use of Matthew's (preexisting) Gospel as he wrote his own. This explains the double tradition. Later on, Mark, with access to both Matthew and Luke as sources, abridged each of them in order to produce his own, shorter version (chopping out the material we now call the double tradition, for example). This then accounts both for the triple tradition and for the places where Mark overlaps with either Matthew or Luke and not with the other.

Looking only at the surface of these things, and invoking the principle of "Occam's razor" (that the simplest solution is best), we might wonder why the two-document hypothesis is a more popular solution to the Synoptic problem than the two-Gospel hypothesis is. After all, why invent a hypothetical document like Q if we don't need to? The answer is that the appeal of the two-document hypothesis—even with Q—increases the more scholars compare the three Gospels in detail. Whether we assume that Mark used Matthew and Luke, or that Matthew and Luke (independently) used Mark, we must logically ask why the "user" made changes in his sources. For most Gospel scholars, the "improvements" that Matthew and Luke would have made to Mark's story seem more historically plausible than the "improvements" Mark would have made to Matthew and Luke. Both Matthew's diction and Luke's are far more polished than Mark's, and Mark's presentation of the disciples, even of Jesus, is less refined, almost more offensive, than either Luke's version or Matthew's. Mark's account of Jesus' family regarding him as out of his mind (Mk 3:19-21), for example, seems more like something Matthew and Luke would have dropped out than like something Mark would have added. While it is not conclusive, this kind of reasoning strongly suggests that Matthew and Luke have actually "improved" Mark, rather than the other way around. That is, on this ground "Markan priority" appears more likely than "Matthean priority." Though scholars still debate the question, the remainder of this chapter will operate from the perspective of the two-document hypothesis (Markan priority). That it matters, and that it matters a great deal, becomes obvious in the next section, which is devoted to *redaction criticism.*

7.4 REDACTION CRITICISM

The term *redaction* is just another, older word for "editing." Redaction criticism of the Gospels is the study of how one Gospel writer edited another Gospel (or other sources) in the process of composing his own. Of course, it assumes that such use truly did occur, and to some degree it visualizes the resulting "new" Gospel as a kind of second edition of the source. That is, according to the two-*Gospel* hypothesis, Luke's Gospel is something like the "second edition" of Matthew, and Mark is an abbreviated second edition of Luke, as well as a "third edition" of Matthew. On the other hand, in terms of the two-*document* hypothesis (the solution followed here), both Matthew and Luke represent independent "second editions" of Mark. Even this, however, is not really the right way to view the matter; none of the resulting Gospels is to be regarded as a second (or third) edition of its source document(s). Each Gospel writer intended to tell the story of Jesus in his own particular way, not simply to fix up the source(s) he used. This is amply clear in Luke's prologue.

7.4.1 Sources and Redactions

But what does redaction criticism tell us, and how does it do so? Suppose I draft a letter for my wife to send to our congresswoman, but my political views and my wife's do not precisely coincide. In the draft, I tell the congresswoman that the government needs to start up the Hanford nuclear facility again real soon, so that we will not experience so many energy crises. My wife, in copying the letter over as a final draft, makes a subtle change or two. When she is done, we now urge that government needs to *clean* up that Hanford nuclear facility real soon, *even though* we will likely experience many *more* energy crises. Leave out a word or phrase here, change a word or two there, and presto! a new message. Anyone with both drafts in hand could compare them with each other and determine the political views of each writer. On the other hand, without knowing which draft came first and which depended on the other, the redaction critic is unable to discern which writer made *conscious* changes from his or her source. This is a significant problem for interpretation, because making such *conscious* changes implies an especially strong motivating interest, one that perhaps stands out from other interests.

So, if Mark's Gospel came first, as in the two-*document* hypothesis, then we have no way of knowing what source Mark himself may have deviated from in order to make a particular point, nor what those particular points would be. Although we have other means at our disposal for discerning his theological intentions, Mark's editorial treatment of a *known source* would not be one of them. It would be similar for Matthew's Gospel, under the two-*Gospel* hypothesis. Yet, again under the two-*document* hypothesis, when we read either Matthew or Luke and compare it with Mark, we are able to deduce special interests in Matthew and Luke from observing the way each makes changes in Mark's story. This is why the choice of a solution to the Synoptic problem implies a big difference in results. Whose consciously made changes are we discerning anyway: Matthew's and Luke's, or Mark's?

The issue with Q, the other source in the two-document hypothesis, is more complicated. Suppose that, in addition to my wife's editorial work, my daughter also made a copy from my original draft of a letter to our congresswoman, making changes in *her* own way—different from the changes my wife made. But suppose she did so after my wife had already mailed hers and without ever having seen her mother's version. Unfortunately for you, my original draft has since vanished. Think of my lost original draft as like Q, and consider my wife's letter and my daughter's letter, both based on my draft, as like Matthew and Luke. Now somewhat later, both my wife's copy and my daughter's fall into your hands. You can discern where their copies agree and where they differ, and somehow you know (pretend with me here, okay!) that they both used the same first draft (mine) as a source. You do not know which one of them made changes from the original, however, since you do not have the original for comparison. My daughter urges that Hanford be returned to the Native American community, while my wife, as you recall, urges that it be cleaned up. Which one made a *special effort* to express her own particular perspective and which one merely followed my lead? Or do both deviate from the original, but in different directions? This is the problem with Q. We do not even know whether Q existed as a written document, let alone what exactly it may have looked like. All we have to go by are the many and various ways Matthew and Luke agree with each other—or sometimes *almost* agree with each other—against Mark. Where Luke and Matthew differ from each other in wording or emphasis in the (shared non-Markan) Q material, we cannot be certain which one follows the presumed original, or whether either one of them does. Things thus remain considerably ambiguous where Q is concerned. This has not prevented Q-scholars from erecting fabulous Q-castles in the air, however.

As responsible exegetes of the Synoptic Gospels, we have little choice but to work from one or another theory of the literary relationship among them. If it comes to a choice between the two-source hypothesis and the two-Gospel hypothesis, then we must pick one or the other. We cannot simultaneously assume that Matthew "edited" Mark *and* that Mark "edited" Matthew. In one sense, it does not much matter which theory we work from, so long as we pick one; we are in good company either way. We will have *more* good company with the two-document hypothesis, but *good* company with either. The results will differ of course, but that only makes for productive conversation among the members of the Body. If it were important to God that we get it absolutely right, I suspect he would have (and could have) made it clearer. The fact that he has not made it clearer than it is means, I think, that it is also important to him that we work together on it.

7.4.2 Redaction as Selection

It will be very helpful to you if you consult a Gospel synopsis as we work through this discussion. A bit later, we will spend considerable time on how to make good use of the synopsis. Meanwhile, if you have access to K. Aland's *Synopsis of the Four Gospels* or its Greek version, *Synopsis Quattuor Evangeliorum*,[2] flip it open to index 1 for easy reference. The following discussion assumes the Aland *Synopsis*.

Once redaction critics have clarified a working model of who edited whom (such as the two-document theory), they analyze a text in terms of *selection, arrangement* and *adaptation*. In other words, neither Matthew nor Luke *select* Mark 3:19-21 (the harsh reaction of Jesus' family to his sense of mission); we could say that they "de-select" it. But they do select most of Mark's other material, though not always the same parts—Matthew (Mt 15:21-28) selects, but Luke de-selects, Mark's story of the Syrophoenician woman, for instance. Moreover, having selected one of Mark's pericopes, Matthew or Luke may then proceed to eliminate (de-select) elements within it or to include additional material selected from the larger Jesus-tradition in circulation at the time (oral or otherwise, even from Q). Mark goes to elaborate lengths to describe Jesus' encounter with the demoniac in the country of the Gerasenes (Mk 5:1-20). Matthew retains the story (Mt 8:28-34), setting it in a slightly different geographical location and adding a second demoniac; but otherwise he cuts it to the bone, de-selecting large chunks of detail preserved by Mark. On the other hand, Matthew and Luke both select the account of Jesus' temptation (Mk 1:12-13). But whereas Mark's version of the event is as lean as it can be without vanishing altogether, both Matthew and Luke work out their "editions" of it with considerable flair and similarly enough to raise the question of Q as a shared source (Mt 4:1-11; Lk 4:1-13). All of this raises the question, *why?* Why does Matthew,

---

[2]K. Aland, ed., *Synopsis Quattuor Evangeliorum*, 13th rev. ed. (Stuttgart: Deutsche Bibelgesellschaft, 1985), and K. Aland, ed., *Synopsis of the Four Gospels*, rev. ed. (New York: United Bible Societies, 1982).

or Luke, choose not to include this or that text from Mark, which, according to theory, lay right there before his very eyes? Discerning an answer to that question moves us along the road toward understanding the motives behind the changes made and thus toward grasping the theological message the evangelist wishes to convey.

7.4.3 Redaction as Arrangement

The second stage of redaction criticism involves analyzing *arrangement*. Luke selects Mark's story of Jesus' hometown sermon, which Mark positions well along in his Gospel (Mk 6:1-6). Luke however places it very early in his Gospel, at the very outset of Jesus' ministry in Galilee (Lk 4:16-30). Matthew also selects this pericope, but he leaves it in relatively the same place Mark has it. Why, we may ask, does Luke rearrange the sequence of things like this? Part of the answer may lie in the way Luke also adds considerable detail to Mark's account of the event, elaborating on what Jesus actually had to say in the sermon. In Luke's hands, the sermon at Nazareth becomes a programmatic statement, a kind of manifesto, for Jesus' mission (and by extension into Acts, that of the early church?).

As is the case with selection, arrangement can be applied not only to a pericope's position within the Gospel's larger framework but also to the elements within a pericope. Luke and Matthew both preserve a genealogy of Jesus; Matthew's comes at the very front of his Gospel, but Luke places his version between the accounts of the baptism and the temptation of Jesus. In addition to these differing "big-picture" arrangements, these two genealogies differ internally by running in opposite directions. Matthew's begins with Abraham and flows downstream, while Luke's begins with Jesus and flows upstream, all the way past Abraham to Adam and God (Lk 3:23-38). It is no accident that Luke takes the reader from there directly to the temptation in the desert. By doing so, Luke presents Jesus as the new Adam, facing a new temptation, and representing all of humanity, Jewish and Gentile alike. Arrangement is a powerful redactional tool.

7.4.4 Redaction as Adaptation

Editors *adapt* their source material to suit their own tastes and objectives. Selection and arrangement are two forms of adaptation, whether on the level of an entire book or on the level of a pericope, but there are other forms of adaptation as well. Matthew selects Mark's pericope on the healing of Peter's mother-in-law (Mk 1:29-31), but he arranges it to follow the Sermon on the Mount (Mt 8:14-15). He also makes certain internal rearrangements to it in order to make it reflect the chiastic shape of the story of the leper (Mt 8:2-4; we will return to this point in chapter eight). In addition, however, Matthew adapts some of the language of Mark's account, changing a word or two here, a pronoun there, until the mother-in-law story quite obviously "matches" the leper's story. This editorial maneuver enables Matthew to bind together three healings as a literary unit (leper, centurion's "son" [Mt 8:5-13] and Peter's mother-in-law) and thereby to embed within them a profound theological statement: Jesus has come to touch the untouchables, even though touching them is apparently not required for healing them.

7.4.5 A Word of Encouragement in This

For many of us, thinking of the Gospels in this way can be confusing and disturbing. If Mark is part of God's Holy Word, it can disturb us to hear that even Matthew or Luke would have dared to treat it in this way. How could the simple act of reading the Gospel story become so confusingly complex? These are understandable concerns, but they come at the matter from the wrong end. *They imply that our assumptions about Holy Scripture are to be preserved in spite of what we may discover about the Scriptures from studying them as they are.* What we ought to do instead is what we usually claim to be doing anyway: we need to allow the *actual* character of the Scriptures to define for us what our assumptions about them should be. If we can trust the God who has given us these documents, can we also trust him to have given us something he approves of? Our responsibility is not to decide in advance what the biblical documents ought to be like, but to *let them be* whatever they actually are. We cannot properly understand them or communicate their message unless we treat them with that kind of respect. We need not fear the search for the truth. That said, we must also admit that the model we have just considered does not necessarily reflect the truth we seek; for now, however (in my view anyway), it makes the best sense of the evidence before us.

7.5 USING A GOSPEL SYNOPSIS

As hinted above (see footnote 2), *the* tool of choice for studying the Gospels this way is the *Synopsis of the Four Gospels*, edited by Kurt Aland. It is available in English (RSV text) and in Greek (with the Latin title *Synopsis Quattuor Evangeliorum*). There are similar tools, but Aland's is the Lamborghini of Gospel synopses. The editorial peculiarities of each individual Gospel are *every bit as much part of the inspired Word of God* as is the Gospel story itself. This means that we can greatly benefit from using a tool like this in the analysis of God's Word. As a tool, the synopsis enables us to be more readily faithful to the Word in its fullness than we could otherwise be, like using a backhoe instead of a hand-trowel to excavate a new basement. Not that it would otherwise be impossible to accomplish the same results; rather, the synopsis makes the job far easier. For that reason, we will spend the rest of this chapter on how to find our way around in the tool and on how to use it. This means that the tone and character of the following discussion will be quite different from the material in sections 7.1—7.4, more a "how-to" than a "what-is" discussion.

7.5.1 Design of the Synopsis

The design of the Aland *Synopsis* can be puzzling. Understanding how it was (apparently) compiled helps us in understanding the way it is laid out. Here is the logic of it. As we go through this, it will be helpful if you keep your copy of the *Synopsis* open to index 1, the "Index of the Gospel Parallels" (pp. 341-55 in the English edition; all page references in the following discussion refer to this edition). The *Synopsis* provides (a) the text of each of the four Gospels arranged in its proper order, start to finish. Simultaneously, for each Gospel's individual pericopes, and in as little space as possible, it also provides (b) any parallel texts from the other Gospels, conveniently laying them side by side in columns. In order to provide these services, the *Synopsis* is designed as follows. Envision a large workroom with four long tables where the cutting-and-pasting process of assembling the *Synopsis* is underway.

1. First visualize each Gospel laid out on its own table and cut up into its separate pericopes. The points of division between pericopes reflect, of course, the editor's form-critical judgment. We are free to challenge any of his decisions in this, but if we do, we need to be able to say why we do and to supply (and justify) an alternative analysis.

2. Next, the pericopes of each separate Gospel (making up the entire Gospel) are laid out in the order they follow in that Gospel, pericope by pericope, all the way through—again, one Gospel per worktable.

3. Many of these individual pericopes, such as those that belong to the triple or the double tradition, reappear in one or more of the other Gospels, though not necessarily in the same order or precisely the same form. From index 1, we can see, for example, that John the Baptist's preaching of repentance—pericope 14, numbered in the left-hand margin—occurs in both Matthew and Luke. Some of these corresponding, parallel pericopes are obviously alternate versions of the "same" story. Others are less obviously so but are close enough in certain respects to be treated as parallels to each other.

4. Then, for each of the four Gospels, one Gospel at a time, copies are made of the parallel pericopes from wherever they occur in the *other three* Gospels.

These copies are then laid out in separate columns on each worktable along-side their parallel counterparts in the "leading" Gospel for that table, with one column for each separate "non-leading" Gospel. Thus, the order of the dupli-cated pericopes from the other three "non-leading" Gospels is often scram-bled in the process. In the *Synopsis,* the "leading" Gospel is whichever one of the four the *Synopsis* is currently focusing on.

5. Now, on each separate worktable in the cutting room (where we are con-structing the *Synopsis*), we have four separate columns of Gospel pericopes— one for each Gospel, one set per table. To change the metaphor slightly, they are like decks of cards, each deck arranged in proper order for that Gospel. In addition, where appropriate, and in parallel columns, we have attached to each pericope (to each card in a deck) copies of all its parallel cards from the other Gospels.

6. Next, all four of these decks are inter-shuffled into *one master deck.* In the process of combining the four decks, we eliminate all redundant cards in or-der to cut down on size and the use of space. Index 1 provides a list made from the combined decks of these pericopes and parallels. Wherever parallel peri-copes occur in the same relative order in their respective Gospels, the separate pericopes for those Gospels appear together in one place, rather than appear-ing in two or three—or even four—separate places. For an example, look in index 1 at pericope 20, "The Temptation." The *Synopsis* arranges the separate Gospel columns relative to each other so that this pericope comes at the same relative place in Matthew, Mark and Luke. Thus, the data for the temptation does not need to appear in three different pericope locations, one for each Gospel; "slot" 20 does the job by itself for all three.

7. Finally, in index 1, and in the rest of the *Synopsis*, we can distinguish the "in-order" (lead) material from the "out-of-order" (parallel) material by whether bold type or plain type is used for indicating the chapter-verse refer-ences. The bold type refers to in-order pericopes for a given Gospel. A plain-type reference indicates a parallel text duplicated and displaced for conven-ient comparison with some other Gospel's "in-order" pericope.

Take a moment now to look over the four Gospel columns in the next few pages of index 1. Try to visualize these four separate lists having been merged, shuffled together like decks of cards, with the adjacent redundancies weeded out. Judging from the information provided in the index at pericope 128 ("The Parable of the Mustard Seed"), determine how many times in the *Syn-opsis* the parallel versions of this pericope will be laid out, and where they are found. (For the answer, after you have figured it out for yourself, see the end of the chapter: Answer 1.)

7.5.2 Navigating in the Synopsis

If we want to find the *Synopsis* treatment of a particular pericope in Luke (say, Lk 4:16-30), we can use three different ways to locate it. (1) We can follow the bold-type references down the Luke column of index 1 until we come to Luke 4:16-30 in bold type. Try it; which number pericope is it and on what page will we find the text? (See answer 2, below.) (2) Or we can use index 2, "Index of New Testament Passages" (pp. 356-61 in the English edition). Try it for Luke 4:16-30. Here, too, the bold typeface indicates in-order references. The references for the out-of-order parallels are not explicitly listed in index 2, but the pericope and page numbers for them are. Note that pericope 139 treats the parallels to Luke 4:16-30 from the perspective of the other Gospels' order, that is, where Matthew and Mark are the "leading" Gospels. The smaller, plain-type verse numbers listed there in index 2 are secondary parallels; we will come back to them in a moment.

3) The third way to find the in-order treatment of Luke 4:16-30 takes us to the main body of the *Synopsis*. Turn to page 207 (which I selected by opening the book at random; if you are using the Greek *Synopsis*, turn instead to p. 323). Across the very top of the page, in the header, we find three sections. In the "gutter," on the left, we see "[no. 240]" (the Greek *Synopsis* uses the German abbreviation *nr.* in place of the English *no.*); this tells us the number of the pericope treated on that page (in this case, the pericope actually starts on the preceding page). On the far right, at the outer margin, is the page number, 207 (or 323), which got you here. This means that we can use either the page number or the pericope number to find our way around in the body of the book, provided we know what they are, as in my telling you to turn to page 207. (Note that on page 206 and other even-numbered pages, the page and pericope numbers are still at the outer margin and in the "gutter," respectively; but margin and gutter are reversed as to left and right.) Turn now to pericope (not *page!*) 184, using just the page headers. What *page* do you end up on? (See answer 3, below.)

However, if we know only the biblical reference of the pericope, such as Luke 4:16-30, we can locate it by using the center portion of the page header, where we find a reference for each of the four Gospels. These references occur in either bold or plain typeface, and there will always be at least one Gospel reference in bold. What do we have in the header for page 170 (p. 267 in the Greek *Synopsis*)? (See answer 4.) What this means is that on any particular page, the header will indicate in bold type which Gospel or Gospels provide the "lead" text(s) for this pericope. In the case of page 170 (or p. 267), Luke's order alone is the "lead." The plain typeface for the other three Gospel references in the header on this page—and get this—indicates the *last pericope treated as a leading text for each of those Gospels*. It is *not* telling us that these texts are treated on *this* page as out-of-order parallels. This means that we can riffle backward or forward through the book, watching the center page headers, until we find the desired passage listed there in bold. Try it for finding Luke 4:16-30 in bold. The process should take you to pages 31-33 (pp. 48-50 in the Greek *Synopsis*). So if we know the biblical passage we want to study in the *Synopsis*, we have three tools to use in order to locate it: the two indexes and the page headers.

7.5.3 Secondary Parallels

In the next section, we will see what the *Synopsis* can show us about the various Gospel writers' editorial activities. First, however, there are a couple more things to observe about its design. In the process of exploring the layout of the *Synopsis*, we noticed text and references printed not just in plain type, but even in *reduced* plain type. Consider pericope 248, for example. This pericope represents John's story of how Jesus heals a man born blind (Jn 9:1-41). For this Johannine pericope, and for the several other Johannine pericopes printed in the immediate vicinity (pp. 206-14 [Greek, pp. 321-33]), there are very few parallels in the other three Gospels. In fact, for pericopes 238-50, the lead texts are all from John's Gospel, and there are *no* primary parallels for any of them. However, for two of them in the English *Synopsis* (nos. 240 and 248) and for four of them in the Greek *Synopsis* (adding nos. 241 and 247), small-print references are provided at the head of the Matthew, Mark and Luke columns; further down these columns, also in small print, we find the texts corresponding to those references. In fact, in pericope 248 there is even an additional small-print text from John. These additional texts are *secondary* parallels. Though not directly parallel to the lead text, they are in some way reminiscent of it and therefore, in the editor's opinion, worthy of note. Often, these secondary parallels will switch on a light bulb in our heads as we think about the meaning of the lead text. Take a moment to read over the lead text of pericope 248, and then read the various secondary parallels that Aland has supplied, not only from the three Synoptics, but from elsewhere in John as well. How do these secondary parallels suggest we might read and understand the message of John 9?

Note also that wherever there has just been, or will now be, a break in a lead Gospel's sequence, each lead pericope text is supplied with the *Synopsis* "address" for the previous and/or the next lead text from that Gospel. Primary parallels pulled *out* of sequence are also supplied with the "addresses" where they occur *in* sequence. As an example, turn to pericopes 16 and 17. Finally, at the end of most pericopes and at the bottom of virtually every page in the main body of the English *Synopsis*, we find two sets of notes. The upper one (where there *are* two) provides alternative translations in other English-language versions of the text. The lower one (again, where there are two) provides other information, such as alternative readings based on various ancient manuscripts, as well as potentially interesting cross-references to other biblical texts. In the Greek *Synopsis*, these marginal notes provide text-critical data for each Gospel (described in chapter two, above) as well as a wealth of cross-references to quotations, allusions and other parallels from outside the Gospels.

7.5.4 Peter's Mother-in-Law

We may use Matthew 8:14-15, the healing of Peter's mother-in-law, as an example of what the *Synopsis* can tell us. Using this particular text implies, first, that we are asking here about Matthew's message, not about Mark's, Luke's or John's. We will therefore turn to the place in the *Synopsis* where Matthew's version of this story appears as the "lead" text. Using index 1, index 2 or the page headers (as described above in 7.5.2) brings us to pericope 87 (English, p. 75; Greek, p. 117). We can see immediately from the layout of pericope 87 that Mark and Luke place versions of this same story relatively earlier in their respective Gospels (both treated as pericope 37 in the *Synopsis*) and that John does not record this event at all. Nevertheless, the versions from Mark and Luke appear here in pericope 87, "out of order," so as to provide easy access to them as parallels to Matthew's version. (The reverse is true at pericope 37.)

Further attention to index 1 reveals that the main difference in arrangement between Matthew and Mark at this point (viewed from the perspective of the two-document hypothesis) is that Matthew postpones this healing story until almost immediately after Jesus delivers the Sermon on the Mount. Once Matthew's Jesus comes down from the mountain (Mt 8:1), his first encounters are with persons whom Mark's Jesus meets in Mark 1, namely the mother-in-law of Simon (Mk 1:29-31) and the leper (Mk 1:40-45). In the process of "selecting" these two stories from Mark 1, Matthew reverses their order and deselects (omits) two other texts Mark includes between them. Matthew then brings in a story (perhaps from Q; cf. Lk 7:1-10) about the healing of the son (or servant: παῖς) of a Roman centurion and inserts it between the two he gets from Mark. The net effect is, in part, that the Sermon on the Mount becomes a kind of programmatic manifesto for Matthew's Gospel (as the Nazareth sermon does for Luke's Gospel), and these three needy persons represent the first people Jesus meets in his active healing ministry in Galilee.

With these preliminary observations on the *selection* and *arrangement* of the mother-in-law pericope (all available to us through index 1), we can turn our attention to the *adaptation* of its internal wording. For this purpose it is almost essential to adopt some system of visually highlighting the agreements and discrepancies between two parallel Gospel accounts. It is easiest to do this directly on the pages of the tool itself, a tool intended for our *use*. The fact that Aland's Greek *Synopsis* is particularly expensive, in contrast to the English-only edition, may make some users reluctant to "mark up" their copies in this way. In that case, users should at least make photocopies of relevant pages and mark *them* up. But marking up even the Greek edition is no worse than underlining text or writing marginal notes in an expensive new Bible. Once you get past making the first mark, the struggle is over, like getting the first scratch on a brand new car.

The particular system we adopt for highlighting the comparisons is not important, so long as it enables us to see clearly how the two accounts compare and contrast. It should highlight (a) text in verbatim agreement between the two parallel accounts, (b) text nearly in verbatim agreement but adapted to some degree, (c) text kept intact but rearranged, (d) text omitted from the parallel, and (e) text added. Some highlighting systems use combinations of solid, dashed and dotted underlining (and its absence) for this purpose; others use contrasting colors. One potentially confusing factor is worth mentioning here, however. Whether we operate from the two-document hypothesis or from the two-Gospel hypothesis, we will need to keep separate how Matthew and Luke individually relate to Mark. In a pericope representing the triple tradition, for example, where all three Synoptic Gospels preserve the pericope in relatively the same location (as in pericope 146, the Feeding of the Five Thousand), the marking-up of Matthew and Mark may interfere with the marking-up of Mark and Luke. See figure 7.2 for a graphic depiction of marking up Matthew and Mark at pericope 87.

In figure 7.2, solid lines underscore material which Matthew (on the two-document hypothesis) has taken over verbatim from Mark. Broken lines underscore what Matthew borrows from Mark, but with certain adaptations, usually grammatical. In one instance an additional line, dotted, indicates that Matthew has moved a piece of text from the spot it occupies in Mark to one more congenial to his own purposes. (Mark's ἤγειρεν "raised" in v. 31 is converted to passive and moved to follow πυρετός "fever" in Mt 8:15; thus it is underscored by *both* a broken line and a dotted line.) Text without underscoring is either omitted by Matthew from Mark's text or added by Matthew to the story. Similar underscorings analyze the English version; but notice that the moving of text (requiring a dotted line) is no longer observable.

Καὶ ἐλθὼν ὁ Ἰησοῦς εἰς τὴν οἰκίαν Πέτρου εἶδεν τὴν πενθερὰν αὐτοῦ βεβλημένην καὶ πυρέσσουσαν καὶ	Καὶ εὐθὺς ἐκ τῆς συναγωγῆς ἐξελθόντες ἦλθον εἰς τὴν οἰκίαν Σίμωνος καὶ Ἀνδρέου μετὰ Ἰακώβου καὶ Ἰωάννου.³⁰ ἡ δὲ πενθερὰ Σίμωνος κατέκειτο πυρέσσουσα, καὶ εὐθὺς λέγουσιν αὐτῷ περὶ αὐτῆς.³¹ καὶ προσελθὼν ἤγειρεν αὐτὴν
ἥψατο τῆς χειρὸς αὐτῆς, ¹⁵ καὶ ἀφῆκεν αὐτὴν ὁ πυρετός, καὶ ἠγέρθη καὶ διηκόνει αὐτῷ	κρατήσας τῆς χειρός· καὶ ἀφῆκεν αὐτὴν ὁ πυρετός, καὶ διηκόνει αὐτοῖς.
And when Jesus entered Peter's house, he saw his mother-in-law lying sick with a fever; ¹⁵ he touched her hand, and the fever left her, and she rose and served him.	And immediately he left the synagogue, and entered the house of Simon and Andrew, with James and John. ³⁰ Now Simon's mother-in-law lay sick with a fever, and immediately they told him of her. ³¹ And he came and took her by the hand and lifted her up, and the fever left her; and she served them.

Figure 7.2. Synoptic view of Mt 8:14-15 (left column) and Mk 1:29-31 (right column), with redaction-critical markings. (Corresponds to Aland, *Synopsis*, pericope no. 87; English: RSV.)

From the highlighted text of pericope 87 (using this underscoring system), we can quickly pick out what Matthew has omitted from Mark and what he has inserted from elsewhere. He omits mention of the synagogue and of Andrew, James and John. He also does not say that anyone drew Jesus' attention to the woman lying sick in the house or that Jesus seized her by the hand and raised her up. Instead, Matthew tells us that on entering the house of Peter (Mark calls him "Simon"), Jesus *saw* the woman, who was lying down and feverish. And instead of grasping her hand and raising her up (as Mark has it), Jesus simply *touched* her hand and she rose up, apparently on her own strength. From both versions we learn that the fever left her and she began to serve, but whereas in Mark she began to serve *them*, Matthew reports that she began to serve *him*, Jesus only.

What, if anything, do all these redactional changes suggest to us about Matthew's intentions? For one thing, Matthew does here what he also does with Mark's material in many other places: he strips away information that he apparently regards as irrelevant to the story at hand. Since Andrew, James and John have no role to play in this scene—as far as Matthew is concerned anyway—out they go. Much more interesting, however, is the way Matthew has rearranged the elements of the story so that they form a seven-part chiasm. As he enters the house,

A. *Jesus* sees *the woman.*

    B. She is *lying down.*

        C. She is *feverish.*

            D. Jesus *touches* her hand.

        C'. The *fever* leaves her.

    B'. She *gets up.*

A'. *The woman* serves *Jesus.*

All these elements are present in Mark's version of the story, but not in this chiastic order. In fact, Matthew has adapted the material as well as having rearranged it. Jesus *sees* the woman, rather than being told about her. He *touches* her hand (ἥψατο) rather than seizing it. Once more on her feet, she serves *him* alone (αὐτῷ), rather than all of them (αὐτοῖς).

The obvious next question is to ask why Matthew has adapted the story in this way. What is he up to? This question leads us into the subject of the next chapter, to which we now turn.

Answers

1. Two places: pericopes 128 and 209, pp. 119 and 188 (pp. 181 and 294 in the Greek *Synopsis*)

2. Pericope 33, p. 31 (p. 48 in the Greek *Synopsis*)

3. Pericope 170 (p. 267 in the Greek *Synopsis*)

4. Only Luke in bold

8

NARRATIVES II

Thickening the Plot

But the angel said to the women,
"Do not be afraid; I know that you are looking for Jesus who was crucified."
MATTHEW 28:5

The preceding chapter ended with an unfinished task. It is one thing—a good thing—to analyze what an author such as Matthew has done with his sources. It is another thing to discern what that author wants to say by means of what he has done with his sources. Most of us are quite used to this process in everyday life. My wife may say to me, "It's been some time since the garbage was taken out." To this rather banal bit of information, I could respond with thanks for her keeping me uselessly up-to-date on the status of various domestic conditions. Of course, that would hardly take into consideration the question *why* she would bother to tell me this at all. In *real* everyday life, I will hear the subtext of her announcement: something like, "Take out the garbage now!" Her more indirect way of issuing this virtual command may reflect a stinging, sarcastic wit or a desire to respect the dignity of my person, or something else altogether. Let's consider this dynamic with regard to Gospel texts.

On the surface of things, Matthew has at least told us in 8:14-15 that Jesus healed Peter's mother-in-law of a fever, as we saw above in section 7.5.4. This "simple" fact is worth knowing for its own sake. It is quite possible that the story circulated as a detached anecdote during the earliest period of the church's existence, perhaps in the form Mark gives it in his Gospel—and perhaps in Aramaic. The question before us, however, is why Matthew wishes to retell the story in the new way we observed earlier. Assuming he had Mark's version to go by, why does he strip various details from it, rearrange it as a chiasm, and make certain changes in vocabulary and pronouns? Why does he place it where he does?

The answer to questions like these cannot be found by restricting our attention to the story itself. The overall coherence of Matthew's Gospel and of the various parts and subparts making it up (things we discussed in chapters three and four!) require us to assume that any given smaller narrative unit has organic ties to its larger literary context. Matthew—or any of the other writers of New Testament narrative—has pursued a narrative *strategy* in telling his story, and he has provided clues for reading the story the way he wants us to read it. Whether we correctly interpret these clues when we catch them (or whether we catch them at all—or whether we "catch" what isn't really there!) is another question, but we are bound to make an attempt if we wish to honor Matthew and his book. Even if we get it wrong, God gives us grace to keep working at it. It is truly unfortunate when we, as teachers of the church, refuse to try for *fear* of being wrong or for fear of finding something we would rather not find. In this regard, it is worth recalling the angel's words to the women arriving at the tomb, seeking the Lord in all the wrong places: "Do not be afraid; I know that you are looking for Jesus who was crucified" (Mt 28:5).

If, then, we cast our net a bit more broadly over Matthew's larger plan, we notice two things about this mother-in-law text. First, it is the third in a row of three healing stories (Mt 8:1-15), directly following the Sermon on the Mount. The second thing we notice is that a summary passage immediately follows it in verses 16-17, describing in general terms further healings Jesus performed that evening. (We will return to the subject of summary passages later in this chapter.) Following the summary passage, Matthew reports several "nonhealing" events. With the Sermon on one side and a series of nonhealing stories on the other, our attention is thus drawn to the triple healings and summary in 8:1-17.

Analysis of the first of these healing stories, the one about the leper (Mt 8: 2-4), reveals that it too is shaped as a chiasm (in fact Mark's version also has it this way):

A. A *leper* comes to Jesus.

    B. He says, "Lord if *you will*, you can *make me clean.*

        C. Jesus stretches out his *hand* and *touches* him.

    B'. Jesus says, "*I will; be clean.*"

A'. The *leprosy* leaves him.

Thus, the middle member of Matthew's chiasm in the story of the healing of the leper is the statement that Jesus "stretched out his hand and touched (ἥψατο) him." Striking, to say the least, is the parallel to the story of Peter's mother-in-law, where (as we saw in section 7.5.4) Matthew deliberately rearranges and rewords Mark's version in order to put Jesus' *touching of the woman's hand* at the center of a newly formed chiasm. We then notice that the center story, regarding the healing of the centurion's servant (Mt 8:5-13), is by far the longest of the three and that its point is, in part, Jesus' ability to heal from afar, *without touching!* When we consider the three persons Jesus encounters here, we recognize that, according to Jewish custom, all three are ceremonially untouchable and that these are the first "needy" people Matthew's Jesus directly deals with at the commencement of his public healing ministry. Factoring that idea into Matthew's message as a whole, we glimpse one aspect of what it means to Matthew that God has returned in Emmanuel, Jesus of Nazareth, to "be with" his people. The story also helps us to see just who Jesus' "people" really are. He touches the untouchables for no other reason than simply to touch them. In fact, by touching them *he* probably "contaminates" *them* with his own cleanness in the same way their uncleanness was thought to contaminate the ritually clean.

There is much more of the same sort to consider even in this short passage, but this much makes it clear that a New Testament storyteller embeds a portion of his message in the very way he tells the story. None of these five narrative documents (the four Gospels and Acts) has been strung together at random. They are all well designed and well executed, and they repay us a hundredfold for our efforts to understand them on their own terms. Yet we can take it for granted that what made sense in this respect to a first-century Jewish writer will not necessarily be what a twenty-first-century Western reader expects to find. Primarily for this reason, we cannot overemphasize the fact that our first exegetical responsibility to New Testament narrative is to let it be whatever it is, rather than to seek in it only what we expect to find there. Jesus is no longer in the tomb; we will find him only where he really is.

With this preliminary acknowledgment of the nature of biblical narrative, we may now turn to specific subtypes and techniques that the authors use to weave their larger stories together. We will consider (1) narrative texts with plot, character and setting; (2) type-scenes and parallel accounts; (3) Old Testament citations and allusions; (4) extended speeches and shorter *logia;* and (5) summary passages.

8.1 STORIES WITH PLOT, CHARACTER AND SETTING

Many excellent books and dictionary articles on the subject of Jesus' parables give advice on hearing them and reading them as their Gospel authors apparently intended. At the same time, recent decades have seen a surge of interest in the way *any* story is told, parable or otherwise. The discipline of "narrative criticism"—with its interest in character, setting, plot, point of view, implied author and implied reader, narrator and "narratee"—has brought fruitful new insight to the reading of biblical stories. Granted certain distinctions between parabolic stories and reports of actual events, such that we can usually tell them apart, there are nevertheless significant similarities between them as categories. Insofar as a parable is a story with a lesson, it is similar to any story in the Gospels or Acts. No account of any event in biblical narrative, we may assume, is told simply to record what happened. Thus, much of what we look for in parables (point, invitation, challenge, warning) we will also find in any Gospel story.

8.1.1 Parables and Events

Not all parables are stories, of course. The Old Testament Hebrew word *māšāl*, frequently translated in the Septuagint as παραβολή "parable," applies to a wide variety of figurative language, not just to narratives. Proverbs, metaphors and similes, songs, pithy aphorisms and riddles all fall within the general category of "parable." We will take up some of these more specialized types below. Here, however, we restrict our attention to parables in story form. Luke's Gospel contains some of the most famous of the New Testament story parables. The good Samaritan (Lk 10:29-37), the prodigal son (Lk 15:11-32), and the Pharisee and the publican (Lk 18:9-14) are well-known examples. Like all good stories, these tales, though short, have cast, setting and plot. We want to know what messages Jesus (or Luke) conveys by the way the characters in these little stories interact with each other and with their settings, and by the way the plots unfold. How many characters are there? Is one or more of them central to the action? Are any of them peripheral, even expendable? How do they relate to each other? Do they speak? If so, what do they say, and how much, and when, and to whom? Is there an implied contrast or a comparison? Is one character more "approved" by the storyteller than another is?

One crucial consideration with respect to author approval (which is similar to author's point of view) is whether the author approves of what the audience would approve of. For example, Luke's Jesus clearly presents the Samaritan traveler as the "good guy" in his parable, and he portrays the priest and the Levite in less than flattering terms. Luke informs us that Jesus told this story to a Jewish legal expert, a man who doubtless would have regarded any Samaritan as fully compromised in the eyes of Jewish law. That fact is a crucial assumption for the larger story in which the parable occurs. This parable is not a lesson about how to be nice to our neighbors but a disturbing reassessment of just who is qualified to "inherit eternal life" (Lk 10:25): even our enemies are.

In this way, Luke reveals his (and Jesus') "point of view" as quite different from that of a typical Jewish scribe.

Or consider a contrastive parable. In the story of the unjust judge (Lk 18:1-8) the contrast that Jesus sets up is not one between a persistent widow and the negligent judge she hounds; instead he contrasts that heartless judge with God, who needs no hounding at all. Thus, the parable is not about constantly begging God to do what we want him to do, but about quiet and persistent confidence in a God who truly cares for his own, *unlike that other judge.* This, in fact, is exactly what Luke says the parable is about in his introduction to it (Lk 18:1). Seeing the story in this light removes the oppressive burden it might otherwise appear to lay on our shoulders, as if it were encouraging us to badger God until, like a beleaguered mother, he caves in.

John's Gospel is devoid of parables in the usual sense, though he has plenty of parabolic metaphors: the Lamb of God (Jn 1:29), the vine and the branches (Jn 15:1-8), the good shepherd and his sheep (Jn 10:1-18), and others. Nonetheless, we do see the parabolic story principle at work in his narration of actual events in Jesus' life. In John 3:1-21 the devout Pharisee Nicodemus comes to Jesus at night, clandestinely but in obvious sincerity. Despite being a teacher of the people (Jn 3:10), however, Nicodemus cannot quite "get" what Jesus tells him. Then, after a short interval dedicated to John the Baptist's testimony (Jn 3:22-36), the Evangelist takes us with Jesus into Samaria. There, in broad daylight this time (Jn 4:6), Jesus meets a Samaritan woman, despised by the Jews and fully conscious of it (Jn 3:9). Her bold, almost "improper" flirtatiousness contrasts strongly with the serious theological concerns of Nicodemus. Yet, also in contrast to that anxious teacher of Israel, this "contaminated" woman "gets it," and she gets it enough to evangelize her own village. Telling the two accounts almost back-to-back like this is part of John's narrative strategy; we need to consider it carefully when we read his story.

Even this is not the end of it. (Why should it be?) The first half of John's Gospel relates a series of seven or eight "signs" (σημεῖα) performed by Jesus, after each of which John "unpacks" its significance through the subsequent events of his larger story. Jesus' turning of water into wine at the wedding in Cana (Jn 2:1-11) is the first of the signs, and the second is the healing of an official's son in Capernaum (Jn 4:46-54; cf. Mt 8:5-13). The paired stories of Nicodemus and the Samaritan woman appear between these first two signs, as if in partial explanation of the first one. As such, they complement Jesus' cleansing of the temple (Jn 2:14-22), which they closely follow. Taken in this context, the stories of Nicodemus and the Samaritan woman illustrate that Jesus has transformed the water of traditional second-temple Judaism into the wine of the Father's glory returned. This "new wine" of Jesus upsets everything, from temple practices to traditional standards of acceptability in the kingdom of God. This may well be what John means in John 1:14 (RSV): "And the Word became flesh and dwelt among us, full of grace and truth; we have beheld his glory, glory as of the only Son from the Father." In Jesus, the long absent Shekinah Glory—God's holy presence—has returned to his tabernacle, to his temple, with "cleansing" consequences for his people. In this regard, there is a thematic similarity to Matthew's interest in God's presence "with us" in Jesus, Emmanuel.

8.1.2 Whose Story Is It, Anyway?

We have been ignoring for the moment a problem raised in chapter seven regarding the peculiar nature of the Gospels as (we might say) stories told about a storyteller. Much of what we have in the Gospels is the story of Jesus telling a story. The parables are good examples of this phenomenon. The same two-level dynamic occurs with Luke's account of the speeches of Peter and Paul in Acts. It poses a delicate problem for us. Put bluntly, the issue is whether what Jesus originally intended by the use of the parable of the Good Samaritan, for instance, matches what Luke intends by it. Do Luke and Jesus use the parable in the same way, with the same intended results? More precisely, does Jesus' original use of the parable match Luke's purpose in *telling the story of Jesus telling that parable?* One of my former professors (R. P. Meye) has argued that Luke deliberately placed this account directly ahead of the story of Martha's frustration over her sister Mary's failure to help out in the kitchen (Lk 10:38-42). Luke did so in order to balance a focus on social action (the example of the good Samaritan) with the call for quiet contemplation (Mary's example). Whether this represents the right way to read Luke's narrative or not (I suspect it is not), it legitimately addresses the potential difference between Jesus' original purposes and Luke's (or those of any of the other Evangelists).

This dilemma (Jesus or Luke?) is closely connected with the question of the relationship between the Jesus of history and the Jesus (or the Jesus*es*) of the Gospels. Again, put bluntly, we want to know how closely the Jesus we meet in any one of the four Gospels resembles the Jesus we meet in any of the other three, or how any or all of those four portraits of Jesus resemble the Jesus who walked the roads of Palestine in the first century. Taking this issue one step further, we may also want to ask how closely any of these depictions resembles the Christ of faith (Jesus as Christians, in various concrete historical-cultural settings, have visualized and worshiped him). The three-dimensional dilemma embodied in this conundrum has evolved into an enormously complex scholarly discussion, which we cannot rehearse here.[1]

For now, it is enough to be aware of the problem. The relationship between Jesus as he was in history and Jesus as portrayed in any of the four Gospels is parallel to the relationship between Jesus as portrayed in the Gospels and the Christ of our faith. In this sense, the Jesus we meet in the Gospel of John is the Christ of John's faith. We may confess (rightly, I believe) that the Holy Spirit superintended the composition of the Gospels, so that they are trustworthy interpretations of the "actual" life and deeds of Jesus. It is of utmost importance, therefore, that we learn all we can about Jesus and his culture as they actually existed together. Nevertheless, in the end, we are committed to hearing the four interpretations of his person and his life as they have come down to us in the canonical Gospels. We need to strive toward faithful interpretations of those Gospel accounts *as we have them* and to structure our understanding of Jesus accordingly, adjusting our own "Christ of faith" as necessary. This can be a painful process when we are thereby compelled to acknowledge that some treasured understanding of Jesus' character has no Gospel support.

8.1.3 Allegory and Allegorization

Occasionally a Gospel presents Jesus as telling a parable to which he adds his own interpretation for the benefit of his disciples. One of the more famous of these is the parable of the sower (Mk 4:1-20, with parallels in Mt 13 and Lk 8). The explanation of the parable (Mk 4:13-20) provides an allegorical interpretation of various elements within the parable: the sower, the seed, the four different kinds of soil, the birds and so on. In other words, this parable is a legitimate biblical allegory. The fact that the assignment of equivalents is not neat and logical does not detract from the allegorical nature of the interpretation. Paul also uses allegory; in the letter to the Galatians, for example, he employs an allegory to make a point about freedom from the law (Gal 4:21-31; especially v. 24).

These biblical examples of allegory have encouraged interpreters down through the ages to try their own hand at allegorical interpretation of Scripture. A celebrated example, often cited in books like this one, is Augustine's

---

[1]N. T. Wright's little book *The Challenge of Jesus: Rediscovering Who Jesus Was and Is* (Downers Grove, Ill.: InterVarsity Press, 1999) introduces the issue clearly and succinctly. The book summarizes the arguments put forth in the first two, massive volumes of Wright's multivolume magnum opus, Christian Origins and the Question of God: *The New Testament and the People of God* (Philadelphia: Fortress, 1992) and *Jesus and the Victory of God* (Philadelphia: Fortress, 1996).

handling of the parable of the good Samaritan.[2] He views the waylaid victim as representing Adam, the thieves as Satan and his angels, the priest and Levite as the Old Testament, the Samaritan as Jesus, the inn as the church, the innkeeper as Paul and so on. Augustine's approach provides an example of *allegorization*, the transformation of what is not an allegory into an allegory. Such an interpretation fails to ask how Jesus' original audience (the Jewish lawyer in this case) could have been expected to grasp the message. ("Paul? Paul *who?*")

The truth is that by means of allegorization, interpreters of parables—or of any story—can make a text mean whatever they wish it to mean. Consequently, during the last century, the long-standing approach was to insist that each parable had one—and only one—main point to make; allegories were systematically excluded from consideration. This is patently a case of overkill, however, since there are, as we have just seen, examples of legitimate allegories in the New Testament, allegories created and used by Jesus and the New Testament authors themselves. Of course, in Galatians 4, Paul *allegorizes* the story of Hagar and Sarah, but then, he was Paul. His practice does not license us to imitate his methods. As interpreters, we will be wise not to treat a text allegorically unless there is good reason to do so, such as when Jesus (or Paul) does. In general, judicious exegesis of stories and parables will avoid *allegorizing* them. Unless we are dealing with a genuine biblical allegory or with other kinds of obviously "multivalent" texts, we should seek instead to understand a story's primary thesis and how it fits into the larger scope of the book in which we find it.

8.1.4 Summing Up for Stories

The chief point to take home from all of this is that the stories of the Gospels and Acts, whether in the form of parables or narrated events, are to be understood as told in a particular way, in a particular context, for a particular reason. As a community of believers, we have the privilege and responsibility to read these stories in such a way that we "see" what the authors have put there for us. We may wish that a writer had been more explicit about his message; we may wonder whether we have understood it correctly or not. But the subtly implicit nature of the Evangelists' presentations makes the discovery process all the more enriching, even thrilling—far more so than when the truth is handed to us in flat propositions, like crackers on a plate. In this, the Gospels reflect God's pedagogy. The ancient, global, Spirit-directed community conversation

---

[2]Peter Cotterell and Max Turner (*Linguistics and Biblical Interpretation* [Downers Grove, Ill.: InterVarsity Press, 1989], p. 311) lay it out in full. The original is in Augustine's *Quaestiones Evangeliorum* 2.19.

ensures not only that there will always be someone to challenge our conclusions, but also that there will always be someone's conclusions to challenge—God's strategy for course correction. We need each other in this task.

8.2 TYPE-SCENES AND PARALLEL ACCOUNTS

As N. T. Wright has said,[3] anyone who watches television news programs realizes that, today, people like the president of the United States can make policy statements from virtually anywhere and expect them to be broadcast to the entire nation—even the world—almost instantly. Jesus did not have that sort of same-day national coverage of his speeches and acts of healing. Thus not only can we assume that Jesus repeated his stories or performed his miracles more than once and in various places, we should actually assume that he did so hundreds of times. This insight makes it a bit less effective when a Gospel scholar superciliously criticizes a Gospel writer for naively preserving what the scholar regards as multiple accounts of a single event. We may in fact be dealing with multiple events in such cases. Setting aside the legitimate historical question of whether reported events are single or multiple, we still need to consider the literary, *interpretive* effect of repetitious narratives. We can divide them into parallel accounts and type-scenes.

8.2.1 Parallel Accounts

Consider two examples, beginning with Jesus' miraculous feedings of the crowds. All four Gospels preserve the story of Jesus feeding the five thousand men (Mk 6:32-44 and parallels; Matthew adds "besides women and children," Mt 14:21). The "problem" arises when both Mark and Matthew a little later on report a similar incident involving *four* thousand people (Mk 8:1-10; Matthew again insists there were actually more people there, if one were to count the women and children, too; Mt 15:38). Admittedly, numerous points of contact exist between the two feeding stories as told by each Evangelist. In both his accounts, Mark mentions Jesus' compassion on the crowds, the disciples' perplexity, the question of how many loaves, the seating of the crowds, the blessing and breaking of the bread, the distribution of food by the disciples, the eating and being satisfied, the gathering up of scraps into baskets, the number of baskets filled and the number of participants—and all in the same order. It is no surprise that some scholars assume that Mark—followed by Matthew (but not Luke)—has been fooled into thinking that there were two separate events here, when in fact there was only one.

---

[3]Wright, *New Testament and the People of God*, pp. 422-23.

Yet to make such an assumption is too easy; it ignores the evidence that Mark and Matthew are otherwise exceedingly skillful storytellers. The *interpretive* question to ask instead is why Mark and Matthew would have each preserved these two stories and placed them so close together. The answer may well lie in the setting each story is given in the text, both literarily and geographically. In both Mark and Matthew, the feeding of the five thousand apparently takes place on Jewish soil. The event symbolizes the return of God to his people. (Reminders of the manna in the wilderness are rife in the account: multiplication of bread, full satisfaction of the eaters, gathering the scraps in baskets.) But in Mark's Gospel, just before the feeding of the *four* thousand, we find Jesus and his followers returning from the Gentile areas of Tyre and Sidon and continuing down the eastern side of the Sea of Galilee into the equally Gentile territory of the Decapolis (Mk 7:31). It is here in the Decapolis, evidently, that this second "feeding" takes place. (This fact, by the way, points up the importance of being familiar with and paying attention to the political geography of Palestine in Jesus' day, as the Gospels reflect it.) Although Matthew omits reference to the Decapolis in his parallel to Mark here, his version of the feeding of the four thousand comes hard on the heels of Jesus' encounter with the pagan Canaanite woman in the district of Tyre and Sidon.

What we have in these two stories, then, is similar to what Luke gives us in his two accounts of the Pentecost experience: one in Jerusalem for the Jewish church (Acts 2) and a second one at Cornelius's house in Caesarea for the Gentile church (Acts 10). In fact, Luke goes to considerable literary lengths to emphasize the *Gentile* nature of Cornelius's household and Peter's initial objections to dealing with them (Acts 9). Similarly, both Mark and Matthew preserve a Jewish and, later, a Gentile manna-in-the-wilderness experience. The kingdom of God and his Messiah have equally salvific significance for all members of the human race.

We can also note in Acts the parallel accounts of a lame man healed. Both Peter in the Jerusalem temple (Acts 3:1-4:22) and Paul in pagan Lystra (Acts 14:8-23) encounter men born lame and raise them to their feet. In their respective situations, both Peter and Paul must immediately deal with awe-stricken crowds and their hostile reactions. In the descriptions of the two lame men and the circumstances of their healings, there are several astonishing parallels, more evident in Greek than in English translation. Taking into consideration the apparently intentional character of these parallels, we may conclude that Luke means to depict Peter and Paul as of equal stature and authority. He presents Peter as the God-sanctioned apostle to the Jewish church, and Paul becomes the apostle to the Gentile church, sanctioned by

God in a similar way. Equality between Peter and Paul in this regard is creatively portrayed in literary terms through these two parallel healing accounts.

8.2.2 Type-Scenes

Visualize a faceless man with a black hat, the setting sun behind him. He bursts through the swinging doors of a saloon in a Western B-movie. How many times have we seen this? Or picture John Wayne, Clint Eastwood or Gary Cooper, striding out into the dusty middle of Main Street for a classic face-off with some snarling desperado. How many times have we seen *that*? We call these type-scenes. They are like symbols, always carrying the same significance for whatever story they occur in. They display expected features, like the ominous clunk of boots on a wooden floor, the clink of spurs and the hushed dread falling over the poker-playing patrons in the saloon. Maybe the barkeeper drops behind the counter, and we get a close-up of a shot glass rolling slowly in a long semicircle across the floor. Imagine what the scene would imply if Black-Hat bursts into the saloon, boots clunking and spurs clinking, and no one even looks up to see who it is. We would have to expect Don Knotts perhaps, or one of the *Three Amigos*. It would change the whole tenor of the film.

Hollywood did not *invent* type-scenes. Consider what happens in Genesis 15:1-6; Exodus 3:1—4:17; Joshua 1:1-11; Jeremiah 1:1-10; Ezekiel 1:1—3:15; Isaiah 6; and Esther 3:1—5:2. All of these passages describe God's initial call and commissioning of an individual to serve him in some way, often as a mouthpiece. Careful analysis of these texts reveals a peculiar pattern (expected features) common to all of them. Each exhibits an introductory remark, a divine confrontation, an objection of some kind raised by the addressee, the commission and a confirmatory sign. These five literary forms, as we can see from examining these seven scenes, do not need to take exactly the same shape or fall in the same relative order in each case, but they all appear nonetheless. Figure 8.1 displays an analysis of these texts. The same pattern is discernible in the story of the annunciation to Mary in Luke 1:26-38. The conclusion to draw is that for some culturally based reason, Jewish tradition liked to use this particular type-scene format for relating a divine call.

Luke makes use of the divine-call type-scene when he describes the Damascus Road experience of Saul/Paul in Acts 9. We can analyze the story as follows (consult your Bible as you work through this paragraph): introduction, Acts 9:1-3a; divine confrontation, Acts 9:3b-4; Paul's objection, Acts 9:5a; divine commission, Acts 9:5b-6, 10-18; confirmatory sign, Acts 9:9, 18-19. In this literary way, Luke connects Saul/Paul with the great prophets of the Old Testament, thereby including him in the line of God's chosen spokespersons. Only

FORM	Gen 15	Ex 3,4	Josh 1	Jer 1	Ezek 1—3	Is 6	Esther 3—5
Introduction	1a	3:1	1a	1-3	1:1a	1a	3:1—4:7
Divine Confrontation	1b	3:2-6	1b-9	4-5	1b-28a	1b-4	4:1-5?
Addressee's Objection	2-4	3:11, 13; 4:1, 10, 13	(implied) 5-9	6	1:28b (implied 2:6-8)	5	4:10-11
Commission	4	3:7-10	(see Con-fron-tation)	9-10	2:1—3:11	8-13	4:8
Confirmatory Sign	5	3:12, 14-22; 4:2-9, 11-12, 14-17	10-11	7-8	3:12-15	?6-7	5:2 (cf. 4:10-11, 16)

Figure 8.1. Type-scenes for prophetic calls

in this case there is a remarkable shift. Here the divine confronter is not God, but the Risen Jesus, who identifies himself with the believers Saul is persecuting. Furthermore, Saul is commissioned to bring the name of Jesus "before Gentiles and kings, and [secondarily?] before the people of Israel" (Acts 9:15). The use of the type-scene of prophetic call places this particular call to go to the Gentiles on behalf of Jesus of Nazareth squarely within the tradition of Old Testament prophecy. Apparently to make sure the readers get the point, as well as to drive home the legitimacy of Paul's apostolic role, Luke repeats this very story *two more times* (Acts 22:4-16; 26:9-18).

A very interesting sidelight on this Pauline call-scene in Acts 9 is the similar "commissioning" of Ananias embedded within the same passage: introduction, Acts 9:10a; confrontation, Acts 9:10b-12; Ananias' objection, Acts 9:13-14; his commissioning, Acts 9:11-12, 15-16; the confirmatory sign, Acts 9:17-19. This provides neat reaffirmation woven right into the midst of Paul's story. No one at all familiar with Old Testament literary forms could possibly mistake Luke's intentions regarding Paul's status in the great parade of God's holy prophets, nor the implied identification of Jesus of Nazareth as the divine commissioner.

In a similar way, scenes of betrothal, intercultural encounters and even divine-human encounters often take place at a community well. The cases of Isaac and Rebekah (through Abraham's mediator, Gen 24), Jacob and Rachel (Gen 29), and Moses and Zipporah (Ex 2:15-22) provide obvious examples.

Recognition of the "meeting-at-the-well" type-scene throws light on Jesus' meeting with the Samaritan woman in John 4. That meeting represents the divine-human encounter, an epiphany in fact. It also represents the clash of cultures (Jewish-Samaritan; male-female; moral-immoral), and it represents the wooing of a "bride." But here the hopeful bridegroom rejects the flirting of the woman and, like Abraham's servant, invites her to betrothal with the One (like Abraham) who sent him: the "Father who seeks" those who will worship him in spirit and in truth. Of course, like Rebekah, Rachel and Zipporah, this Samaritan woman runs "home" and tells all about it, and the home folk come out to invite Jesus to stay. On the other hand, recognition of this narrative artistry does not need to imply doubt about the historicity of the narrated event. It simply acknowledges *the way* in which the writer has told the story, by choice, and strives to "read" what is implied beneath the surface through that very way of telling it.

8.3 OLD TESTAMENT CITATIONS AND ALLUSIONS

The use of type-scenes in New Testament narrative is one form of allusion to Old Testament texts. Less stylized forms of such allusions include the way a Gospel writer may weave selected Old Testament echoes into his narratives. Both Mark and Matthew, for example, comment on John the Baptist's diet and clothing in a way that brings 2 Kings 1:8 to mind, at least for astute readers with concordances in their heads. (For the rest of us, marginal cross-references come in extremely handy in cases like this.) In 2 Kings 1, emissaries sent by Samaria's King Ahaziah to inquire of the god Baal return with disturbing news. A strange man met them on the road, they say, and sent them back with a sarcastic message for the king. They describe the man as hairy and wearing a leather belt. Much annoyed, Ahaziah responds, "It is Elijah the Tishbite." When Matthew describes John the Baptist as wearing "clothing of camel's hair with a leather belt around his waist" (Mt 3:4), readers familiar with the Old Testament story will understand who John is, or rather, what his role is. He is "Elijah the Tishbite," the forerunner of Israel's returning God (cf. Mal 3:1; 4:5).

Matthew is particularly adept at this sort of thing. Echoes of Abraham and the birth of Isaac pepper the text of Matthew 1:18-25, suggesting that Jesus, the newborn son of David, is just as much the newborn son of Abraham (cf. Mt 1:1) and thus the pathway of God's blessing upon all the nations. In Matthew 2, numerous allusions to the exodus from Egypt (e.g., Egypt itself, the death of the babies, flight from one "who seeks the child's life") put readers in a frame of mind to see Jesus in the light of Moses. This primes them to understand his work as that of bringing about a new exodus. Echoes of Moses' final speech in Deuteronomy appear in the story of Jesus' temptation in the wilderness (Mt 4:1-11; cf. Deut 8:3; 6:16, 13), suggesting that the commencement of Jesus' public ministry is somehow parallel to Israel's entry into the promised land to possess it. Fragments of God's words of encouragement to Joshua (Josh 1) show up in the Great Commission (Mt 28:19-20), leaving readers to suppose that the call to possess the "land" has now been placed upon the church (the new Israel), and that the promised land is actually the entire world.[4]

Implied in an author's use of this technique is his confidence in the readers' ability to detect the echoes and allusions. This confidence is in part what narrative critics mean by the phrase "implied reader"; a text's implied reader will "get" every allusion, grasp every innuendo. Of course, there is no such person, even among narrative critics. The idea of such a person is merely the counterpart to the "implied *author.*" Since we cannot get into the head of the *actual* biblical author, we infer his intentions from what the text implies about them, and presto! the *implied* author materializes before us. The point of going to all this trouble is the recognition—once again—that in one sense the text is what we have. The idea of the implied reader is relevant in the present connection, however, because it serves to reassure us twenty-first-century exegetes that we will *not* be likely to catch everything there is to catch. In my own case, for example, it was only when I noticed the cross-reference to 2 Kings 1:8 in the margin of my Greek New Testament beside Matthew 3:4 (and looked it up!), that I began to make the connection between John the Baptist's "ensemble" and that of his predecessor Elijah the Tishbite. I do not have a concordance in my head. If Matthew had dressed John in a blue jumpsuit and given him a white hat, black mask, silver bullets and a white horse, I would have had no trouble with the allusion: "That man was the Lone Ranger!"[5] I did not grow up drenched in the Old Testament texts, however, nor have most of those who listen to our sermons.

We can probably take it for granted, however, that many of the first readers of the Gospels were as familiar with the Septuagint (or the Hebrew Scriptures) as many of my generation are with the lyrics of Beatles' tunes or lines from *The Princess Bride* ("Hello. My name is Inigo Montoya. You killed my father. Prepare to die!"). The novels of Chaim Potok[6] (not to mention the research of Scandinavian scholars like Birger Gerhardsson)[7] point to the prodigious feats of

---

[4]For this last point, see Wright, *New Testament and the People of God,* pp. 388-89.

[5]Readers younger than I am may identify more easily a man wrapped in a scalloped black cape, wearing headgear with pointy black ears on top and driving a jet-propelled "batmobile."

[6]E.g., Chaim Potok, *The Promise* (Greenwich, Conn.: Fawcett, 1969).

[7]E.g., Birger Gerhardsson, *The Reliability of the Gospel Tradition* (Peabody, Mass.: Hendrickson, 2001).

memory performed by both ancient and modern Jews (as is also the case for many other cultures). For those of us who have not committed great stretches of Old Testament text to memory (let alone great stretches of Septuagint text), detecting echoes of that material in the Gospels and the rest of the New Testament will be challenging indeed. We are not helpless, however; we have access to concordances to assist us. An electronic concordance to the Septuagint, for example, helps us to see that the Greek text of Matthew 1:21 is a nearly verbatim quotation of Genesis 17:19, linking the birth of Jesus to the birth of Isaac. It also suggests the value of scouring Matthew 1:18-25 for other links to the story of Abraham; they are actually there in force. Consider, for example, the way in which both Abraham and Joseph are addressed in a vision or a dream, both are told not to be afraid, both are designated as "righteous," and so on.

This highlights another feature of the use of the Old Testament in the New. Lacking the handy chapter and verse divisions we use today, the New Testament writers had to employ other means for citing texts. In many cases, the quotation of a short text is apparently intended to draw the readers' attention to the larger context in which that smaller piece occurs. Matthew (somewhat loosely) quotes Jeremiah 31:15 (38:15 in the LXX), for example, as the depressing climax to his account of the slaughter of the innocents (Mt 2:18). Yet if we read the larger context of Jeremiah 31, we discover that this entire chapter is upbeat, a thoroughly optimistic expectation of Israel's return from her exile in Babylon. In fact, throughout the entire run of the discourse in Jeremiah 31, verse 15 is the only truly discouraging note. Observing this fact raises at least two questions for exegetes: (1) What role does this larger theme of return from exile play at this point in Matthew's story? (2) Why does he select this particularly unhappy text to make the connection? Wrestling with questions like these, which arise naturally from the text as Matthew apparently designed it, can lead to surprising insights into the perspective from which Matthew (or any other writer) presents his material. The fact that such questions *arise naturally from the text* helps to reassure us that, though we may be getting it wrong somehow, at least we are trying to be true to the text as we have it. "Do not be afraid; I know that you are looking for Jesus who was crucified"; that is the goal of exegesis.

8.4 SPEECHES AND *LOGIA*

Anyone who has ever looked at or used a "red-letter" edition of the New Testament is aware that reports of what Jesus says, as opposed to what he does, occupy a heavy percentage of the Gospel text. Add to that the reports of what other characters say in the New Testament narratives, and we soon realize that a variety of utterances (*logia* "sayings"; in the singular, *logion*) and extended speeches makes up a very important subtype of narrative material. Somewhat artificially, we can divide such texts into precisely these two categories: shorter *logia* and extended speeches. But before making a few remarks on interpreting these texts, we need to view them within their context.

Consider once more Luke's parable of the unjust judge (Lk 18:1-8). In it we hear the judge grumbling to himself about the persistent widow: "Though I have no fear of God and no respect for anyone, yet because this widow keeps bothering me, I will grant her justice, so that she may not wear me out by continually coming" (Lk 18:4-5). Of course, it is Jesus who actually speaks these words as he tells the story; the judge himself is not really there. The judge's speech is a speech within a story. But even that parabolic story about the judge, told by Jesus, is related to us the readers as part of a much larger story about Jesus, told by Luke. In other words, what we have in Luke 18:4-5 is a speech set within a story, which itself is part of a longer speech set within a larger story. Several observations significant for exegesis can be made on the basis of this literary phenomenon. Unless we adopt something like the perspective represented in the following observations, we are in danger of misusing and abusing Gospel speeches, short or long.

For one thing, some stories make their point in a speech, while some speeches make their point with a story. A speech can make its point either by argumentation (like letters do) or by telling a story (like Gospels do), or both. Similarly, some letters make a point by telling a story (Gal 1—2), and some stories make a point through an argument (Mt 22:23-33). In a sense, anything is possible. Second, and in more or less the same vein, parables typically have a particular point to make and often sum up that point, or lesson, in a pithy remark made by one of the characters or by the teller of the parable (usually Jesus). The account of a real event, however, can function the same way a parable does in this regard, as in the case of Jesus' encounter with the centurion (Mt 8:5-13). The conversation between Jesus and the centurion occupies the heart of the story and in fact assists the reader to see just what Matthew means to teach by rehearsing the scene: the faith of an "untouchable" Gentile is as acceptable to God as anyone else's faith is. Third, the embedding of the unjust judge's soliloquy within the parable told by Jesus (Lk 18:4-5) and the embedding of this parable within Luke's "travel narrative" imply Luke's artistry. Luke has decided not only which stories about Jesus to use in his Gospel (selection) but has chosen where to place them (arrangement) and how to tell them (adaptation).

The upshot of these three observations is that even in the case of conversations, speeches and the sayings of Jesus, *we cannot ignore the larger contexts in which we find them.* It makes no exegetical sense to quote the popular exhortation Jesus uses in John 3:7 (KJV): "Ye must be born again" (or "anew" [RSV], or "from above" [NRSV]), if we do not simultaneously connect it with the rest of his midnight remarks to Nicodemus (Jn 3:1-21). We do not have exegetical license to apply it however we like simply because Jesus himself uttered it. Its meaning is determined by its larger context.

8.4.1 Shorter Logia

With these preliminaries, we can turn to a brief look at the shorter sayings, most of them spoken by Jesus. Classical form-critical treatments of Gospel material categorized these texts according to a classification more suited to Greco-Roman literature than to anything that Jesus and his audiences would have recognized. In the Old Testament, as we have already seen, the Hebrew term *māšāl* applied to a wide variety of these figurative speeches, including not only story-form parables but also very brief sayings. The long chain of parables in Matthew 13, for example, includes quick similes of the form, "The kingdom of heaven is like X." Though they are not "stories," they are indeed parables; they lead us to ask in what respect the kingdom of heaven is like a bit of yeast, or like a grain of mustard seed. In some cases, the answer will be that it is not like a mustard seed at all, but it operates like the life cycle of the mustard plant. Even though the text may literally say that the kingdom of heaven is *like a merchant* searching for fine pearls, we realize that it is actually the "one pearl of great value" that the kingdom is like. The mention of the merchant is simply the point of entry for the parable; the merchant himself is in fact the one overcome by the kingdom (Mt 13:45). In other words, we should not insist that these formulations be worded as precisely as we might want them to be. We are dealing with evocative literature, not with legal documents.

Frequently, a story will end in a short saying, summing up the point. Jesus' debate with the Pharisees over harvesting grain on the sabbath (Mk 2:23-28) ends in his provoking declaration, "The sabbath was made for humankind, and not humankind for the sabbath; so the Son of Man is lord even of the sabbath" (Mk 2:27-28). We may take this to be Mark's way of both telling his readers the meaning of the encounter and providing them with a real-life illustration of the principle embodied in the *logion.* The story does not justify a Saskatchewan wheat farmer in firing up the combine on a Sunday (nor does it prohibit it); it simply warns against blind obedience to formal tradition in the face of basic human need; it reminds us of God's abiding sovereignty over all his creation.

There is much more that could be said about short sayings in the Gospel material, but what needs to be kept in mind with them can be summed up as follows: (1) we must read them in context, and (2) we must read them with sympathy. We must not extract them from their literary settings as if they are somehow universally valid in whatever context we may wish to use them. We must not insist that they operate like a string of computer language. They are creative, dynamic, fluid and unpredictable. They demand that we think and that we give them the chance to *interpret us*.

8.4.2 Extended Speeches

In addition to short sayings, and even to medium-length sayings like story-parables, both the Gospels and the book of Acts also contain a number of extended speeches. The Sermon on the Mount (Mt 5—7) and its counterpart, the Sermon on the Plain (Lk 6:17-49), are two obvious examples. So are four other major "discourses" in Matthew (chaps. 10, 13, 18, and 23—25). The Farewell Discourse in John's Gospel (chaps. 14—17) is equally well known. To these we may add the various speeches of Peter, Stephen and Paul scattered throughout the book of Acts. There are several things to notice about reading these texts.

One of these is that comparing Matthew's Sermon on the Mount with the parallel texts from Mark and (especially) Luke strongly suggests that Matthew has woven the Sermon together from many individual pieces. Very few of the Sermon's parts appear in Mark, and those that do appear there occur in random order by comparison. Much more of Matthew's Sermon reappears in Luke, and Luke arranges the Sermon on the Plain to a great degree in the same order as Matthew has arranged the Sermon on the Mount. (This raises the question whether these sermons might therefore come from Q.) Yet a great deal of Matthew's Sermon is absent from Luke's Sermon on the Plain, though it appears elsewhere, "randomly," throughout Luke. We could cogently argue that Jesus preached these sermons, or parts of them, on various occasions, but before we decide whether we gain anything by doing so, we should consider a second phenomenon.

Luke tells us in Acts 20 that one evening Paul talked on into the night so long that a young man nodded off and fell out of a window. Though we grant that Luke attributes Paul's long-windedness to the fact that he intended to leave the next day, we may nevertheless assume that Paul was not usually as succinct a speaker as we might judge from the length of his recorded speeches. Most of these, like the Areopagus address (Acts 17) and his defense before Agrippa (Acts 26), can be read aloud in a matter of two or three minutes. Acts scholars often cite the candid testimony of Thucydides (c. 460-400 B.C.), Athenian general and author of *The Peloponnesian War*, regarding his treatment of speeches in that account. He admits (1.22) that he cannot provide verbatim transcripts for the speeches, but that he summarizes the gist of each instead, putting into the mouths of the speakers the words that seem to him, the author, to convey their basic messages (and, we might surmise, to suit his own purposes). The fair assumption is that Luke has done the same for the speeches of his main characters.

Considering these factors, third, we find ourselves once again faced with the issues of context and redaction. The authors of the Gospels and Acts tell their stories to the best of their abilities (which are considerable), selecting, arranging and adapting their "speech" material in ways that convey the theological significance of the speeches they preserve (no less than of the events they portray). We may wish to regard Matthew's version of the Sermon as an accurate "court-reporter style" transcript of a presentation, one distinct from the one preserved in Luke 6. (On the principle mentioned above, that Jesus likely repeated his speeches—and deeds—numerous times throughout his ministry, this is entirely possible.) Alternatively, we may wish to regard Matthew 5—7 as the author's attempt to present Jesus theologically as a new Moses delivering a new "law," doing so by modeling Jesus' five extended discourses according to the five books of the Pentateuch. Either way, we must now interpret the texts *as we have them*. The concerns that guide the analysis and interpretation of these speeches in the Gospels and Acts are virtually the same as those outlined above in chapter six, which guide responsible interpretation of New Testament letters. Context and structure, rhetoric and content, as well as the "occasion," the culture and the audience—including the original *reading* audience—guide us in how we should understand these speeches.

8.5 SUMMARY PASSAGES

In the introduction to this chapter, we observed that Matthew closes off the story of Peter's mother-in-law with a summary passage (Mt 8:16-17). In doing so, he follows Mark (Mk 1:32-34); Luke does the same (Lk 4:40-41). The term *summary passage* refers to a short text characterized by a concentration of generalizing statements. That is, rather than treating Jesus' activity in connection with a specific person or situation, a summary statement will mention the general sorts of things he did in a certain vicinity or over a period of time. Often, imperfect tense-forms predominate among the verbs, as if the author were painting a typical scene.

Consider Mark 1:32-34: "That evening, at sundown, they brought to him all who were sick or possessed with demons. And the whole city was gathered around the door. And he cured many who were sick with various diseases, and cast out many demons; and he would not permit the demons to speak, because they knew him." The timing is specific ("that evening, at sundown"), but the details are generalized ("they" brought to him "all" who were sick; the "whole city" was gathered; he cured "many" who were sick with "various" diseases). Several of the verbs are in the imperfect: ἔφερον "were bringing"; ἦν ἐπισυνηγμένη "was gathered"; ἤφιεν "would [not] permit; ᾔδεισαν "[did not] know" (actually a pluperfect, but used "imperfectly"). Matthew's version employs more aorist verbs, but Luke increases the number of imperfect verbs in his parallel.

Texts like this occur at odd intervals throughout the Synoptic Gospels and Acts. In one respect, they are rather inconspicuous compared to the specific and detailed stories they punctuate. We may easily pass them over as intrinsically less arresting and less interesting. They play an important role in the Gospels, nevertheless. Otherwise we could reasonably assume they ought to have been left out altogether. They function a little like rest stops along a highway. Travelers pull off the road, have a cup of coffee and check the map. They see at a glance where they have been and take a quick look at where they are headed. Maybe there is a display illustrating the various attractions and typical wildlife of the immediate area. Refreshed and reoriented, the travelers hit the road again, headed toward some distant destination.

Summary passages offer readers the same sort of service, and wise readers will pay attention to them. We have been insisting all along that each biblical narrative has its own structure and design and that any one portion of it fits within that organized context. If this is true, then we can take it for granted that the biblical authors have built into their narratives various signposts to guide their readers. Summary passages provide one very important form of such signposts. (Others include the several structural patterns and repetitions, conjunctions, and other "markers" discussed in chapter three, especially in section 3.2.2.) Matthew 4:17 and 16:21, for instance, constitute summary statements of what is *about to* happen: "From that time, Jesus began to proclaim" the kingdom of heaven, and later he "began to show his disciples" that he must shortly die in Jerusalem. These two (matching) statements provide us orientation in Matthew's overall story; they help us to see how all the parts fit together into a coherent whole.

In terms of getting a sense of the unity and direction of a particular Gospel, or of Acts, it would be a worthy exercise to read it through, cover to cover, identifying and isolating its various summary statements. We could then make a list of them, in their proper order, and analyze the progression they represent. That analysis ought to provide a significant piece of evidence, drawn directly from the text itself, for establishing the author's intended message. It cannot be overemphasized how important it is to let the text speak for itself; summary passages provide one useful means for doing that.

Taking to heart all the advice offered in this chapter may threaten to overwhelm us. The point is not to overwhelm, however, but to make aware. Adeptness at using the skills implied here grows with experience. We can only begin where we are and experiment. One suggestion for the process is to use colored pencils or highlighters to mark up the text on a photocopied page. Coordinating colors for various "signposts," themes, repeated vocabulary and other patterns can cause structure and texture (no pun intended) to spring out in bold relief. There is no "right" way to do this; we are free (and encouraged) to do our own explorations and to see what we find. When we do find something, we are encouraged to bring it to the table of the Grand Conversation. Meanwhile, we turn now to another New Testament genre, the strange world of apocalyptic literature.

9

APOCALYPSE

Alternative Education

Then I saw another portent in heaven, great and amazing:
seven angels with seven plagues, which are the last,
for with them the wrath of God is ended.

REVELATION 15:1

And though St. John the Evangelist saw many strange monsters in his vision,
he saw no creature so wild as one of his own commentators.

G. K. CHESTERTON, *ORTHODOXY*

One Sunday morning after worship, I began to converse with an elderly saint whose Norwegian-born parents had immigrated to South Dakota in the nineteenth century. I asked her if she had ever read Rølvaag's *Giants in the Earth*, since it paints a vivid picture of the struggles endured by early Scandinavian pioneers on the Great Plains. She fixed me with a look of mixed sorrow and horror. "I never read novels," she said. "I only have time for spiritually edifying books." Oh.

To my way of thinking, one of the best sources of spiritual edification is good fiction. For some reason I tend to respond deeply to stories, whether or not they are "true." I often find myself thinking of things in terms of a novel or short story I have read or of a movie I have seen. I visualize divine retribution, for instance (and perhaps wrongly!), in terms of Nicholas Nickleby's thrashing of vicious schoolmaster Wackford Squeers or of that other schoolmaster who gets free "boxing lessons" in the old Roddy McDowell film *How Green Was My Valley*. I do not wish to belabor this, especially since I have been a schoolmaster myself. The point is simply that we human beings have differing learning styles. Thus, even in Scripture, God apparently approaches us on a variety of levels intending to reach us in whatever way we respond to best. This, I believe, is a useful perspective to take in considering the exegesis of that strange piece of work at the end of the New Testament. It represents a kind of alternative education.

9.1 WHAT IS IT?

We are talking about the book of Revelation, or the Apocalypse of John the Theologian, as many ancient manuscripts title it (and not to confuse it with a noncanonical book under a very similar name). It is indeed a strange piece of work. A friend of mine told me about a man who said that he had read the entire New Testament and had understood it just fine "except for that bit of science fiction at the end." To modern readers, Revelation truly is a daunting and intimidating book. In principle, we have little trouble with letters, or with stories or sermons—even prophetic sermons. But what is this that we find in Revelation? Images of beasts and monsters, ghastly horsemen on the order of Sauron's Nazgul, frightening enough to make Washington Irving's headless impostor laughable by comparison. What is this hoard of human-headed locusts or this harlot seated on seven hills?

There has been no shortage of speculation about these things. I sometimes picture us, scholars and lay readers alike, picking at Revelation as the Israelites picked at the bread from heaven on the morning it first appeared like dew in the desert (Ex 16:15). "What is it?" they asked. *Manna?* This is a good thing to do, of course. Any time we encounter something puzzling in Scripture, it is a good thing to try to figure it out. But doing so requires a willingness to draw whatever conclusions a careful consideration of all available evidence might lead us to. Not that we are each individually responsible to examine all that evidence! Rather, we are part of the Grand Theological Conversation, part of a studying community. We work *together* in the grand project of understanding the ancient texts, and this implies that we listen to each other and critically evaluate each other's opinions with care, sympathy and grace.

We can assume first of all that Revelation was not *intended* to be daunting or intimidating reading for its first addressees. As with any other biblical book, if we want to understand this one, we need to begin by recapturing its original setting as well as we can. But this can be a little tricky. Some enormously popular views on Revelation risk giving little or no attention to the circumstances out of which the book arose in the first place. Many people are taught to regard the book of Revelation as God's detailed, chronologically sequenced blueprint for their own rather immediate future. Without ever trying to understand the book for themselves, they devotedly follow various expositions of it sensationalized in highly imaginative (and lucrative) novels and films. These colorful "takes" on Revelation are based, of course, on the legitimate assumption that the entire Bible, Revelation included, is still relevant today. It is an assumption I also make in this present textbook. Ironically (in my own experience anyway), some who have never personally studied or perhaps even read Revelation, but who are intimately familiar with popularized interpretations of it, confidently reject alternative interpretations. They sometimes even impugn the very Christianity of those who propose alternative interpretations. On the other hand, I myself am guilty of assuming that the view of things I subscribe to is the only "intelligent" one. There is no greater fool than a theological fool.

Clearly, if we are to benefit from this book as a portion of Christian Scripture and to rise above strife and division over it, we must let it speak for itself. And if we are to let it speak for itself, we must read it in the same text-and-context-sensitive way we use in reading all other New Testament books. We will naturally need help in this, but we should not be so fearful of the peculiar strangeness of the book of Revelation that we let others do *all* of our thinking about it for us. This chapter, then, takes up the task of reading New Testament apocalyptic literature, Revelation in particular, on its own terms. With that, we come back to the *manna* question: "What is it?"

9.1.1 The Book of Revelation in Its Genre

In volume three of the *Cambridge History of Judaism*, Christopher Rowland draws our attention to a pertinent text in the Mishnah (the collection of Jewish rabbinic teaching compiled in the early third century A.D.).[1] Tractate *m. Ḥagigah* 2.1 reads in part:

> The forbidden degrees may not be expounded before three persons, nor the Story of Creation before two, nor the [chapter of the] Chariot before one alone, unless he is a Sage that understands of his own knowledge. Whosoever gives his mind to four things it were better for him if he had not come into the world—what is above? what is beneath? what was beforetime? and what will be hereafter? And whosoever takes no thought for the honour of his Maker, it were better for him if he had not come into the world.

The angst underlying this passage is apparently born of reverence for the inscrutable things of God, things beyond normal human ken. The Genesis account of creation and Ezekiel's mystical *merkabah* (holy chariot) experience,

---

[1]C. C. Rowland, "Apocalyptic: The Disclosure of Heavenly Knowledge," in *The Cambridge History of Judaism;* ed. W. Horbury et al. (Cambridge: Cambridge University Press, 1999), 3:784.

All Indians Must Dance

All Indians must dance, everywhere, keep on dancing. Pretty soon in next spring Great Spirit come. He bring back all game of every kind. The game be thick everywhere. All dead Indians come back and live again. Old blind Indian see again and get young and have fine time. When Great Spirit comes this way, then all the Indians go to mountains, high up away from whites. Whites can't hurt Indians then. Then while Indians way up high big flood comes like water and all white people die, get drowned. After that, water go away and then nobody but Indians everywhere and game all kinds thick. Then medicine man tell Indians to send word to all Indians to keep up dancing and the good time will come. Indians who don't dance, who don't believe in this word, will grow little, just about a foot high, and stay that way. Some of them will be turned into wood and burned in fire.

Wovoka, the Paiute Ghost Dance Messiah (1854?-1932) (quoted in Sherman Alexie, *The Lone Ranger and Tonto Fistfight in Heaven* [New York: Atlantic Monthly Press, 1993], p. 104)

described in the first chapter of his prophecy, for example, fascinating though they may be, invite hubris in those who are unqualified to pierce the veil hanging between this world and God's world. It is better, say the rabbis, to honor our Maker by leaving such things alone.

What is especially interesting here, however, is the list of four subjects the rabbis regarded as off limits for study: things "above" and "beneath," and things "beforetime" and "hereafter." We will come back to this in a moment. For now we can note that Rowland and others consider this remark a reference to the many Jewish (and probably Christian) apocalypses in circulation during the three or four centuries straddling the turn of the era. The book of Revelation is *only one of a large number* of similar works from this period. Together, these many literary pieces—including Revelation—form a genre, somewhat loosely defined, one that scholars today prefer to call the genre of "apocalypse." (The term *apocalyptic,* used as a noun, was often applied to this genre up until the later decades of the twentieth century. In commentaries and other works, you may well run into the word *apocalyptic* used this way: "Jewish apocalyptic," for instance. That usage is less common today.)

Some of the more famous of these other apocalypses include portions of biblical books: Daniel 7, Zechariah 1—8 and, differently, 9—14, Mark 13 and its parallels, are all examples. Apocalypses from outside the boundaries of canonical Scripture include *4 Ezra, 2* and *3 Baruch,* large sections of the various *Books of Enoch, The Shepherd of Hermas, The Testament of Abraham, The Apocalypse of Abraham, The Apocalypse of James* and many, many others. Apocalypses are not limited to Judaism and Christianity; scholars have studied Persian, Babylonian, Roman and other ancient Mediterranean examples as well. Nor are they limited to the ancient world. Medieval examples have been identified (Dante's *Divine Comedy* has apocalyptic elements), and even today we have our own versions of the genre. The popularized interpretation of Revelation in the Left Behind series of books and films itself embodies a contemporary apocalyptic viewpoint. That series and other publications like it claim to provide an accurate portrayal of what Revelation predicts; but insofar as they misrepresent the message of Revelation (*if* they do, of course) they constitute a new apocalypse for the twenty-first century. The sidebar on page 182 presents an example of a nineteenth-century Native American apocalypse. But what is it that makes these apocalypses recognizable as apocalypses?

9.1.2 Characteristics of an Apocalypse: The Shape of the Genre

Coming to a consensus on this question has not proven easy; it remains elusive today. This is why we said above that the genre of apocalypse is "loosely defined." Imagine a thousand wooden blocks of many kinds, colors, sizes, shapes, décor and on and on. Your job is to sort them into classes of similar blocks. You start out with color—blue, for example. But you notice that among the solid blue ones there are other blue blocks with red polka dots and still others with green polka dots. No matter. You put all those blue blocks, with or without polka dots, into category one. Next you find all the smaller blocks and divide them from the larger blocks. But wait a minute. Some of the blue blocks, already in category one, are small and some of them are large. So you pull the large ones out and put them with the other larger blocks into category two. But that defeats your criterion for category one.

It is something like this with deciding what makes an apocalypse. Given, say, ten literary analysts, we will likely have ten different but partially overlapping lists of documents proposed for the distinction of fitting into the category (or genre) of apocalypse. Each of the ten analysts will have a particular set of criteria for deciding which documents do and which documents do not qualify as apocalypses. One analyst will count as essential a criterion that another analyst sets aside as nonessential. No matter which way the cuts are made, someone's favorite apocalypse (if it *is* an apocalypse) falls off the list. There is circularity in this process: from a given selection of documents we develop a list of criteria; from that list of criteria we decide which documents belong in the selection. Nevertheless, in spite of the fluidity of the present state of the discussion, we can operate for now with the following oft-quoted definition of apocalypse. It emerged from a 1979 symposium facilitated by John J. Collins, the results of which were published under the title *Apocalypse: The Morphology of a Genre*. This definition has found widespread support, since it succinctly sums up the essential elements of most, if not necessarily all, apocalypses.

> "Apocalypse" is a genre of revelatory literature with a narrative framework, in which a revelation is mediated by an otherworldly being to a human recipient, disclosing a transcendent reality which is both temporal, insofar as it envisages eschatological salvation, and spatial, insofar as it involves another, supernatural world.[2]

This definition of Jewish apocalypse has five main elements, all of which also characterize the book of Revelation. In the first place, apocalyptic literature is *revelatory literature*. It is not literature in the sense of a history of Rome, an entertaining short story, a letter of recommendation or a Gospel account. Instead, it is literature designed to reveal certain secret information previously concealed. The revelation of this secret information comes only to a select audience, however, not to humanity in general. It thus presupposes—and reinforces—an inner circle of the privileged few. Second, the information an apocalypse reveals is set within a *narrative framework;* the revelation is conveyed in a sequence of events. There is a protagonist of sorts to whom various things happen (John in the case of Revelation; Dante himself in *The Inferno*); the story of the seer's amazing experience, and often the structure of what is revealed in that experience (the account of things yet to come, for example) progresses from stage to stage, like a plot.

The third and fourth elements involve the actors: there is an *otherworldly mediator* of the revelation and there is the *human recipient*, the seer. Ordinarily, in Jewish apocalypses, the human recipient is one of the illustrious heroes of Israel's religious past: Adam, Abraham, Enoch, Ezra or Baruch, for example. This implies something that Collins's definition does not mention: that the typical apocalypse is *pseudonymous*, that is, falsely (or better: fictitiously?) attributed to a famous person from antiquity long dead at the time of writing. In Revelation, the recipient is John, a venerated leader of the Asian churches at the end of the first century. Most of Christendom, including many scholars, re-

---

[2]J. J. Collins, "Introduction: Towards the Morphology of a Genre," in *Apocalypse: The Morphology of a Genre*, Semeia 14 (Chico, Calif.: Scholars, 1979), p. 9.

gards this "John" of Revelation (whoever he is) as speaking for himself and thus do not consider his apocalypse pseudonymous like other apocalypses. Whether he is in fact John the son of Zebedee or another of two or three persons who were named John and affiliated with the ancient Ephesian church is harder to say. The other standard figure in an apocalypse, an otherworldly guide and mediator of the revelation, is often an angel sent by God to explain everything to the human seer. In Revelation, of course, one of the mediators is identified in the very first chapter as the "living one" who died and is alive forever and ever (Rev 1:18), that is, he is the Risen Lord himself. But he is no less "otherworldly" for that. "One of the elders" encircling the throne of God serves John as another mediator (Rev 5:5), as does an angel who shows up from time to time (Rev 1:1; 10:9; 17:7; 19:9; cf. 22:6, 16).

The fifth element in the Semeia definition regards the content: apocalypses reveal *transcendent reality*. This reality can be presented from one of two perspectives, sometimes from both. It may be a *temporal* reality. The seer may be instructed in the progress of Israel's future among the world of nations; from the perspective of the readers of such an apocalypse, this prophesied future will actually constitute Israel's past. That future historical progression is typically "periodized," divided into successive epochs, often according to the world-domination of such current and coming powers as Assyria, Babylon, Persia, Greece or Rome. The book of Daniel is a good example of this type of apocalypse. The angelic mediator (in Daniel's case, a heavenly "attendant," Dan 7:10, 16) helps the seer to understand how the power of God prevails throughout the course of history. Apocalyptic mediators assure the seers that it will continue to be so until God's will for his people is reasserted—often permanently, and usually with (and through) Israel's vindication and elevation.

But the revealed transcendent reality may also be presented from a *spatial* perspective. The seer may be led on a journey out of earth and into the heavenly abode of God, or he may be taken below the earth into the netherworld, like Dante. The book of *2 Enoch* (also known as the *Slavonic Apocalypse of Enoch*), chapters 1—68, provides a good example of an "ascent" apocalypse, in which Enoch travels the seven heavens. Either way, the seer's angelic guide interprets for him the significance of what the seer sees there. Some apocalypses combine the temporal and the spatial types. The Revelation of John is one of them; in addition to hearing "what must soon take place" (Rev 1:1; 22:6), John is both taken up into the throne room of heaven (Rev 4:1) and, later, permitted a glimpse into the bottomless pit (e.g., Rev 9:1). We may now recall the objection raised in the Mishnah against unqualified persons prying into the dimensions transcending this world, whether spatial (above or below) or temporal (beforehand or hereafter).

These five elements, according to the Semeia definition, constitute the essence of a Jewish apocalypse. Although there is room for plenty of variation among apocalypses (we can tell them apart, after all), most of them have these five characteristics in common. But what else can we say about them? We can approach that question from the angles of function and method in apocalyptic literature.

9.1.3 The Function and Method of Apocalypses

Subsequent tinkering with the Semeia definition has produced statements of the purpose or function of apocalypses. One of these suggests that apocalyptic literature is "intended to interpret present earthly circumstances in light of the supernatural world and of the future, and to influence both the understanding and the behavior of the audience by means of divine authority."[3] But apparently not all apocalypses have the same function; some are more urgent than the word *influence,* used above, might suggest. James VanderKam would therefore like to substitute the word *exhort,* or at least *encourage,* for the word *influence.* Because of this and because the proposed "function" extension could be applied just as easily to the definition of other religious literature (Paul's letters, for example), it has met with less approval than the original definition by itself.[4] VanderKam's two hesitations about the added purpose statement are certainly understandable, to a point anyway. Even if we may consider them a bit overblown, they do help us to think about this particular aspect of apocalyptic literature. Let us begin with its function, or purpose, and then take up its method.

Function. Part of the function or purpose of an apocalypse, according to the additional Semeia statement, quoted above, is "to influence both the understanding and the behavior of the audience by means of divine authority." This does indeed apply as well to other kinds of religious literature, as VanderKam claims, making it less than effective as a distinguishing mark of apocalypses. But that fact needs to be regarded as a problem only if we wish to use it to distinguish apocalypses from other religious literature. Yet if it is in some sense a true statement of purpose for apocalypses, then it simply demonstrates that

---

[3]A. Yarbro Collins, "Introduction: Early Christian Apocalypticism," in *Early Christian Apocalypticism: Genre and Social Setting,* Semeia 36 (Decatur, Ga.: Scholars, 1986), p. 7.

[4]J. VanderKam, "Apocalyptic Literature," in *The Cambridge Companion to Biblical Interpretation,* ed. J. Barton, Cambridge Companions to Religion (Cambridge: Cambridge University Press, 1998), p. 311.

apocalypses have the same fundamental purpose and function as do Paul's letters, Old Testament prophecy or the Synoptic Gospels. All of these genres aim, we could say, to guide their readers into a faithful and thoughtful obedience to God in the midst of whatever circumstances they face. It is true that the audiences of some apocalypses find themselves in politically more desperate straits than Paul's Corinthian readers do. These circumstances may involve distress from current persecution (as with the books of Daniel and Revelation) or from ongoing theological agony over God's injustice in the wake of the events like those of A.D. 70 (as with *4 Ezra*). The danger of assimilation to the culture of "this world" may provide the motivating force behind an apocalypse; the letters to the seven churches of Asia (Rev 2—3) are filled with warnings against succumbing to this sort of thing.

Not all apocalypses display such urgency, though; some that portray otherworldly journeys may be less interested in bearing up readers subjected to political oppression or the temptation to assimilate, and more interested in simply satisfying natural curiosity about things beyond human ken (*The Testament of Adam* may be one of these). On the other hand, it is entirely possible that severe political persecution plays just as large a role for the readers of Matthew's Gospel or 1 Peter as it does for the readers of Revelation. Matthew's story of the transfiguration, for example, may be aimed at encouraging Jewish Christian readers not to abandon their allegiance to Jesus for a return to the cultural safety of Moses (Mt 17:1-8). All biblical genres in fact deal with their audiences' circumstantial crises by appealing to the authority of God in some way and by interpreting the readers' world in terms of God's world. They do this in order to provide their readers with a clear-headed view of what really counts in life, a long theological perspective from which to act. The book of Revelation is no different from the rest of the biblical literature in this regard.[5]

That kind of theological perspective, whether it is framed in terms of spatial transcendence (the reality of that other world) or temporal transcendence (the inevitability of the coming eschatological judgment), is intended to give *contemporary* readers the wherewithal for making godly choices and adopting godly principles, even if it means they die. That is to say, the focus of biblical literature—in all of its various genres—is *on the present*. Its foremost concern is for the welfare of its original readers. Even apocalyptic literature is primarily concerned about those for whom the authors first wrote. Though it frequently

---

[5]We can just as cogently argue that apocalyptic thinking pervades all of the New Testament and is not restricted to Revelation. Cf. M. E. Boring, *Revelation*, Interpretation (Louisville: John Knox, 1989), p. 44.

appeals to the future, it does so with the original readership in mind. In this it is just like Paul's letter to Rome or the Gospel of Mark. We who interpret the book of Revelation today need to keep this point firmly in mind if we wish to be faithful to the text. If our exegesis results in something irrelevant to the original readers, it is automatically suspect for that very reason. Matthew was concerned about believers in (perhaps) Antioch of Syria; Paul about believers in Rome, Corinth and elsewhere; John the Seer about believers in the Roman province of Asia. If this is so, then the difference VanderKam is rightly looking for will not be so much in the function of an apocalypse as in its method of revealing the supernatural world and the future.

Method. The Gospels reveal the transcendent world by means of narrative, in the form of the person of Jesus of Nazareth. In the stories of his words and deeds, the Gospel writers demonstrate that the kingdom of God has come "among" human beings in Jesus himself (e.g., Lk 17:21). In a similar way, the book of Acts (Luke, volume two) carries out the same theme, but now that transcendent Presence is manifest in the activity of the Holy Spirit and his handiwork, the church. The letters and sermons of the New Testament represent a more rhetorically based method. Argument and assertion establish the theological foundation on which a writer like Paul or the author of the letter to the Hebrews proceeds to lay out an ethical program, usually in the context of some particular problem.

An apocalypse, however, appeals to the imagination.[6] It aims at the same goal as a Gospel or an epistle does, but rather than using reports of Jesus' earthly words and deeds or rhetorical argumentation, it employs heavenly journeys and creative interpretations of history projected into the future. These journeys and predictions are frequently couched in the imagery of fantastic metaphor and symbolism. Rather than straightforward references to known people, places and events, we hear instead of hideous beasts, bloodthirsty harlots and colossal battles between the forces of evil and the armies of God. In place of structured logical arguments, we are treated instead to layer upon layer of heavenly realms, to secret numbers, great portents in the skies, cataclysmic earthquakes and giant fireballs crashing into the sea, turning it to blood.

---

[6]As J. J. Collins argues in *The Apocalyptic Imagination: An Introduction to Jewish Apocalyptic Literature*, 2nd ed. (Grand Rapids: Eerdmans, 1988). The emphasis this chapter lays on the use of imagination as a method of communicating a vision is not meant to imply that the vision John saw was not real. Instead, what is meant is that the book of Revelation is not likely a verbatim transcript of John's experience, but a literary composition making full use of the genre to which it belongs. For my part, I have no doubt that the book preserves a faithful rendering of the content and burden of what John the Seer saw.

One likely reason for this way of communicating is the simple fact that what the author of an apocalypse usually wants to depict concerns a reality lying beyond human experience; it cannot be conveyed *without* recourse to imagination. Paul himself simply refuses to attempt a description of what he experienced in the "third heaven," excusing himself by claiming that he is not permitted to say anything more about it (2 Cor 12:4). Apocalyptic writers, however, have no such scruples. They describe the indescribable and express the inexpressible. Another reason for the heavy use of metaphor and symbolism may have been the need to conceal from state authorities what those authorities would surely have regarded as seditious teaching. John disguises the bold prediction of the Roman Empire's destruction in the garb of Old Testament prophecies of the downfall and desolation of Babylon and other cities, including Jerusalem (compare Rev 18:2 with Is 21:9; 34:11-15; Jer 50:39). Nevertheless, it is hard to see how an astute Roman reader would not have recognized the empire symbolized in the harlot seated on *the seven hills* (Rev 17:9).

Much of the imaginative imagery used in apocalypses is drawn from a great reservoir of standard forms. To give just a few examples, John's colorful depiction of the Risen One's voice as sounding like "the sound of many waters" (Rev 1:15; 14:2) corresponds to the description of the "full, resounding voice" that "Ezra" hears announcing the end of the world. To Ezra its sound was also like the sound of many waters (*4 Ezra* 6:17). The angel Iaoel, sent by God to "Abraham" to reveal the truth about God, is portrayed as having a body "like sapphire," and "the aspect of his face was like chrysolite, and the hair of his head like snow" (*Apocalypse of Abraham* 11:2; cf. Rev 1:14). Very frequently the tree of life appears (e.g., *1 Enoch* 24:4—25:7; *4 Ezra* 8:52; *Apocalypse of Elijah* 5:6), which we meet as well in Revelation 2:7; 22:2, 14, 19.

Images of beasts, bears, oxen, lions, eagles and leopards—often boasting seven heads, ten horns, six wings, diadems and eyes front and back—commonly represent the great dominating nations of history or the living creatures surrounding the throne of God (e.g., Dan 7; Ezek 1:10; 10:14; *4 Ezra* 11; cf. Rev 4:7; 13:1-2). What we are here describing as a reservoir of standard forms and images is not all that different from what political cartoonists have at their disposal today. Party politics in the United States of America frequently appear in the shape of elephants and donkeys. During the Cold War, a bear with a sickle and hammer painted on his flank signified the Soviet Union. The mystery that cloaks Revelation (and other apocalypses) arises partly from our lack of familiarity with that ancient reservoir of images.

The panoramic history of the Old Testament provides the source for many of these images. From creation and the flood, through the exodus, the conquest, the monarchy and the fall of Jerusalem at the hands of the Babylonians, apocalyptic literature mines the pages of Holy Writ for the vocabulary of its imaginative vernacular. The book of Revelation is no exception in this. Bruce M. Metzger has calculated that over two-thirds of the verses in Revelation allude to the Old Testament in some way.[7] In addition to the mention of the tree of life (Rev 2:7; 22:2), we hear of hidden "manna" (Rev 2:17), the tribes of Israel (Rev 7:4-8), a scroll sweet in the mouth and bitter in the stomach (Rev 10:9; cf. Ezek 3:1-3), blasphemies attributing to the first beast what belongs to God alone (Rev 13:4 ["Who is like the beast and who can fight against it?"]; cf. Ex 15:11; Ps 113:5), fire called down from heaven (Rev 13:13; cf. 1 Kings 18:38), plagues of judgment (Rev 16; cf. Ex 7—12), and many other examples. Such allusions abound, as a quick review of the marginal references and italicized texts in NA[27] will show.

The point of what we have been rehearsing just now is that Revelation presents us with the same sort of imagery as we encounter in a whole host of ancient Jewish apocalypses. If we are to understand this book, we must allow it to be one of them and to learn from them something of its nature. Only then will we be able to treat it on its own terms. But before we turn to a few examples of interpreting New Testament apocalyptic literature, we need to consider one more feature of the genre: the nature of its view of the future. We need to address the relationship between eschatology and apocalypticism.

9.1.4 Apocalyptic Eschatology

We have used the term *eschatological* (or *eschatology*) a few times already in this chapter, but what does it mean? Formed from the Greek adjective ἔσχατος (*eschatos*) "last," it is typically defined (by *Webster's New World College Dictionary*, for example)[8] as "the branch of theology, or doctrines, dealing with death, resurrection, judgment, immortality, etc." That is, eschatology deals with the "last things," including the ultimate fate of the world as we know it. But this is not necessarily the same thing as either "the future" or apocalypticism. Since terms like these, and the concepts lying behind them, are easily confused, it is well worth making the modest effort to consult a good biblical dictionary for an orientation. Consider it an important element of the exegetical task.[9]

---

[7] *The New Oxford Annotated Bible with the Apocryphal/Deuterocanonical Books*, New Revised Standard Version, ed. B. M. Metzger and R. E. Murphy (New York: Oxford University Press, 1991, 1994), p. 364 NT.
[8] "Eschatology" in *Webster's New World College Dictionary*, 3rd ed. (New York: Macmillan, 1996).
[9] Articles in *Dictionary of New Testament Background [DNTB]*, ed. Craig A. Evans and Stanley E. Porter (Downers Grove, Ill.: InterVarsity Press, 2000), for instance, draw several helpful distinctions.

David Aune calls attention to the difference between prophetic eschatology and apocalyptic eschatology.[10] Prophetic eschatology is fundamentally optimistic, expecting that the promised future resolution to a present crisis will arise out of the present course of history; it looks forward, for example, to the renewal of Israel's status as a leading world power under a messianic king like David. Apocalyptic eschatology, on the other hand, is fundamentally pessimistic. It looks for a cataclysmic invasion of the future into the present, destroying or radically altering the present world and replacing it with a new creation. In a somewhat similar way, John Collins distinguishes four kinds of biblical eschatology.[11] *Political* eschatology expects a final king and kingdom in this present world; one day, Israel's messiah will return to set her free from foreign domination. Political eschatology is more interested in the corporate fate of the larger group (Israel, Judaism, the church) than in that of an individual person. *Realized* eschatology, too, is more focused on this present world as the scene of salvation; it shows up in the Gospel of John (e.g., Jn 5:24), as well as in Qumran literature and Gnosticism. But it is very often interested in the fate of the individual rather than that of the group. *Cosmic* eschatology and *personal* eschatology, in their turn, are oriented toward the life beyond this one. Personal eschatology concerns the nature of life after death for the individual. Where does the soul go to dwell (assuming it survives)? What is the nature of resurrection or of the judgment of individuals? While personal eschatology does not necessarily entail a new creation, cosmic eschatology most definitely does. It presumes that following the divine, cataclysmic destruction of this present world and the final judgment, God will re-create the heavens and the earth for the dwelling place of his redeemed people.

If we align "apocalyptic eschatology" with the personal and cosmic varieties, in that they involve judgment after death and a radical end to the world as we know it, then we will have to admit that some documents we might otherwise categorize as apocalypses are not really eschatological. They show little or no real interest in describing the final judgment or the end of the world. *Third Baruch* (also known as *The Greek Apocalypse of Baruch*) and possibly the *Testament of Abraham* fall into this category. Of course, this dilemma presupposes defining the categories of both apocalypse and eschatology, which takes us back to our problem with the wooden blocks. Still, the importance of being alert to these distinctions, however we define them, is, once again, that it helps us to allow Revelation and other New Testament apocalyptic literature to be whatever it actually is.

---

[10]D. E. Aune et al., "Apocalypticism," *DNTB*, pp. 45-58; see p. 47.
[11]J. J. Collins, "Eschatologies of Late Antiquity," *DNTB*, pp. 330-37.

9.2 Reading the Apocalypse Now: Avoiding the Extremes

Perhaps the toughest question facing readers of Revelation today is whether this document legitimately speaks to their own generation and culture, and if it does, how it does. I am convinced that although we must recognize the primacy of the original circumstances lying behind Revelation, the book's relevance is no more *restricted* to its ancient audience than the relevance of Paul's letters or of the Gospels is restricted to theirs. We no longer face the fury of Roman emperors who insist that all their subjects worship them as gods, on pain of death. But even in the West, we have plenty of opportunity to betray our commitment to God in Christ by succumbing to the pressures of cultural conformity. And in other parts of the world, no less today than at any other period of Christian history, people must choose between (a) political or religious conformity, in defiance of their faith in Jesus Christ, and (b) death for remaining faithfully committed to him. There is no sure reason why challenges of this kind might not someday engulf the West as well. In a way, we are living on borrowed time.

The fundamental message of Revelation is as powerfully effective for us today as it presumably was for the churches of ancient Asia two millennia ago. That message is that there exists another world beyond this one— God's world—and that a time of divine judgment is coming to vindicate God's people against those who oppress them. For us as Christians and exegetes, however, it is extremely important how we define who God's oppressed people are, and who their oppressors are. Our understanding must conform not to current fashion, political or religious, but to the values expressed in Revelation, as well in the rest of Scripture. The depiction in Revelation 17—18 of the great whore and her judgment sounds disturbingly like business as usual in Western Christendom. Some of us (older!) North American readers of Revelation remember a day not so long ago when the now defunct Soviet Union was expected to play the role of leading the forces of evil against God and his armies at Armageddon. Since 1989, we may smile at that reading, having learned a lesson about being careful. But we must be correspondingly careful not to equate the armies of God in any way with the West—whether with Great Britain, Canada, the United States (or "America") or any other European country. No matter how we may wish, as democratic Western nations, to compare ourselves with other nations in terms of human rights, we have such an enormous consumer's appetite that we can just as easily see ourselves in terms of the great whore of Revelation 17. Whether that reading actually fits or not is an exegetical and hermeneutical question, but the possibility that it does fit should give us pause as we think about (and preach!) this text.

Perhaps the greatest danger to avoid in reading Revelation for the benefit of contemporary audiences—apart from assuming its irrelevance or its impenetrability—is the temptation to seek the book's message as if it were embedded in the symbols and metaphors themselves, rather than in the realities they point to. We must avoid the extremes of unnecessary fear and intimidation, or simple dismissal, on the one hand, and of inordinate fascination and undue speculation on the other hand. For rather than presenting its message in the form of factual narrative or of rhetorical argument, apocalyptic literature paints a mood instead. It stimulates the imagination through the use of primordial imagery and biblical allusion, and through a standard library of signs, characters and literary pictograms. It creatively combines these raw materials in ways that conjure up a sense of the indescribable, the inexpressible, a sense of the truth about God and his ultimate control over the affairs of humanity. Out of this sense of God's inalterable plans for judgment and renewal comes the inward confidence needed to remain faithful to him in all circumstances, however severe. For this reason, striving to attach specific correspondences to the details of Revelation's many symbolic and metaphorical portrayals—especially when the corresponding entities exist only in the twentieth or twenty-first centuries—makes of an apocalypse like Revelation something it was likely never intended to be. What could it possibly have meant to the brothers and sisters in Pergamum, who witnessed the martyrdom of their friend Antipas (Rev 2:13), that someday a horde of Huey or Apache attack helicopters would take part in the great battle at the end of the age? Yet that is how some late twentieth-century interpreters understood the cloud of locusts in Revelation 9:3, 7. They may be right nonetheless, but it is a topic well worth discussing.

The bottom line with Revelation and other biblical apocalyptic literature is threefold. For one thing, we must insist on its relevance: it is not so remotely anchored in the past that it has nothing to say to us today; yet neither is it so engrossed in the coded prediction of modern phenomena that it had no relevance for its first-century readers. Second, we must be willing to listen to it and work with it, even if at first its bizarre nature seems impermeable to our understanding. Although there is much about ancient apocalypses that eludes us now, there is by the same token much we have learned. We may indeed feel *duly* intimidated by what, for now, remains beyond our reach. But the tools for informing ourselves about those ancient settings and about the means and methods of apocalyptic literature lie ready for us to pick up and put to use. And third, we must permit this literature to be what it is, hearing it on its own terms and steadfastly resisting the temptation to make of it something it is not. We should strive to avoid speculative interpretations that make concrete connections between the ancient symbols and contemporary persons, nations or other artifacts irrelevant to the ancient readers. How might these recommendations look if we apply them to the New Testament?

9.3 A Look at Some New Testament Apocalyptic Literature

We can now take several apocalyptic texts from the New Testament in order to see how some of these guidelines play out in practice. The texts we will use are 2 Corinthians 12; 1 and 2 Thessalonians; Matthew 23—25; and Revelation 13.

9.3.1 2 Corinthians 12

We can begin with an apocalyptic text that never got off the ground, so to speak. In the midst of a passionate self-defense against his detractors in Corinth, Paul alludes to something he had experienced fourteen years earlier, in which he was "caught up to the third heaven" (2 Cor 12:1-4). There, in "Paradise," he heard things "no mortal is permitted to repeat." This experience sounds like just the sort of "journey" an apocalyptic writer might have taken. Paul, however, does not attempt to reveal the secrets of God's world that he presumably heard there, as a journey-apocalypse would do. He only reluctantly refers to the event at all as a means of demonstrating that he does have something to boast about, even if his opponents deny it and even if he has been given a thorn in the flesh all these years to keep him from getting a big head over it (2 Cor 12:5-10). In other words, this may not be an apocalyptic text itself, but it certainly could have evolved into one, had Paul not been instructed otherwise.

9.3.2 1 and 2 Thessalonians

Likewise, if Paul had not been otherwise instructed about his visit to the third heaven, we might be tempted to think that a few years prior to writing 2 Corinthians he had already divulged to the Thessalonian believers some of that strange experience. For if any of his surviving correspondence can be considered apocalyptic, it is 1 and 2 Thessalonians.[12] The setting is clearly one of oppression and persecution (e.g., 1 Thess 2:2, 14; 3:4; 2 Thess 1:4-5). Paul had been forced to flee Macedonia (in which Thessalonica is situated) and was now in some anxiety as to whether this newly planted community of believers

---

[12]For the present point, we can ignore questions that scholars raise about the integrity of 2 Corinthians as an originally complete letter and about the authorship of 2 Thessalonians.

would remain faithful in the midst of their troubles. He therefore sent Timothy back to see how things stood (1 Thess 3:1-3), and Timothy has returned with a good report (1 Thess 3:6). Although much relieved and overjoyed, Paul does not leave the matter there; he writes the Thessalonian church a letter reiterating the ethical teaching he had laid down when he was among them (1 Thess 4:1-12).

Then, in 1 Thessalonians 4:13, he turns to a question they have sent back to him with Timothy. Apparently, since Paul left, some of their people have died (perhaps from persecution), and the surviving believers are confused about the fate of these who now "sleep." In response, Paul waxes apocalyptic; he formally declares, "by the word of the Lord" (1 Thess 4:15), that both the dead in Christ and those believers still alive at the return of Christ will be taken up together, alive, to meet the Lord in the clouds of the air and to be with him forever. He adds for good measure the colorful details that the Lord will descend with a great shout,[13] accompanied by the archangel and with a mighty trumpet blast (1 Thess 4:16). He refuses to give any more specific information, however, claiming this is all they need (1 Thess 5:1). But he does stress the fact that the actual timing of this anticipated "Day of the Lord" (1 Thess 5:2) cannot be predicted; instead it will come unexpectedly, "like a thief in the night." The only way to be prepared for it is to remain busy in an everyday life of righteous obedience (1 Thess 5:12-22). Paul evidently intends that this declaration of what is yet to come will comfort the believers in their confusion, even if what he expects remains for now beyond human experience.

Clearly it did just that (2 Thess 1:3). Yet, although the first letter brought comfort, it also inspired in the Thessalonian believers a new anxiety (2 Thess 2:1-2): had the Day of the Lord *already* come? In order to reinforce his earlier point, Paul returns in a second letter to the image of the Lord's descent from heaven, adding now the new element of a flaming fire of vengeance, God's righteous judgment against those who persecute God's people (2 Thess 1:5-10). Paul seeks to comfort this worried flock by appealing to apocalyptic images, images he had imparted to them even in the days he was there among them. The Day of the Lord has *not* come. In fact it will not come until a certain sequence of rebellion takes place (2 Thess 2:3-12), in which the man of lawlessness or the son of perdition (cf. Ps 88:23 LXX) asserts himself in the place of God and leads many astray. For the moment, something is keeping this development at bay, and the Thessalonians will re-

---

[13]See C. A. Evans, *Noncanonical Writings and New Testament Interpretation* (Peabody, Mass.: Hendrickson, 1992), pp. 186-88, for an interesting connection here with Ps 47:5.

call what it is, for Paul told them about it when he "was still with [them]" (2 Thess 2:5-7). We who read this text today usually feel a little annoyed at Paul's failure to be more specific, but our annoyance is not an excuse to fill in the blanks as we please! What he does go on to say, however, is that once the lawless rebel is revealed, the returning "Lord Jesus will slay him with the breath of his mouth" (2 Thess 2:8). This sounds amazingly similar to the Rider on the white horse in Revelation 19:11, out of whose mouth comes a sharp sword to smite the nations (Rev 19:15), as well as to other apocalyptic or "pre"-apocalyptic texts (e.g., Ps 52:2; Is 11:4; *Pss Sol* 17:24; Wis 18:15-16; *4 Ezra* 13:8-11). In other words, Paul once more comforts and reassures the Thessalonian believers with apocalyptic imagery, drawing upon the reservoir of resources available to him from Jewish apocalyptic tradition. His main concern in all of it is to ensure that the members of the church, even in the midst of difficult times, remain faithful to their Lord; he has simply appealed to the coming judgment and to a reassuring apocalyptic eschatology to reinforce his instruction.

9.3.3 Matthew 23—25

Paul deals with a familiar tension in the Thessalonian letters. On the one hand he encourages the suffering believers to look forward to the ultimate solution, which he refers to as the Day of the Lord. On the other hand, he must tone down undue anticipation of the Day of the Lord, both by rebuking some "idlers" who refuse to work (probably because they expect the end at any moment; 1 Thess 4:11; 5:18; 2 Thess 3:11-13) and by reassuring others that they have not been left behind. This same tension is evident in the apocalyptic portions of the Synoptic Gospels. We can look briefly at Matthew's Gospel to see it in operation.

The Gospel of Matthew contains five major discourses: (1) the righteousness of the kingdom (Sermon on the Mount; Mt 5—7), (2) the proclamation of the kingdom (Mt 10), (3) the mystery of the (formerly hidden) kingdom (parables of Mt 13), (4) family relations within the kingdom (Mt 18), and (5) the cosmic crisis of the kingdom (Olivet [Eschatological] Discourse; Mt 23—25). This structure suggests that the main purpose of Matthew's Gospel is to declare everything his audience ought to know in view of the appearance of the kingdom of God in the person of Jesus the Nazarene. This purpose is especially directed to Jewish believers—perhaps in Syrian Antioch during the last two decades of the first century—believers who were caught between reluctant membership in an increasingly Gentile movement, on the one hand, and separation anxiety in view of a Jewish community that condemned them as deserters and traitors, on the other. Many of them may well have been refugees from the destruction of Jerusalem in the year 70. Add to this the strong likelihood that Christians and Jews alike were subject to persecution by the Gentile population in the wake of the Jewish War. In some measure, then, Matthew's readers may have found themselves in circumstances appropriate for apocalyptic encouragement.

Matthew 23 presents Jesus' scathing criticism of a hypocritical form of Judaism espoused by certain scribes and Pharisees; it includes the famous list of "woes" (Mt 23:13-36; cf. the parallel "Beatitudes" in Mt 5). Jesus' remarks reflect the emptiness of second-temple Judaism. The fact that Matthew now rehearses these woes to his own readers suggests that he sees a similar emptiness and hypocrisy among the Jewish leadership in Antioch (assuming it is Antioch). The strongly anticlerical (not anti-Semitic) tone of Matthew 23 sets the stage for Jesus' prediction of the Jerusalem temple's destruction in Matthew 24:1-2; the disciples' questions to Jesus in 24:3, posed later on the Mount of Olives, are based on this prediction. The disciples want to know three things: (a) when the temple will be destroyed, (b) what will be the sign of Jesus' coming as king, and (c) what will be the sign of the end of the age. Taking these together, we get the impression that for the disciples the destruction of the temple and the end of the age would occur simultaneously; for them, life without the temple was unimaginable.

Jesus' answer to these questions fills up Matthew 24—25 and falls into two main parts: a discursive portion full of warnings and further predictions (Mt 24:4-36) and a supportive, supplemental section devoted to various parables, some of them quite long (Mt 24:37—25:46). What is remarkable about Jesus' reply is that it contains a great deal of material dealing with a coming catastrophe and a great deal more designed to *quell* apocalyptic enthusiasm.

Intermingled in this discourse, then, are *two sorts of statements*, both of which must be considered within this larger context. The first sort is composed of predictions and descriptions of disaster and apocalyptic "resolution." Matthew 24:5-14 warns of wars and rumormongers, false messiahs, international crises, persecution and betrayal. The distressing prospect continues in Matthew 24:15-28 with expectations of desolation and sacrilege, warnings to flee and warnings of false messiahs and false prophets. Much of this can easily be understood as referring (from Matthew's perspective) to the recent events in and around Jerusalem (A.D. 66-70). But threaded throughout is a cosmic theme, which comes to the fore in Matthew 24:29-31. There we hear of the coming of the Son of Man, of portents in the sun and the moon, loud trumpets and great mourning.

Even within this first group of texts, then, Matthew's readers are apparently left with the sense that Jesus is talking about two things at once. On the one hand they hear of (a) the now very familiar catastrophe that had occurred in Jerusalem some ten to fifteen years earlier. They now know that life continues without the temple after all. On the other hand, they continue to hear of (b) the still expected "end of the age," to be heralded by the appearing of the Son of Man in the clouds of heaven and accompanied by great astrophysical events, reminiscent of the undoing of creation (Mt 24:29). Both events are cataclysmic. One is "real" history by now. The other, more far-reaching, is yet to be. The first is a type of the second.[14]

This sort of statement, accentuating the seriousness of the hour, is balanced by the second sort, intending apparently to exercise a calming influence, to forestall any enthusiastic irresponsibility arising in response to the apocalyptic character of this material. Thus the second group of texts includes warnings not to be led astray (Mt 24:4); the coming of the Son of Man will be unmistakable (Mt 24:27), as well as unpredictable, for no one knows the hour when the end will come—not even the Son himself (Mt 24:36). The readers are called to endure and to be vigilant to the end (Mt 24:13). The parabolic material at the end of Matthew 24 and the three long story parables in Matthew 25 all speak to the need for calm-headedness and faithful, steady patience. The times may be dire and distressing, but there is a job to do while the Lord tarries in carrying out his re-creation of all things.

Thus, there are three things to notice in this discourse, all interwoven with one another: (1) historical references, (2) apocalyptic references, and (3) delay passages (downplaying enthusiastic apocalypticism and encouraging perseverance in the face of trouble). It is the same tension we saw in the Thessalonian letters. Like Paul, Matthew wants his readers to be mentally and spiritually prepared for whatever may happen, but to keep their heads with respect to what any of it may mean for the final day. They still have work to do, and the Lord remembers them. The point is a demand for faithfulness to one's God-assigned tasks, ethics and mission in the intervening period of delay.

---

[14]It is by no means impossible, of course, that this imagery of portents in the sun and moon and of the Son of Man returning in the clouds to retrieve his own from all corners of the earth (Mt 24:29-31) simply expresses metaphorically the heightened emotional impact of the events of A.D. 70. I am not completely uncomfortable with this level of "reduced" interpretation in this context. However, for now at least, it feels to me like too much of a stretch—or shrinkage. Cf. N. T. Wright, *Jesus and the Victory of God* (Philadelphia: Fortress, 1996), chap. 8, esp. pp. 339-68.

9.3.4 Revelation 13

Interpreters have sometimes drawn distinctions among four main approaches to Revelation. One approach, the so-called preterist view (that is, having to do with the past), relates the book exclusively to the ancient setting. Another, the futurist view, understands it almost exclusively, at least from chapter four onward, in terms of the setting relevant to the modern readers and their future. A third approach regards the progressive unfolding of the revelation as a prediction of the progressive unfolding of history (usually Western history), typically up to the time of the contemporary reader; this is called the historicist approach. (Of course, the results of the futurist and historicist approaches change with the passing years, shifting from reader to reader.) The fourth of these interpretive approaches, the idealist, despairs of the other three and views Revelation as historically nonspecific, concerned with universal principles of God's truth rather than with genuine historical phenomena.

Each of these four approaches has its strengths and weaknesses. What is recommended in this textbook is a judicious blending of at least three of them. An interpretation of New Testament apocalyptic literature will be rooted above all in a careful analysis of the original circumstances lying behind the ancient text. But it will also pursue a thoughtful reading of the interpreter's own circumstances in light of that text. Whether or not that process will lead to positive identification between the ancient symbols and particular modern persons, nations or events, or whether it will imply more general principles of life, is less certain. But it should at least result in contemporary Christians becoming convinced that their God is still in ultimate control of the universe. No less now than at the end of the first century, he remains intimately concerned with the behavior and the fate of the human race, and he is committed to particular ethical and social values; it is important to him how we treat each other and how we regard him. He will not be mocked forever. With these thoughts in mind, we may close this chapter with a look at Revelation 13.

The preterist interpretation of apocalyptic literature, totally determined by the situation contemporary to the writer of the book, commonly views the first beast (Rev 13:1) as the Roman Empire and the second beast (Rev 13:11), whose mark is 666 (Rev 11:18), as Nero Redivivus (that is, "Nero come back from the dead," like some people's expectations for Elvis and JFK).[15] The message of Rev-

---

[15]Alternatively, the first beast may be seen as Nero and the second as a Neronic faction urging Christians (and others) to pin their hopes on the overthrow of Rome by the armies of Parthia under the leadership of Nero *redivivus*. Cf. A. J. P. Garrow, *Revelation* (London: Routledge, 1997), pp. 88-92.

elation is then completely fulfilled in the fifth century A.D. with the fall of Rome.

The strength of this approach is that it keeps the book relevant to the original readers, who were facing the rise of emperor worship and the consequent persecution of those who refused to comply. To be assured that the persecuting powers were doomed would have given added courage to the readers to remain faithful to Jesus Christ. Its weakness, however, is that in it the entire message of the book of Revelation is not really fulfilled; the final overthrow of Satan (the dragon, Rev 13:2) and of evil (so clearly portrayed) did not actually occur in the original readers' lifetime, nor with the collapse of the empire some three to four centuries later. Approaching Revelation from a strictly preterist perspective would imply that the author pursued his purpose—at least in part—by falsely or mistakenly comforting his persecuted people.

Futurist approaches in our day have often regarded the first beast as representing the nations of the European Union; the second beast is the coming world ruler sponsored by the EU. The conflict and conflagration described in later chapters portray the Great Tribulation, which will culminate in the Battle of Armageddon, and are preceded by the rapture of the church. Interpreting Revelation in this way is common among dispensationalists.

The strength of this way of reading Revelation, of course, is its focus on the end of all things. It takes seriously the *world* scale of the matter and the *final* answer to the problem of evil. Where the preterist approach leaves unresolved the ultimate fate of Satan, since he did not vanish with the fall of Rome, the futurist approach acknowledges that the end is yet to come. Its weakness, however, is that it would have been only remotely relevant to John's original readers, if relevant at all. How would knowledge of the future EU, for example, or of Moscow, or of swarms of helicopters, have been comforting to Christians suffering under Emperor Domitian (or Nero)? It would assume that those first-century believers could have somehow known the significance of the EU. And what are we to make of futurist interpretations popular prior to the fall of the Soviet Union in 1989?

As we have seen, popularized futurist readings of Revelation are themselves apocalyptic literature for a new time and place. During the East-West Cold War, when Soviet communism was understood as the primary threat to the Western way of life, futurist explanations of Revelation were oriented along the Moscow-Washington/London polarity. Since 1989, and especially since   9/11, the orientation has shifted in the direction of a polarity between London/Washington and Near Eastern terrorism. In other words, many Christians in the West become consumers of an ever-evolving apocalyptic, the proponents of which see their own political concerns directly reflected in an ancient text written to first-century Christians in Asia Minor. We may certainly be grateful that these twenty-first century Christians are thus encouraged to maintain trust in God for their future (though we may have doubts about the passivity that such an approach can inspire in them). Yet we must be careful not to assume that such readings of Revelation necessarily represent accurate and appropriate *exegesis* of the text.

The historicist approach views Revelation as a prediction of events up to the interpreter's own time in later Western history. Why it should be restricted to *Western* history is a mystery in its own right. In any case, churches inheriting the outlook of the Reformation, for example, might view the first beast as the Roman Catholic Church and the second beast as the pope.

Of course, the strength of this approach is that it makes Revelation truly prophetic of later Christian history and therefore immediately relevant for Christians of that later period. But, as with the futurist approach, the obvious weakness is its openness to subjective and shifting application. It would be just as legitimate for proponents of the sixteenth-century Roman church to regard the first beast as the Protestant movement and the second beast as Martin Luther or John Calvin. Or the second beast might be a multi-headed amalgam made up of Luther, Calvin, Zwingli, Melanchthon and a host of others. Cartoon-like propaganda from the period is rife with such depictions. In any case, why would John the Revelator feel inclined to inform his first-century Christian church in Asia regarding the coming battles of the European Reformation? Or why should this view on Revelation apply only to Western Christianity? Why would it not have been just as legitimately speaking of the seventh-century African church in its encounter with Islam?

Those who despair of the previous three approaches may turn to a fourth, one that neatly avoids the pitfalls facing the others. According to the idealist (or timeless) approach to reading Revelation, the first beast of Revelation 13 can be understood perhaps to represent fallen human nature and the second beast taken as representing self-centeredness.

The obvious strength of this moralistic interpretive procedure is the way it concerns itself with overarching ethical principles relevant to any readers in any situation. It encounters none of the problems arising from attempts in other approaches to match up symbols with actual historical events and personages, past or future. It has two major weaknesses, however. For one thing, the correlation of moral ideals with specific metaphorical representations in the text is as open to interpretive abuse as is the allegorizing method we discussed above in chapter eight in connection with Gospel parables. There are no reliable guidelines for knowing what ideal or principle John had in mind with the beasts of Revelation 13, for instance. In the second place, such a message, even if correctly discerned, would be far too divorced from the desperate historical situation the original readers were presumably facing. It lacks the assurance of a final vindicating consummation of all things. In a typical apocalyptic situation, such as the threat of death for failure to confess that Caesar (not Jesus) is lord, would a "seer" like John have comforted his people with a symbolic moralistic essay on, say, self-centeredness? Of course if we prefer the idealist approach, we can always abandon the assumption that Revelation was written for a people in apocalyptic distress. To do that, however, would raise a host of new exegetical problems.

The fact that we have at least these four diverse approaches to reading Revelation suggests that there is no firm consensus about which one is to be recommended. Probably the best approach will appreciate the strengths in all of them and attempt to avoid their weaknesses. The exegetical perspective represented by the guidebook you now hold in your hands puts a very high value on acknowledging the primacy of a biblical text's original setting. That setting forms the beginning place for sound exegesis. Minimizing the value of that setting for understanding a text opens the door to manipulating the text into meaning whatever we may wish it to mean. On the other hand, it is clear that we cannot exhaust the message embodied in the book of Revelation by restricting its application to the first century. Its scope and grandeur burst the bounds of the ancient situation.

In order to strike a reasonable balance between original relevance and subsequent applicability, the "best" approach to the exegesis of New Testament apocalyptic will probably appeal to type and antitype. John speaks of Rome as a "type" of God's concern with the eschatological beast. Jesus (or Matthew) in the Olivet Discourse (Mt 24) speaks of the fall of Jerusalem as a "type," while God in the Olivet Discourse speaks to future readers of the "antitypical" fulfillment at the end of the age. It is important from an exegetical point of view to identify the historic "types" represented metaphorically in the original setting of Revelation or of the Olivet Discourse (Rome, Domitian, the destruction of Jerusalem etc.). But we have neither need nor justification for insisting that the antitypes implied for some later situation represent this or that *specific* event, institution or personage recognizable to us in our own settings (such as the pope or Protestantism or the European Union).

In any generation, in any historical setting anywhere in the world, various specific entities may play the roles assigned to the antitypes implied in Revelation, just as Rome and its Caesar once did in the original setting. But the identities of the *final* players, let alone the dates of their appearance, remain veiled to us, hidden in the mist of the future outworking of God's purposes. As exegetes of New Testament apocalyptic literature, we must say all we can, but no more than we can. This is, I think, what Paul means in 1 Thessalonians 5:1-2: "Now concerning the times and the seasons, brothers and sisters, you do not need to have anything written to you. For you yourselves know very well that the day of the Lord will come like a thief in the night." Eagerness to know more than has been revealed is perhaps what the Mishnah warns against in *m. Ḥagigah* 2.1. We do not need to know the details; we only need to be constantly ready.

9.4 CONCLUSION

I close this chapter by summing up its fundamental message. Jewish-Christian apocalyptic literature provides the church an alternative style of communication, not unlike fiction could have done for my elderly friend if she had been open to it. As an alternative *style* of biblical communication, apocalypses simply employ alternative forms and methods to convey the same message conveyed by all of Scripture: "God lives and is in control of his creation and its fate; though it may not seem so just now, it is true nonetheless. Therefore remain faithful to him, and he will right all wrongs in his own good time." Interpreting Revelation is not so much a matter of divining the blueprint of the future as it is a matter of understanding the present in terms of God's reign—whether conceived of as already here, or yet to come, or both—and of learning to read the symbolic and metaphorical "language" in which that reign is described.

10

MOVING ON

What Do We Do Now?

Tí οὖν ἐροῦμεν πρὸς ταῦτα; So, what shall we say about these things?
ROMANS 8:31

So, what *do* we do now? That is a reasonable question to ask at this stage. It is also important not to get the wrong idea from it. Asking this question—and asking it now—does not somehow imply that we can never do anything at all until we reach this point. In order to discuss the procedures covered in this book, it has been necessary to organize them in some logical way, taking them one by one and analyzing them step by step. Yet, in real life, at the everyday level, we will seldom have the luxury to operate as methodically as that. It would be nice, in theory, to choose a text, translate it from Greek (or Hebrew), consider the textual tradition, analyze structure, literary form, historical setting, narrative and rhetorical strategy, and so on—more or less in that order and more or less thoroughly. Only then (in this theoretical world) would we begin to formulate a contemporary message based on that text. For a privileged few biblical scholars, that may be how it works. For the rest of us, however, the phone rings, the kids need a ride to soccer practice, and the water heater springs a leak. Then we hear that Ward and June Cleaver are splitting up and need immediate intervention counseling. By the time we sit down to prepare the Sunday morning sermon, it is already Friday afternoon. Weeks when we lack enough time to do the ideal job far outnumber the weeks when we have all the time we need.

This is true in part because there is simply no end to what we *could* do, if only we had enough time. There is always some other commentary to check, another ancient primary source to consult, or one more word analysis to carry out. In reality, however, our work will be more a matter of refining a hunch that has been building within us for months than a matter of working up something entirely new, from scratch. For this reason we must avoid the temptation to beat ourselves up when we cannot do the full job of exegesis we would like to do, or that we think our professors would have expected us to do. Otherwise, we will begin to convince ourselves that the task of regular exegesis is too big, too demanding, too unrealistic. This can lead us into the habit of neglecting, rather than pursuing, the task as much as possible. But for those who are called by God to feed his flock, as well as for that flock itself, neglecting exegesis like this is nothing less than tragic, since without solid and nourishing food, the Body withers.

What I am trying to say is this: exegesis is a *lifetime* employment, not a weekly one. It is a bit like keeping a ball rolling by giving it regular nudges, rather than each time starting it up fresh from a complete stop. Sometimes the nudge will be a mere tap, and at other times a powerful shove, but the ball keeps going, almost of its own accord, unless all nudging, tapping and shoving stop. This crude analogy may help to release some of us from an absurd burden of false guilt and a crippling sense of our insufficiency. We may work on specific texts one at a time, but over time, we progressively build up insight, understanding and confidence. Our call is not to do everything we *should* do (anyway, who determines what that is?), but to do everything we *can* do, given our constantly shifting circumstances. The trick is never to let the ball stop completely, even if at times—even many times—we can give it no more than a mere nudge, a single tap.

With that caveat, this final chapter attempts to draw conclusions for benefiting from the fruits of responsible New Testament exegesis. The work of exegesis is not an end in itself. Even if some people treat it that way, they probably—at least—make a living from it! But most of us who are called to the ministry of the Word of God recognize that exegesis and the results it produces play an enormously important role in the life of God's people and the world. Unfortunately, so does the neglect of exegesis.

10.1 Exegesis in Its Context

Although I have focused on exegesis in this book, I nevertheless acknowledge both sides of the interpretation coin: exegesis and hermeneutics, or meaning and significance, or "what the text meant" and "what the text means." The underlying assumption, or confession, has been that the Bible preserves in written form the authoritative Word of God to humanity, not just for the original audiences of its various portions, but for all humanity of all cultures in all conceivable historical settings. (We see the apostle Paul taking something like the same attitude in Rom 4:23-24.)

Set within its larger context, exegesis leads us to be always forming and reforming our understanding of biblical revelation. That process, in turn, has implications for life, faith and practice. Personal transformation, interpersonal relationships, teaching and preaching, leadership, values-assessment and the setting of priorities—all these things and more are subject to the results of careful exegesis and thoughtful, patient dialog about the significance of those results for any contemporary situation. In terms of the "big picture" diagram provided in chapter one (and keeping in mind the caveat mentioned just a moment ago), I am speaking now of the transition from exegesis to hermeneutics. We are "ready" (perhaps as much as we can be for now) to feed the exegetically reconstructed ancient message into the "hermeneutical grid," doing so in order to relate the ancient context to some contemporary one. This will enable us, as far as possible, to recast that ancient message in terms that make appropriate sense to contemporary audiences in their own contexts. Some people refer to this stage of the process as "application"; provided we are careful to define our terms, *application* is a useful word in this connection.

10.1.1 What We Mean by Application

In fact, there are dangers to avoid in using the term *application* in this context. By acknowledging the legitimacy of using it, I am not suggesting that this maneuver is a simple matter of deducing biblical "principles" and of "applying" them to our lives. The will of God is not a piece of computer software with which we analyze the database of our circumstances in order to find out what we should do in some particular situation. Nor is Pastor Bob or your mother the computer techie who runs the program for us, giving us on Sunday something amounting to the "seven principles of successful Christian prayer," or of stewardship or of raising children.

What we are after rather, in my view, is a *comprehensive understanding of the person of God* insofar as he has revealed himself to us. This revelation comes packaged primarily in the life and words of God incarnate in Jesus Christ, and secondarily in the history of his dealing with humanity (particularly with Israel and the early church) and in the words of his prophets and apostles. The fundamental question (again, I admit, as it seems to me) is always about what Jesus would do, how he would think, act, behave and speak, if he were in the situation we find ourselves in. Although there is danger lurking here, too, this is what I mean by "applying" the scriptural message to a contemporary situation. The danger lies in the temptation to decide "what Jesus would do" on the basis of what we ourselves would do. This, however, only reinforces the importance of exegesis. As the human manifestation of God, Jesus did not come to us with a list of principles and procedures, but with a life and a heart. Biblical exegesis seeks to tell us what that life and heart were like in the ancient settings. Hermeneutics seeks to tell us how that life and heart "apply" to our own settings, how they presumably manifest themselves here and now. God is so interested in the success of the endeavor that he has endowed the church with his Spirit to guide us in figuring it out. Still, even under this restricted definition, application is not necessarily the same thing as *authoritative* application. We need to consider this for a moment.

10.1.2 Authoritative Application: Personal Obedience and Servanthood

Many who read this book already hold positions of authority within a congregation, or they someday will. They may preach sermons, lead Bible studies, conduct committee work and hold offices. If we are reasonably modest (that is, if we have a *healthy* self-image), it may amaze us how often people look to *us* for authoritative answers to questions about life and doctrine. It can and should be frightening, for the responsibility is enormous. Fortunately, these same people will also tend to ignore the answers we give them. The authority we assume as leaders in the church must not be assumed lightly and certainly not as a means of alleviating our own insecurities. Here are two considerations for enhancing our effectiveness and our confidence as "authoritative" leaders among the people of God.

Servanthood. We are called to be more concerned with our people's welfare (including, first of all, that of our own families) than we are with our own. That is, we can govern our lifestyle with the assurance that Christ's own self-sacrificing example (Mt 16:24; Phil 2) not only bears no threat to our existence but also carries its own unshakable promise of reward. Adopting this concern and living it out will cause our trustworthiness to blossom.

Obedience. We are encouraged to remember that we represent Jesus Christ. We are Christ incarnate—or at least members of Christ incarnate. When we speak the Gospel, when we visit the sick, when we condemn or pardon sin, we do so with the authority of and on behalf of the Creator of the universe. Obedience in being repentant, above all else, is true righteousness and genuine dependence on God. If we suffer for it, we, like Paul, complete the sufferings of Christ (cf. Col 1:24).

In a nutshell, the greatest of all our *hermeneutical* endeavors is seen in the way we speak and live. Exegesis provides the raw material for thinking about these issues. As such, it packs enormous power for transforming us according to that incarnational model; it will affect all aspects of our lives. The incarnation, in fact, epitomizes God's determination to channel his message to humanity *through* humanity. If our people are to hear that message, they will hear it through us, or through someone just as human as we are. In a very important sense, even the Bible is written and preserved through human effort. Therefore, if we want our people to hear God's message with clarity and accuracy—that is, with "authority"—there is no better way to accomplish our desire than by reflecting the results of our exegesis in our own thinking and behavior. Exegesis, hermeneutics and leadership are all of one cloth: Christ-centered integrity.

10.2 EXEGESIS AND THE BROADER THEOLOGICAL CONTEXT

Granted its more general implications, exegesis nevertheless has a particular relevance for the especially "verbal" or "academic" aspects of ministry. One of these aspects is the process of developing a more comprehensive understanding of the larger biblical-theological picture. There is no universal consensus on whether that larger picture exists at all as a coherent unity (let alone on what it looks like if it does). But the concepts of divine inspiration and "canon" imply that such a unity does exist; and assuming it does, we can stop a moment here to think about the relationship between an at least theoretically comprehensive biblical theology and the exegetical task.

10.2.1 Context and Reciprocity

We have seen on several contextual levels that there is a circular or reciprocal semantic relationship between smaller and larger units of those levels. The meaning of a word, for instance, is in part determined by the meaning of the sentence in which it occurs; but, reciprocally, we understand the sentence's meaning more adequately when we know the meanings of the words that make it up. We saw in chapter three that this very principle holds all the way "up" to the level of entire books. We took it to cover even larger bodies, such as Paul's letters or the Pauline "corpus," and we can now apply it "canonically." That is, this reciprocity holds even at the level of the relationship between an individual biblical book and the New Testament (or the entire Bible) itself.

Christian biblical theology as a whole is constructed from the various theologies embedded in the individual biblical books, each with its own historically determined special concerns and emphases. Reciprocally, the individual theologies of the several books in the canon cannot be fully understood outside the theology of the whole canon. Of course, this assumes that the Christian biblical canon is the product of the inspiration of God's Spirit, both in its content and in its collection into a unified whole. Not every biblical scholar is convinced of this. I am, but you will have to make up your own mind about it.

10.2.2 Letting the Scripture Speak for Itself

Here, however, we need to draw a rigorous distinction between (a) the canon's unified theology as it *really is* (again, assuming there actually is one) and (b) our own notions and traditions as to what it is—that is, *what we think it is.* The very multitude of conflicting systems of Christian theology proves that some of these systems—undoubtedly all of them—are wrong in certain respects in the ways they attempt to frame biblical doctrine. Precisely for this reason, we must *keep on listening and re-listening* to the messages of the individual books of the Bible. It is far too easy to read back into them what we expect them to say (or have been told to expect them to say), based on our own ideas of what they, as Christian books, ought to say. To the contrary, our ideas of what they ought to say must be determined by what in fact they do say. If, for example, we read the book of Revelation through the system recently popularized in the Left Behind series of novels and films, it will sound very much like a clear-cut blueprint for the future. If we read it without that system, it sounds quite different altogether. Our problem is that we can never come without some system or other, some paradigm, some set of questions to ask, some scheme of reality we expect to find. That is not bad; otherwise we could not come at all. Our task, however, is to let *the Bible* always be *revising* our ideas of what the Bible says.

10.2.3 Hearing the Canon as a Whole

It is vitally important to let a given book's individual point of view guide us in forming (and reforming) our theological system. It is equally important to let Christian theology—drawn from the *canon as a whole*, and as understood by the church as a whole—test and temper extremist interpretations of individual passages. We may safely assume that the authors of New Testament books wrote what they wrote within the context of the community of believers and of the traditions handed down from the days of Jesus' earthly ministry. Each author had his (or her?) own particular contribution to make. Yet there was (so evangelicals confess) a kind of community conscience, a nascent *regula fidei*— we might identify it with the Holy Spirit—that prevented maverick or renegade theology while at the same time permitting a prophetic criticism of various "human" interpretations of the traditions.

So we have then a tension or balance between (a) the *individual theologies* of the various authors and books of the Bible and (b) the *unified voice* of the canonical Christian Scriptures. We must never slight one in favor of the other. We must allow each to criticize and adjust *our ideas* of what the other teaches. On this perpetual, balanced interplay between the canon as a whole and the

individual books within the canon rests the health, spiritual growth and edification of the church. On its neglect, some portion of the church has often
been shipwrecked: Gnostics and docetists in the Johannine community, judaiz-
ing legalists and Gentile antinomians in the Pauline communities. Who would
it be today? We ourselves are not immune.

We need a good way, then, to bring this issue to bear on "everyday" exegesis.
In fact, there are two concerns. One of them is to determine as well as we
can—on our own—what the Scripture actually teaches on some matter we are
interested in, say, the "antichrist." The other concern is at some level to join in
the ancient and worldwide discussion of the subject, the one that has been underway in the church for centuries.

10.2.4 The Idea of (the) Antichrist

Take as an example the subject of the antichrist. The recent spate of Christian
publications and films focused on the "end times" has intended to be faithful
to Scripture. How far it has succeeded in this intention is open for debate, as
it is of course for any other Christian publication or film on the same subject,
or any subject. Even the far-fetched predictions we heard about the return of
Christ on a specific date around the recent turn of the millennium belong to
this age-old discussion. Each voice in the discussion deserves at least one hearing by someone somewhere, even the voices of those who themselves refuse to
listen to any voice but their own. Still, it would not be possible for some lone
individual to listen to every voice on every issue. For most of us, it will likely be
impossible to listen to every voice on even one issue. We must imagine instead
an almost infinitely complex web of discussion and dialog extending across
the centuries and around the world. There is no way to master it all, but if we
wish to be faithful to the Spirit's lead, it is essential that we join it to whatever
degree we are able.

Popularized expositions of the "end times" give enormous prominence to
an evil figure of world-scale power, known as the antichrist (or simply, Antichrist, as if it were his [her?!] proper name). This figure is sometimes portrayed as identical with one of the eschatological beasts of Revelation 13 and
is expected to exercise absolute dominion over the earth in the last days before the Great Judgment. Having read an exposition of this kind, we may wish
to consult the Bible for ourselves in order to decide how much we can rely on
this portrayal. By checking a concordance, we find four New Testament occurrences of the term ἀντίχριστος "antichrist": 1 John 2:18, 22; 4:3; 2 John 7. The
concordance will tell us also that this term occurs nowhere else in Scripture,
not even in the book of Revelation.

An examination of the term's use in 1 and 2 John tells us at least the following. (a) The believers have been taught to expect the antichrist as a sign of the "last hour" (1 Jn 2:18; 4:3). (b) They know him by that title, *antichrist.* (c) But in fact the antichrist has already come in John's own day, and thus John can say it is the last hour now (that is, in the first century! 1 Jn 2:18; 4:3). (d) The antichrist's coming is manifest in "many" representatives who have "gone out into the world" (1 Jn 2:18; 2 Jn 7). (e) He and they are also known as "deceivers" (2 Jn 7). (f) His (their) chief characteristic is the refusal to recognize that the man Jesus is also the divine Christ—tantamount in John's eyes to a denial of both Father and Son (1 Jn 2:22)—and the refusal to confess the divine Christ's humanity and incarnation (1 Jn 4:2-3; 2 Jn 7). (g) This latter point is also attributed to the *spirit* of the antichrist (1 Jn 4:2-3), which explains how there can be *many* antichrists/deceivers.

Taking a cue from these data, we can move on to trace the idea of "deception" in the Johannine letters. (a) First John 4:6 identifies the "spirit of error" (the deceiving spirit—probably equivalent to the spirit of antichrist; 1 Jn 4:3) with the refusal to listen to sound doctrine. (b) First John 2:26-27 may suggest that "those who are deceiving" the community are claiming a special anointing from their (proto-Gnostic?) god. (c) First John 3:7-8 seems to suggest that these deceivers are likewise teaching a freedom of behavior that John equates with sin and the devil's work. It is no doubt in contrast to this that he urges "genuine love" (2 Jn 1). Finally, (d) the reference to false prophets who have gone out into the world (1 Jn 4:1) belongs here too, since it heads up the whole section on the spirit of the antichrist.

From this quick analysis of the only biblical occurrences of the term *antichrist,* we get the impression that it refers to one who opposes ascribing divinity to the man Jesus of Nazareth. This may also imply a gnosticizing of the idea of the Christ, altering it from the earthly messianic role understood in Palestinian Judaism to a heavenly, divine role more in line with proto-Gnostic expectations. Such expectations kept the human and the divine in sharply distinct categories, on the assumption that anything material or earthly could have no part in anything divine or spiritual. For John, separating Jesus the human being from Christ the eternal incarnate God destroys the heart of the gospel. In John's own historical-social context, drawing this distinction perhaps represents the ultimate opposition to God and his purposes. It would not have required a long stretch for later exegetes to connect the antichrist with the ultimate God-opponents described in Revelation, especially if it was assumed that the author of the Johannine epistles and the author of Revelation were one and the same person.

Articles on "antichrist" in Bible dictionaries can point us to other biblical treatments of figures like the antichrist; it is one of the chief services that such articles offer us. Thus, besides references to Revelation 13, we may find others to Ezekiel 38—39 (Gog of Magog) or to Daniel's "abomination of desolation" (Dan 9:27). We may be referred to the "many false prophets and false christs" in Mark 13 and Matthew 24, or to Paul's "man of lawlessness/son of perdition" in 2 Thessalonians 2. Likewise mentioned will be numerous relevant extrabiblical traditions, both Christian and Jewish. Such articles may also trace the idea through subsequent history of Christian theology. From all this there is discernible a fairly common thread of an eschatological figure who opposes either God, or the returning Christ (the antichrist), or who sets himself up as God or as the Christ (false christ). This distinction in roles is perhaps what lies behind the two beasts of Revelation 13. At any rate, these can be seen as eschatological figures.

For John the letter writer, too, the antichrist is an eschatological figure, expected at the "last hour," but in his opinion, the last hour has already arrived. In his view, anyone brash enough to deny the incarnation and thereby sever God from humanity has to be the antichrist, especially when such a heresy is making successful inroads into his own congregations. In fact, he regards the spirit of the antichrist as present among the antichrist's followers in the same way as the Spirit of Christ (the "anointing," 1 Jn 2:27; perhaps in contrast to proto-Gnostic claims to being anointed) is present among Christians. In this, John is like the man who called in on a radio talk show to say that he thought the state police should spend more of their energies chasing down super-speeders and lane-weavers than in ticketing people who drive sixty miles per hour in a fifty-five-miles-per-hour zone. As it turned out, the caller had been ticketed three times recently for the latter. We often attribute universal significance to our own personal issues. The interesting thing is that the Spirit of inspiration honors John's sense of frustration and challenges us to see how his "outburst" functions in fact as the inspired Word of God to us in our own situations.

For John, then, we see that, while there may well come a last day when the antichrist *par excellence* will appear, this evil figure has already appeared in spirit in those who oppose sound Christology and ethics. In this sense, we who live in the post-Easter era are already living in the last days. We thus apparently have biblical warrant for identifying spirits of antichrist among us today. The point here is simply that before we absolutize a particular result of "localized" exegesis, we need to broaden the base and compare that result with other texts touching on the same or similar issues, and to consult the broader "conversation" on the subject. The Spirit reveals himself to the church, not just to isolated individuals within the church.

10.3 EXEGESIS, PREACHING AND TEACHING

In addition to gathering an expanding sense of the larger biblical-theological context, we also acknowledge the special relevance exegesis has for sermons and teaching. It is important to devote space to this dimension of biblical interpretation as well. We can do this in the form of providing some suggestions for communicating exegetical results through preaching and teaching.

10.3.1 Find the Word of God for Your People

First and above all else, observe the discipline of prayer, meditation, openness and silence, as fundamental to knowing what God wants you, his spokesperson, to proclaim to his people on his behalf. In other words, *do not be afraid to ask.* On the other hand, this does not necessarily mean that you cannot devote the next six months, perhaps, to a systematic study of Matthew or of Romans, just to keep the exegetical ball rolling.

Second, *choose a biblical text.* Why should we choose a text? It is important to proclaim a biblical text, because in the context of the church, people need to hear the Word of *God,* not just the musings of other people. Of course, in a sense, preaching and teaching is a kind of musing, but it is intended to be a disciplined musing aimed at understanding what *God* has to say in the Scripture. There are at least three common ways to proceed in the business of choosing texts.

1. *Consider some specific need* you sense that your people have, and with this *topic* in mind, *search for an appropriate text.* The topic must *not* be some obnoxious one that obviously pertains to one person or one group within the congregation whom you wish to flog. To do that is to court disaster. It ought rather to speak to broad but important issues that affect the life and calling of the entire community. For example, such topics as marriage and family relationships, guilt and shame, self-esteem and world hunger are likely candidates. Avoid haranguing the congregation on your pet peeves or fanning your people's collective prejudices by harping on topics about which you and they already agree (like the anti-communism sermons of past decades or the anti-secular-humanism sermons of more recent times).

Do not be deceived however; this is a very difficult endeavor. It is not as easy as you might think to select texts that are *appropriate to your topic.* The challenge is to choose texts dealing directly with the topic, if possible; if none can be found, then choose texts that deal directly with the deeper issues involved. *Never* use a text that only secondarily touches on the subject, or worse, has nothing at all to do with the subject, but that contains a word or phrase reminding you of some aspect of the subject. Your message must focus on what the text itself focuses on! Such a message, or a series of such messages, requires careful, long-range planning.

2. Pursue a *through-the-book* series. This technique is extremely good discipline, since it forces the treatment of the *whole* Word of God (at least as it appears in that book). One of its chief problems is that it is not always easy to adjust it to the church year (if that is important to you). Likewise, it is not always appropriate to congregational need (although a typical congregation has many needs), and it can get tedious if not handled properly. Nevertheless, preaching through a particular book keeps the pastor/teacher from growing stale with the same old message week after week. Above all, it contributes to the growth of the saints, not just their conversion.

3. *Lectionaries* (often in three-year cycles) come down to us as a rich and beautiful worship tradition, geared to the church year and unfortunately often ignored in evangelical churches. Offering weekly selections from the Gospels, Epistles, Old Testament and Psalms (with extras for special days), they lend themselves to a unified theme each week, around which one can plan an entire worship service. They are seasonally appropriate, if not always appropriate to the congregational need (but there are four texts to choose from each week). Disciplined use of a lectionary forces us to treat passages we might otherwise ignore. Why, for instance, do we hear so few Christmas sermons on the slaughter of the innocents in Matthew 2:16-18? On the other hand, I have to admit that not one of the several lectionaries I use from the Lutheran tradition includes Matthew 2:16-18! Lectionaries do not necessarily use all Gospel parallels either. Still, using one does solve the ongoing problem of "what to preach on this week," which can eat up so much of a person's study time in the pastorate. As a discipline, try sticking to the Gospels one year, epistles the next year, and so on.

10.3.2 Apply Your Exegetical Results with Care

Once you have a text, carry out an exegesis of it in order to decide what it *meant*. Sound and careful exegesis, of the sort we have been studying in this book, provides the essential control on application. These exegetical results are what you should now seek to make relevant to the people.

1. In the first place, *determine how culture-transcendent or how culture-bound your exegetical results are*. Determining which element or feature belongs in which of these two categories, or to what degree, will always inspire debate. Issues such as human nature, God's character and God's plan for redeeming the world are arguably culture-transcendent. But Paul's concern for his cloak and parchment (2 Tim 4:13), instructions about slavery, his view of the status of women

in Corinth and the wearing of head coverings in church will likely need to be regarded as more culture-bound. When Paul says in 1 Corinthians 11:16 that he and the churches have "no other practice," it is reasonable to assume that he may mean *cultural* practice. The importance of this distinction is simply that what is fairly determined to be culture-transcendent can be applied across cultures more or less without adaptation. What is fairly determined to be culture-bound will need to be adapted to other cultures, if in fact it is applicable there at all. We may agree that on some level "all scripture is . . . useful for teaching, for reproof, for correction, and for training in righteousness" (1 Tim 3:16). That does not necessarily mean, however, that all of it is useful in the same way or to the same degree. Besides, when those words were first penned, they probably referred only to what we now know as the Old Testament. That does not mean that the New Testament is *not* useful for these things, but only that we need to be careful how we understand what we read in Scripture.

2. Second, seek and then teach or preach the *main point of your biblical text.* In the parable of the good Samaritan (Lk 10:29-37), the point is the definition of "neighbor"—and in the context of what it takes to inherit eternal life— rather than what one should do for a neighbor, even though the Samaritan does model neighborliness. The main point of a text may be the principle underlying a time-bound cultural variable. Paul's constraints on teaching by women, for example, may well have been intended to eliminate an unnecessary cultural hindrance to the gospel; some women were perhaps letting their newly found freedom carry them away in a manner culturally offensive to the larger community. The situation is presumably quite different in contemporary Western culture(s). The important theme to preach in that case would be the avoidance of unnecessary cultural obstacles to the church's mission, whether affecting men or women, and not particular rules and regulations for women's leadership in the church. Focus only on what the text itself focuses on. If your text does not focus on what you want to address, find a text that does, or change *your* focus.

3. *Know your people.* In a sense, exegetically analyze your audience. Be conscious of the common humanity your people share with the original audiences and authors. Both groups experience such things as fear, insecurity, pride, lust, anger, greed, hope, love, dreams and more. On the other hand, be equally conscious of differences in cultural settings and issues. Television, nuclear war, off-shore drilling, suicide bombers, labor strikes, cigarettes, ecological destruction and so on either played no role in the first-century world at all, or if they did, they may not have carried the same connotations for Christians then as they do today. Remember that your people are like you. Remember that you

need to speak to the real issues of *their* lives, and therefore you need to *know* your people. Do not think you can justify always isolating yourself in your study. On the other hand, you cannot expect to feed your people *without* regularly isolating yourself in your study. It's a two-sided hermeneutical task requiring effective balance. It is not easy, but neither is it impossible, and it is essential for the health of the church.

4. Apply the Word of God to *the situation your people and you are facing*. On the one hand, avoid presenting a merely exegetical study without reference to your people's need; on the other hand, avoid merely addressing people's need without responsible application of exegetical results. We need a message, but we need a message from *God*. One of my first sermons after finishing my seminary work was on Luke 1:1-4; I delivered a brilliantly irrelevant and stunningly boring lecture on the introductory issues of authorship, date, historiography, Synoptic problem and so on. It was an exquisite disaster. Be careful to "comfort the afflicted and to afflict the comfortable." Some traditions call this the distinction between law, which demands, convicts and offers no hope, and gospel, which forgives, resurrects and offers nothing but hope. Avoid comforting the comfortable and afflicting the afflicted—which is the methodology of hell. Be candid; let your people see you as a fellow sinner. This frees them to admit *their* sin and failure. "If the pastor isn't perfect, why do I have to pretend I am?" One of the most potent killers of a ministry's effectiveness is a posture of pastoral perfection. Be vulnerable and transparent, assuring your people they do not need to become as good as you are in order to find grace with God. Neither do you, for that matter.

10.3.3 Package Your Sermons Effectively

One of the more tragic things in the contemporary church is the packaging of good solid biblical exposition and teaching in dull, rationalistic, propositional, lecture-style, three-point sermons. You may possibly reach people's heads with such presentations—eventually, and that's not bad. But preaching seeks to motivate response of heart and will. Storytelling is often a far more effective means of accomplishing that purpose. In view of this, I recommend the following as one possible way to structure a sermon.

1. Open with a well-told story from your own life, especially a funny one, using it to illustrate the main point of the sermon (which itself should correspond with the main point of your text). It is not necessary that the connection between your story and the text be immediately obvious. Be careful to be discreet and to avoid embarrassing anyone in your audience (like your spouse or children), but show yourself as human and vulnerable.

2. Explain the text more or less exegetically. Avoid being too technical, and do not try to cover everything. Develop the main point from the perspective of the original readers, concluding with the "distilled" core of the text, the one-sentence logic-content statement (see chapter six) in interesting dress. Use imaginative descriptions (Jesus' brown eyes, dusty garments). It is often effective to "re-mythologize" the text in your explanations, talking, for instance, about Pilate as a three-pack-a-day man, puffing away in the back of a limousine on his way to work (to cite an example from Frederick Buechner).[1] "Re-mythologizing" the Scripture is something like the literary technique of "switching" (as when *Romeo and Juliet* is redone as Bernstein's *Westside Story,* or *Cyrano de Bergerac* reappears as Steve Martin's *Roxanne*). This can be effective, provided your audience sees the new "myth " as relevant, that you do not lose sight of the seriousness of your purpose, and that you do not overdo it. Like maple syrup on a Belgian waffle, use it sparingly.

3. "Apply" the teaching of the text to the various situations of the congregation in their own life setting. Tie it in with the opening illustration and call for a response (or at least imply a call for response). This "call" may simply be an encouragement to have confidence in God's utterly free and no-strings-attached grace, or it may be a genuine altar call.

4. Supply your sermon with a catchy, intriguing title. One method of holding your people's attention is to keep them guessing for a while, until you "satisfy" them with the resolution. Start with the title. Titles like "Mr. Potato Head," "The 'Real' Nowhere Man," "Singing to Hell's Angels," "My Lover Is Coming in a 1940 Packard," and "Raising North Dakota," may help to stir up curiosity and expectation. One of my favorite sermon titles (it's not mine!), used for a message on the Gadarene demoniac, is "Giving the Pigs a Permanent Wave." Provided the connection between the title and the message becomes clear at some point, the audience experiences a certain sense of satisfaction just from that. Remember that color, candor, humor and human interest get through to people far more effectively than straight-laced, didactic lectures. Take a lesson from Jesus' own style.

10.4 EXEGESIS FOR LIFE

We can round out this chapter, and the book, with some "realistic" suggestions for a lifelong practice of regular, responsible exegesis, a lifetime of keeping the exegetical ball rolling. The "trick" is to maintain a balance between aspira-

---

[1]Frederick Buechner, *Telling the Truth: The Gospel as Tragedy, Comedy, and Fairy Tale* (New York: Harper & Row, 1977), p. 9.

tion and reality, between expectation and ability. We might want to do an intense structural analysis of Hebrews 2—6, but a series of tragedies in the church family has made that impossible this month; it will have to wait until next month. The reality of our own life-circumstances may not always (or ever) allow us to attain the level of exegetical productivity to which we may aspire. Our abilities at a given stage of our ongoing development may not enable us to satisfy the exegetical expectations *others* may have for us. We are who we are, and we must not agonize over it if we are not what we, or those others, wish we were. That sort of agony cripples us, preventing us from doing even what we are indeed able to do. Be content to do whatever is realistic for you. Keep the exegetical ball rolling with a tap now, with a nudge next week, and if you are lucky, with a genuine shove the week after that—only, keep the ball rolling. The following ten suggestions, listed in no particular order, may provide some guidance in this respect. Pick any or as many as work for you. Add others not listed, if you find them. Above all, maintain a balance between persistence and realism. As you persist, at whatever level you can, you will find yourself growing in ability and skill, absorbing life from the Word of Life, and passing it along to your people, always. Exegesis is for life.

1. Be forever working with some biblical book. Study Galatians for six months perhaps. Set a boundary, and either budget out the book within that boundary, or pursue the study in as much detail as you wish, but quit when you reach the boundary you set for yourself.

2. Treat yourself to reading through one or two significant noncanonical primary texts each year, perhaps at some special occasion like Lent or your birthday. This will keep you dabbling in the ancient world of the Bible, making you perpetually aware of its importance and making you increasingly familiar with its character. You will be surprised how even this "little" exposure will begin to enlighten your understanding of biblical texts.

3. Do not be discouraged if you cannot attain your goals. Simply accept the fact, reset your goals, and start fresh. There is no limit on the number of times you may start over.

4. If you have studied the biblical languages, do a little Greek or Hebrew reading each week, or at least each month. You probably spent an enormous amount of effort and time (not to mention money) in learning those languages. Your professors certainly did in teaching them. Many signals of a text's structure and of its interrelationship with other texts are embedded in the peculiarities of the original language, often in ways that do not readily translate into English. Keep yourself conversant with the original languages at least at some level.

5. Read a significant (heavy-duty) exegetically based book every year or two. N. T. Wright's major volumes on Christian origins and the question of God represent some good examples.[2] Or work through a classic treatment of New Testament theology, such as George Eldon Ladd's.[3]

6. Use commentaries sparingly, unless you have the temperament for that genre. My own experience, which may well be atypical, is that reading through a commentary soon becomes tedious, making me even less motivated to pursue the exegetical task than I may already be as a result of my own laziness. On the other hand, there is scarcely a better, more accessible source of "dialogue" on an exegetical point than what we might find among a good commentary's remarks on a particular passage. In any case, *always* give yourself a chance to understand a text before you resort to commentaries. You have as much native ability to understand, given the tools of the trade and your own common sense, as does any published commentator.

7. Browse randomly in biblical dictionaries. Sit down occasionally and read for an hour, dipping here and there into an article on Capernaum or something on dragons or the metaphorical image of the community well. The wealth of information at our fingertips in dictionaries is astonishing. Get into the habit of nosing around in it, even just for fun.

8. Join a study group. It may be a group of people who want to read Greek or Hebrew. It could be a collection of lay people from your church, who meet for breakfast weekly at Bob's Big Boy and discuss the sermon text for the coming week. It could involve other local pastors who covenant to preach from the same text each week. Consider gathering an online group of far-flung preachers for the same purpose. In any of these or similar cases, the benefit is an incarnated manifestation of the Body of Christ, whose members listen to each other and struggle together with the Word of Life.

9. As you can afford it, obtain a good electronic Bible research program, perhaps one of the three mentioned in chapter two (section 2.3 on concordances). Keep it open and running in the background of your computer whenever you are at work, so that if a question pops up, you can immediately check it out. It is amazing what we can learn with just a few keystrokes. In a promotional blurb for one of these programs, New Testament scholar Craig Evans once said that his electronic Bible software was the first thing he turned on in

---

[2]N. T. Wright, *The New Testament and the People of God* (Minneapolis: Fortress, 1992); *Jesus and the Victory of God* (Minneapolis: Fortress, 1996); *The Resurrection of the Son of God* (Minneapolis: Fortress, 2003).

[3]George Eldon Ladd, *A Theology of the New Testament*, rev. ed. (Grand Rapids: Eerdmans, 1993).

the morning and the last thing he turned off at the end of the day.

10. Take a refresher course. Perhaps a seminary in your vicinity offers special rates for local pastors. Consider traveling every couple of years to take in an exegetical conference or seminar in some distant place, perhaps at your alma mater. Even if you attend something based on an exegetical approach that makes you uncomfortable, rejoice in the fact that your mind is being stretched. Either way, fresh ideas will stimulate your thinking and provide periodic rejuvenation for your lifelong calling to be an expositor of the Word of God.

Just remember never to overload yourself but always to keep the ball rolling, however slowly. Carve out a little "exegetical" time for yourself each week, however short, and stick to it determinedly. Strive not for perfection, but for persistence. I can almost promise you that perfection will never come, depending on how you wish to define perfection. No matter how you define it, you will approach it only through persistence. I won't go so far as to apply to the exegetical task the hackneyed phrase, "there is no higher calling." That would beg a whole host of questions, like "no higher for whom?" Nevertheless, I am convinced beyond all doubt that faithful exegesis of Scripture is indispensable to the full-bodied life of the church, at least on this side of Jordan. If the trained exegetes will not supply it, who will—or rather, who *is* supplying it? It is a frightening question. There may or may not be any "higher calling," but it is high enough. If God has called you to be an exegete, be an exegete for life.

GLOSSARY

allegorization. The transformation of what is not an allegory into an allegory

allegory. An interpretation of a story that makes elements within it represent entities outside it

alternative variant. A form of a text rejected by an editor in favor of the editor's preferred reading

annotated outline. An outline containing brief "annotations" for each section and subsection

autographs. The (now lost) originals of biblical books

chiasm. A literary device organizing a text as a series of mirrored elements, as in A, B, C, C', B', A'; a kind of literary palindrome

clause. A coherent sentence fragment with a verbal element at its core

cluster. One or more linguistic units, of a particular level, joined together in a meaningful way

coherence. Consistency and unity within a text

comment. *See* predicate.

complex sentence. A sentence with at least one independent clause and one dependent clause, often connected with a subordinating conjunction

compound sentence. A single sentence constructed of at least two independent clauses connected with a coordinating conjunction

context. The larger framework and environment in which a phenomenon, such as a text, occurs

contextualization. The adaptation of a message in terms meaningful in a particular context

coordinating conjunction. A word, serving as a syntactical signal, conjoining two or more elements of the same level in the same grammatical function

criticism. The process of discernment in analysis

cultural determinedness. The effect of contextualization on a message and its text

culture-bound. Applicable only to a particular culture

culture-transcendent. Applicable across cultural lines

dependent clause. One that requires additional text in order to be grammatically complete; also called "subordinate" clause

discourse. Any complete, self-contained act of communication

etymology. The study of the history of words

exegesis. The "science" of discovering what a communication, such as a biblical text, meant to its original author and readers

extratextual. Related to phenomena outside of a particular text

form criticism. The analysis of the history, shape and function of texts in the early church

genre. A type (or subtype) of literature, often requiring a particular interpretive approach

gloss. A simple substitution of a word or phrase in Language A for a word or phrase in Language B

govern. The function of a linguistic unit when it controls or determines the role of other units "under" it

grammatically complete. Describing an utterance that can meaningfully stand alone, having an independent clause at its core

hermeneutics. The "science" of understanding the significance for a new audience of a text originally intended for a different audience

historical criticism. Analysis of a text's general and specific historical contexts

inclusio. A literary device in which the beginning of a text is matched by its ending

independent clause. One that is "grammatically complete"; also called "main" clause

interpretation. The process of discovering the significance of a text, including both exegetical and hermeneutical analysis

leading Gospel. In the Gospel synopsis, the Gospel in relation to which parallels from the other Gospels are brought forth for comparison at a particular point or pericope

logion (pl., logia). Saying(s) of Jesus preserved in the Gospels and elsewhere

macrostructure. The larger literary context in which a given text occurs

main clause. *See* independent clause.

meaning. The message of a text, whether as intended by its sender or as perceived by its receptor

microstructure. The internal structure of a given text

multivalent. Having multiple values, or meanings

noun clause, phrase. Any clause or phrase that functions as a noun in another sentence

occasion. The specific historical situation producing or addressed by a text

pericope. A defined coherent portion of a text, often a paragraph

phrase. A coherent sentence fragment that lacks a verbal element

predicate (*n*). The portion of a sentence that comments on the subject or topic; also called "comment"

preferred reading. The form of a disputed text preferred by an editor

prepositional phrase. A noun phrase introduced by a preposition in order to function as an adverb or an adjective

Q. A hypothetical source document containing material common to Matthew and Luke, but missing from Mark (name abbreviated from German *Quelle*, "source")

reciprocal, reciprocity. The quality of mutual effect; A affects B and B affects A

recursive. The quality of being repeatable, or repeated, at successive levels of complexity

redaction criticism. Analysis of the editorial activity of a text's author or compiler

rhetorical criticism. Analysis of a text according to ancient rhetorical conventions

rhetorical question. A question to which the questioner knows the answer and therefore asks only for effect

second-temple Judaism. The period of postexilic Jewish history from roughly the fifth century B.C. to A.D. 70

semantic domain. A constellation, or field, of related concepts and meanings, often reflected in the way a language organizes its vocabulary

sentence. Any minimally complete thought, consisting of at least one independent clause

Sitz im Leben. German phrase that refers to the actual historical situation behind a text

source criticism. Analysis of the sources from which a text was developed

structure. The shape of a text, including the relationship among its constituent parts

subject. The portion of a sentence announcing the topic it comments on; also called "topic"

subordinate clause. *See* dependent clause.

subordinating conjunction. A word, serving as a syntactical signal, that makes the clause it introduces into a dependent clause

switching. Retelling a story with a new setting

synopsis, Gospel. A tool laying out the texts of the Gospels in parallel columns for easier comparison

syntactical signals. The means used by a language to indicate syntactical relationships (conjunctions, case endings, verb forms, etc.)

syntax. The way a language puts elements of a sentence together in meaningful ways

task-oriented theology. Theology developed and discussed in response to a particular "occasion"

textual apparatus. The "footnote" material provided in an edition of a reconstructed text, showing the editor's rationale for the reconstruction

textual criticism. The "science" of recovering the original wording of a document from conflicting copies

textual problem. Wording in a text for which there are two or more conflicting variants

textual variant. One of two or more conflicting readings for a particular text

topic. *See* subject.

utterance. Any stretch of speech, oral or written

variant reading. *See* textual variant.

witness. In textual criticism, a document preserving some form of the New Testament text, "witnessing" to its possible originality

ANNOTATED BIBLIOGRAPHY

The following annotated bibliography lists a very few, selected New Testament exegetical resources and classifies them in two directions. First, it sorts them according to categories of the exegetical task (there will inevitably be some crossover in this). Then, within those categories, it lists resources according to levels of appropriateness *for beginning exegetes:* essential [E], nonessential but useful [U], and nonessential and advanced beyond the beginning stage [A]. Of course, as a beginner gains skill and moves to new levels of competence, some items marked here as nonessential become increasingly essential. The literature on biblical exegesis and interpretation, including the professional tools for its practice, is increasingly vast, especially in English. The items listed here merely hint at what is "out there," but they seem to me to be among the most helpful in the beginning stages. Unfortunately, not all of them remain in print, but those that are not can usually be found in libraries.

General Guidance

Carson, D. A. *Exegetical Fallacies.* Grand Rapids: Baker, 1984. [A] Although negative in its approach, this little book is packed with timely warnings against common errors in exegesis. A handbook of "what not to do."

Danker, F. W. *Multipurpose Tools for Bible Study.* 4th ed. Minneapolis: Fortress, 1993. [U] Helpful survey of available tools and their most productive use.

Fee, Gordon D. *New Testament Exegesis: A Handbook for Students and Pastors.* 3rd ed. Louisville: Westminster John Knox, 2002. [A] Perhaps the first book to purchase and use for advancing beyond the beginning stages. The list of resources is up-to-date and stretching.

Fee, Gordon D., and Douglas Stuart. *How to Read the Bible for All Its Worth.* 2nd ed. Grand Rapids: Zondervan, 1993. [U] Engrossing, accessible discussion of biblical study, aimed at the general educated reader and covering both testaments.

Hagner, Donald A. *New Testament Exegesis and Research: A Guide for Seminarians.* N.c.: n.p., 1993. [U] Comparable to Fee's *Handbook* in its aim, and like Fee, it gives detailed advice for writing an exegesis paper.

Kümmel, W. G. *The New Testament: The History of the Investigation of Its Problems.* Nashville: Abingdon, 1972. [A] Classic account of (mostly German) New Testament scholarship. Provides historical context for doing contemporary exegesis.

Neill, Stephen, and N. T. Wright. *The Interpretation of the New Testament 1861-1986.* 2nd ed. New York/Oxford: Oxford University Press, 1988. [A] Does for the wider and more recent world what Kümmel does for his subject.

Tate, W. Randolph. *Biblical Interpretation: An Integrated Approach.* Peabody, Mass.: Hendrickson, 1991. [A] Helpfully views the interpretative task from three perspectives: behind the text, within the text and in front of the text.

Dictionaries

The title of each of the following seven entries (selected from among many) defines the area it covers. It is essential [E] to have *at least* a single-volume dictionary covering *at least* the entire New Testament, or (better) a set that covers the same territory in more detail.

Achtemeier, P. J., ed. *The HarperCollins Bible Dictionary.* San Francisco: Harper-SanFrancisco, 1996. [E]

Evans, Craig A., and Stanley E. Porter, eds. *Dictionary of New Testament Background.* Downers Grove, Ill.: InterVarsity Press, 2000. [U]

Freedman, David N., ed. *Anchor Bible Dictionary.* 6 vols. New York: Doubleday, 1992. [U]

Green, Joel B., et al., eds. *Dictionary of Jesus and the Gospels.* Downers Grove, Ill.: InterVarsity Press, 1992. [E]

Hawthorne, Gerald F., et al., eds. *Dictionary of Paul and His Letters.* Downers Grove, Ill.: InterVarsity Press, 1993. [E]

Martin, Ralph P., and Peter H. Davids, eds. *Dictionary of the Later New Testament and Its Developments.* Downers Grove, Ill.: InterVarsity Press, 1997. [E]

Reid, Daniel G., ed. *The IVP Dictionary of the New Testament: A One-Volume Compendium of Contemporary Biblical Scholarship.* Downers Grove, Ill.: InterVarsity Press, 2004. [E] This "compendium" compiles into one volume selected articles from the three preceding entries.

Texts

Novum Testamentum Graece: post Eberhard et Erwin Nestle. Revised by K. Aland et al. 27th ed. Stuttgart: Deutsche Bibelgesellschaft, 1993. [E] Known as NA[27].

Either this or the next entry is as mandatory for exegesis as a lawn is for mowing.

The Greek New Testament. Edited by B. Aland et al. 4th ed. Stuttgart: United Bible Societies, 1993. [E] Known as UBS[4]. See preceding entry.

Rahlfs, A., ed. *Septuaginta: id est Vetus Testamentum graece iuxta LXX interpretes.* Two vols. Stuttgart: Württembergische Bibelanstalt, 1935. [U] The standard edition of the Greek Old Testament, the "Bible" of the New Testament authors.

Aland, K., ed. *Synopsis of the Four Gospels.* Rev. ed.. New York: United Bible Societies, 1982. [E] Synoptically arranges the RSV text of the Gospels.

Aland, K., ed. *Synopsis Quattuor Evangeliorum.* 13th rev. ed. Stuttgart: Deutsche Bibelgesellschaft, 1985. [E] Synoptically arranges the Greek text of the Gospels. A synopsis is essential for responsible Gospel exegesis.

Lexica

Bauer, W. *A Greek-English Lexicon of the New Testament and Other Early Christian Literature.* Edited by F. W. Danker. 3rd ed. Chicago: University of Chicago Press, 2000. [E] The absolutely essential lexicon for New Testament exegesis; expensive but indispensable and long lasting.

Louw, J. P., and E. A. Nida. *Greek-English Lexicon of the New Testament Based on Semantic Domains.* 2 vols. 2nd ed. New York: UBS, 1989. [U] Fascinating and enlightening alternative arrangement of New Testament vocabulary.

Concordances

A concordance of the Greek New Testament, printed or electronic, is essential [E] for exegesis in that it permits us to locate vocabulary, patterns of text, semi-remembered passages and so on. English concordances usually cover the entire Bible. Since the advent of the personal computer, electronic concordances have made the work of searching texts almost instantaneous, although (like printed versions) they often contain errors in their data. One way or another, beginning exegetes need access to a search-tool of this kind.

Bachmann, H., and H. Slaby, eds. *Computer-Konkordanz zum Novum Testamentum Graece von Nestle-Aland, 26. Auflage, und zum Greek New Testament.* 3rd ed. Berlin: Walter de Gruyter, 1980. Very expensive.

Hatch, E., and H. A. Redpath. *A Concordance to the Septuagint and the Other Greek Versions of the Old Testament (Including the Apocryphal Books).* 3 vols. in 2. Grand Rapids: Baker, 1983; original: Oxford, 1897. [U] Still the standard hard-copy tool for the Septuagint.

Kohlenberger, John R., III. *The NRSV Concordance Unabridged: Including Apocry-*

phal/Deuterocanonical Books. Grand Rapids: Zondervan, 1991.

Moulton, W. F., and A. S. Geden. *A Concordance to the Greek New Testament According to the Texts of Westcott and Hort, Tischendorf and the English Revisers*. Edited by I. Howard Marshall. 6th rev. ed. Edinburgh: T. & T. Clark, 2002. This formerly standard work may in fact be more available than Bachmann-Slaby, and it is still useful.

Three mutually comparable electronic Bible-concordance programs: Gramcord®, Logos® and BibleWorks®. [E] All three are expensive, but they all provide enormously powerful tools for researching the texts of the Hebrew and Greek Old Testaments as well as the Greek New Testament, with many modern translations and other ancient texts besides. Gramcord® works best with Macintosh; either of the other two is a better choice for Windows. Further information is available on the Internet: <www.gramcord.com>, <www.logos.com>, <www.bibleworks.com>.

Textual Criticism

Aland, K., and B. Aland. *The Text of the New Testament*. 2nd ed. Grand Rapids: Eerdmans, 1989. [A] A thorough and complex treatment of the task of reconstructing the New Testament text.

Black, David Alan. *New Testament Textual Criticism: A Concise Guide*. Grand Rapids: Baker, 1994. [U] "Concise" is the right word for this tiny book, but the work provides a handy, readable orientation to the issue.

Metzger, B. M., and B. D. Ehrman *The Text of the New Testament: Its Transmission, Corruption, and Restoration*. 4th ed. New York/Oxford: Oxford University Press, 2005. [A] Classic account; more readable than Aland and Aland, and often rather entertaining.

Metzger, B. M. *A Textual Commentary on the Greek New Testament*. 2nd ed. Stuttgart: Deutsche Bibelgesellschaft, 1994. [E] Strongly recommended, even to beginners, as an over-the-shoulder look at the editorial process behind UBS[4]. A great way to "learn" textual criticism.

Biblical Linguistics and Semantics

Barr, James. *The Semantics of Biblical Language*. Oxford: Oxford University Press, 1961. [A] Watershed iconoclastic assessment of the semantic abuses of the day, including a devastating critique of the famous Kittel theological dictionary. Dated and harsh, but still worth reading.

Beekman, John, and John Callow. *Translating the Word of God*. Grand Rapids: Zondervan, 1974. [A] Excellent and practical treatment of grammatical and other linguistic features of the New Testament. Written primarily with concerns of translators in mind, but equally helpful for exegetes, of which translators are a subset.

Black, David Alan. *Linguistics for Students of New Testament Greek: A Survey of Basic Concepts and Applications:* Grand Rapids: Baker, 1988. [U] Helpfully brings home to all New Testament students the ins and outs of basic linguistics.

Cotterell, Peter, and Max Turner. *Linguistics and Biblical Interpretation.* Downers Grove, Ill.: InterVarsity Press, 1989. [A] Instructively applies to biblical texts insights drawn from the science of linguistics.

Silva, Moisés. *Biblical Words and Their Meaning.* Rev. and expanded ed. Grand Rapids: Zondervan, 1994. [A] One of the very best treatments of "word study" for biblical literature.

Wallace, Daniel B. *Greek Grammar Beyond the Basics: An Exegetical Syntax of the New Testament.* Grand Rapids: Zondervan, 1997. [E] The current "standard" second-year grammar of New Testament Greek. Responsible exegetes cannot depend on their beginning grammars any more than advancing exegetes can depend solely on the present introductory text for exegetical method!

Structure and Discourse

Beekman, J., J. Callow and M. Kopesec. *The Semantic Structure of Written Communication.* Dallas: SIL, 1981. [A] Describes the complex system of discourse analysis lying behind the "Semantic Structural Analyses" (SSAs) of particular biblical books, published primarily for Bible translators by the Summer Institute of Linguistics. Somewhat technical, but very instructive.

Black, David Alan et al, eds. *Linguistics and New Testament Interpretation: Essays on Discourse Analysis.* Nashville: Broadman, 1992. [A] Like the Reed and Porter volume listed below, contains helpful (and sometimes difficult) essays illuminating the application of discourse analysis to biblical texts.

Louw, J. P. *Semantics of New Testament Greek.* Philadelphia: Fortress, 1982. [A] Discourse-analytical approach to exegesis. Creative and stimulating.

Reed, J. T., and S. E. Porter, eds. *Discourse Analysis and the New Testament: Approaches and Results.* Sheffield: Sheffield Academic, 1999. [A] See above, Black et al., *Linguistics and New Testament Interpretation.*

Historical Backgrounds

Achtemeier, Paul J., Joel B. Green and Marianne Meye Thompson. *Introducing the New Testament: Its Literature and Theology.* Grand Rapids: Eerdmans, 2001. [E] Recent "introduction" to the New Testament literature. At least one good introduction to the New Testament is an essential tool of exegesis.

This one is excellent.

Barrett, C. K. *The New Testament Background: Writings from Ancient Greece and the Roman Empire That Illumine Christian Origins.* Rev. ed. New York: HarperSan-Francisco, 1987. [U] Provides tantalizing snippets of ancient literature relevant to the New Testament world.

Bruce, F. F. *New Testament History.* Garden City, N.Y.: Doubleday, 1969. [A] Wonderfully readable account of the historical setting in which the New Testament arose.

Charlesworth, James H., ed. *The Old Testament Pseudepigrapha.* 2 vols. Garden City, N.Y.: Doubleday, 1983-1985. [A] Two fat volumes, packed with the full translated and annotated text of the most important nonbiblical religious documents of Second Temple Judaism. Does not include Qumran texts.

Collins, J. J. *The Apocalyptic Imagination: An Introduction to Jewish Apocalyptic Literature.* Rev. ed. Grand Rapids: Eerdmans, 1998. [A] Excellent discussion of the nature of ancient Jewish apocalyptic literature.

Esler, P. F. *The First Christians in Their Social Worlds: Social-Scientific Approaches to New Testament Interpretation.* London/New York: Routledge, 1994. [A] Short and useful guide to the method and benefits of a sociological look at the New Testament.

Evans, Craig A. *Noncanonical Writings and New Testament Interpretation.* Peabody, Mass.: Hendrickson, 1992. [U] Handy guide to the wide range of ancient literature relevant to New Testament study.

Hanson, K. C., and Douglas Oakman. *Palestine in the Time of Jesus: Social Structures and Social Conflicts.* Minneapolis: Fortress, 1998. [U] Enlightening orientation to the sociocultural issues (family, economics, religion, power) latent within the New Testament Gospels.

Helyer, Larry R. *Exploring Jewish Literature of the Second Temple Period: A Guide for New Testament Students.* Downers Grove, Ill.: InterVarsity Press, 2002. [U] Like Evans, above, but wholly devoted to Jewish literature and more thorough.

Hennecke, E., and W. Schneemelcher, eds. *The NT Apocrypha.* 2 vols. Philadelphia: Westminster, 1963-1964. [A] Translations of and comments on much of the sometimes strange literature that arose in the early centuries of the church.

Kennedy, G. A. *New Testament Interpretation Through Rhetorical Criticism.* Chapel Hill: University of North Carolina Press, 1986. [A] Serviceable introduction to reading New Testament literature in light of first-century rhetoric.

May, Herbert G., ed., with assistance of G. N. S. Hunt and in consultation with R. W. Hamilton. *Oxford Bible Atlas.* 3rd ed. New York: Oxford University

Press, 1984. [U] Most Bibles contain maps of ancient Palestine and the Roman world among their end papers. But a full atlas provides much more information.

Marshall, I. Howard, Steven Travis and Ian Paul. *Exploring the New Testament: A Guide to the Letters and Revelation.* Downers Grove, Ill.: InterVarsity Press, 2002. [E] Second of two volumes introducing the New Testament (see following entry). Excellent alternative to Achtemeier, Green and Thompson.

Wenham, David, and Steve Walton. *Exploring the New Testament: A Guide to the Gospels and Acts.* Downers Grove, Ill.: InterVarsity Press, 2001. [E] First of two volumes introducing the New Testament (see preceding entry). Excellent alternative to Achtemeier, Green and Thompson.

Witherington, Ben, III. *New Testament History: A Narrative Account.* Grand Rapids: Baker, 2003. [A] Not as readable as Bruce, above, but readable enough and more up to date. Tells the engrossing "story" of the New Testament era, from the Maccabean wars onward. Gives insight into the personality quirks of the great players.

Wright, N. T. *The New Testament and the People of God.* Minneapolis: Fortress, 1992. [A] Along with the following two entries, constitutes the first volumes in a projected multivolume work reassessing the historical circumstances of the New Testament story, setting it within the larger story of God's dealing with humanity and "his people's" role in it.

———. *Jesus and the Victory of God.* Minneapolis: Fortress, 1996. [A]

———. *The Resurrection of the Son of God.* Minneapolis: Fortress, 2003. [A]

Literary Issues

Alter, Robert. *The Art of Biblical Narrative.* New York: Basic Books, 1981. [A] Devoted to the Old Testament narrative but wonderfully creative (and readable!) and applicable to New Testament narrative.

Caird, G. B. *The Language and Imagery of the Bible.* Philadelphia: Fortress, 1980. [A] Richly rewarding treatment of the literary resources of ancient writing, especially as they appear in the Bible.

Longman, Tremper, III. *Literary Approaches to Biblical Interpretation.* Grand Rapids: Zondervan, 1987. [A] Short but suggestive survey of the subject.

Powell, M. A. *What Is Narrative Criticism?* Guides to Biblical Scholarship. Minneapolis: Fortress, 1991. [A] Excellent introduction to reading the New Testament narratives as stories.

New Testament Theologies

Summaries of the various "theologies" of New Testament writers help exegetes to get a bigger picture of the ideas regarding God, Christology, humanity, the nature of salvation and so on, as they are presented—or taken for granted—in the New Testament literature. The following two are representative of many available. It is essential [E] to have access to at least one such summary, in order to keep the larger picture in view.

Caird, G. B., and L. D. Hurst. *New Testament Theology*. Oxford: Oxford University Press: 1994. [E]

Ladd, George Eldon. *A Theology of the New Testament*. Edited by Donald A. Hagner. Rev. ed. Grand Rapids: Eerdmans, 1993. [E]

Hermeneutical Theory

Green, Joel B., ed. *Hearing the New Testament: Strategies for Interpretation*. Grand Rapids: Eerdmans, 1995. [A] Collection of essays on wide-ranging approaches to interpreting the New Testament. Of mixed quality and readability, but overall informative.

Noll, Mark A. *Between Faith and Criticism: Evangelicals, Scholarship, and the Bible in America*. 2nd ed. Grand Rapids: Baker, 1991. [A] Discerning and helpful discussion of the apparent conflict between faith and scholarly analysis of Scripture.

Thiselton, A. C. *The Two Horizons: New Testament Hermeneutics and Philosophical Description*. Grand Rapids: Eerdmans, 1980. [A] Important, often difficult discussion of the philosophical issues inherent in New Testament interpretation.

Walsh, Brian J., and Sylvia C. Keesmaat. *Colossians Remixed: Subverting the Empire*. Downers Grove, Ill.: InterVarsity Press, 2004. [A] A creative approach to the text of Colossians, reading it in the context of ancient Roman culture and in the context of contemporary Western culture. One example of a twenty-first-century message thoroughly grounded in responsible exegesis of a first-century original. Hermeneutics at its best.

Subject Index

Note: This index operates as a kind of modified concordance; occurrences of the specific listed words on the listed pages serve as markers for the various places where the relevant subject is mentioned or discussed. A particular discussion may continue on other pages not listed, but the listed pages should drop the reader into the near vicinity.